AN INTRODUCTION
TO THE STUDY OF JEREMIAH

D1599841

Other Titles in the T&T Clark
Approaches to Biblical Studies series include

AN INTRODUCTION
TO THE STUDY OF JEREMIAH

C. L. Crouch

Bloomsbury T&T Clark
An imprint of Bloomsbury Publishing Plc

B L O O M S B U R Y
LONDON · OXFORD · NEW YORK · NEW DELHI · SYDNEY

Bloomsbury T&T Clark
An imprint of Bloomsbury Publishing Plc

Imprint previously known as T&T Clark

50 Bedford Square
London
WC1B 3DP
UK

1385 Broadway
New York
NY 10018
USA

www.bloomsbury.com

**BLOOMSBURY, T&T CLARK and the Diana logo are trademarks of
Bloomsbury Publishing Plc**

First published 2017

© C. L. Crouch, 2017

British Library Cataloguing-in-Publication Data
A catalogue record for this book is available from the British Library.

ISBN: HB: 978-0-5676-6573-7
PB: 978-0-5676-6572-0
ePDF: 978-0-5676-6574-4
ePub: 978-0-5676-6576-8

Library of Congress Cataloging-in-Publication Data
A catalog record for this book is available from the Library of Congress.

Cover image: The Church of Pater Noster, 1615
© Photograph by Zev Radovan

Typeset by Integra Software Services Pvt. Ltd.
Printed and bound in India

you know

CONTENTS

ACKNOWLEDGMENTS

There is a great deal of provocative and insightful work on the book of Jeremiah which has appeared in the last few decades but does not appear in this *Introduction*. The limitations of the form, together with the structure I adopted, left me able to mention only a handful of recent works in the text and footnotes, though some of those whom I have neglected do appear in the Further Reading. Despite their general anonymity, these and many others have exerted their influence on my thinking about the book of Jeremiah and thereby on the substrata of this introduction to it. In lieu of footnotes—and with apologies to those for whom citation metrics are the currency of the day—I would like to express here my appreciation to the many and varied members of the Jeremiah guild, both those for whom the book(s) has been a lifetime companion and those who have entered its ranks on a more occasional basis.

Acknowledgment is due also to the Alexander von Humboldt Stiftung/Foundation, whose award of a research fellowship for a related project gave me access to the library of the Theologische Fakultät of the Georg-August-Universität Göttingen, without which this would have been a much slower and more difficult task. The students of the Vacation Term for Biblical Study held at Robinson College, Cambridge, provided the impetus for the book and a welcome trial audience. My second- and third-year students in the Department of Theology and Religious Studies took the announcement that we would be spending an entire semester on the book of Jeremiah with remarkable stoicism and then proceeded to prove themselves an invaluable sounding board for its contents. A number of colleagues have generously donated of their time in reading various drafts.

Finally: to you who have helped make the present shine more brightly than the past. You know who you are.

C. L. Crouch
Nottingham
St Dominic 2016

ABBREVIATIONS

AB	Anchor Bible
AIIL	Ancient Israel and Its Literature
BBB	Bonner biblische Beiträge
BEATAJ	Beiträge zur Erforschung des Alten Testaments und des Antiken Judentums
BETL	Bibliotheca ephemerides theologicae lovanienses
Bib	*Biblica*
BIS	Biblical Interpretation Series
BZAW	Beihefte zu Zeitschrift für die alttestamentliche Wissenschaft
DSD	*Dead Sea Discoveries*
FAT	Forschungen zum Alten Testament
FRLANT	Forschungen zur Religion und Literatur des Alten und Neuen Testaments
HBM	Hebrew Bible Monographs
HSM	Harvard Semitic Monographs
ICC	International Critical Commentary
JBL	*Journal of Biblical Literature*
JSOTSup	Journal for the Study of the Old Testament, Supplement Series
JTIS	Journal of Theological Interpretation Supplements
LHBOTS	Library of Hebrew Bible/Old Testament Studies
NRSV	The Bible (New Revised Standard Version)
OTL	Old Testament Library
OudSt	Oudtestamentische studiën
SBL	Studies in Biblical Literature
SBLDS	Society of Biblical Literature Dissertation Series
SBLMS	Society of Biblical Literature Monograph Series
SSN	Studia Semitica Neerlandica
VT	*Vetus Testamentum*
VTSup	Supplements to Vetus Testamentum
WMANT	Wissenschaftliche Monographien zum Alten und Neuen Testament
ZAW	*Zeitschrift für die alttestamentliche Wissenschaft*

Chapter 1

INTRODUCTION

The book of Jeremiah is not an easy book. Its first impressions are overwhelming; unlike many of the other books of the Hebrew Bible, in which a reasonable degree of textual integrity, a relatively consistent canonical order, and a semblance of thematic coherence provide their readers with a relatively stable interpretive ground from which to work, the book of Jeremiah has persistently defied attempts to draw a neat line around or under its contents, its development, or its meaning. It contains a bewildering array of poetry and prose, its Hebrew and Greek versions reflect unabashedly distinct trajectories in the development of the book, and its theological intentions are difficult to sum up in any straightforward way. This complexity has rendered the book of Jeremiah the focus of intense interpretive scrutiny, as scholars and lay readers alike have tried to make sense of the book's origins, intentions, and interpretation.

The variety of different kinds of material in the book of Jeremiah means that a major focus of interpretation has been the attempt to understand how all these different materials ended up in this one, admittedly large, book—and then what they were meant to be doing once it got there. Unlike Ezekiel, for example, which progresses in a reasonably neat, dated order, or Isaiah, which preserves material from at least two and perhaps three or more different major authors but keeps each of their contributions reasonably self-contained (hence we can talk about First Isaiah and Second Isaiah, and perhaps Third Isaiah), the book of Jeremiah hops around chronologically, switches from poetry to prose and back again in the space of a few verses, includes extensive narrative material focused on the prophet, of a genre which has little if any parallel elsewhere, and—to make matters even more interesting—is preserved for us in two quite different versions: a Hebrew version, which is underneath the translations in NRSV and most other English Bibles, and a Greek version, which is about one-seventh shorter and has the oracles against the nations (OANs) in a different place. As a result of this, the questions "How did we get this?" and "What is it doing?" have been especially prominent in the minds of Jeremiah's interpreters.

At first sight, attempts to answer these questions may appear—like the book itself—to be a chaotic agglomeration of diverse scholarly endeavors. These are dominated by an unruly collection of methods, approaches, and interests, sometimes seeming to work at cross-purposes and resulting in apparent disarray in their disparate assemblage of results. Rather than a reflection of failure or interpretive futility, however, the many voices chiming into the discussion of the book of Jeremiah should be understood to reflect its rich interpretive possibilities. Recognition of these possibilities has put the book of Jeremiah at the forefront of recent biblical scholarship. Indeed, though the situation in Jeremiah may be somewhat extreme, interpretation of the book over the course of the last thirty years or so has closely mirrored changes across the wider discipline. This is especially the case with respect to historiographical concerns, as well as in an expansion of the range of approaches through which the biblical texts are engaged. The study of the book of Jeremiah, therefore, represents in microcosm many of the challenges and opportunities of recent work in biblical studies. To master the twists and turns of recent research on the book of Jeremiah is to gain not only an appreciation of this one book, but an appreciation of and a facility with the trajectories of contemporary biblical scholarship more widely.

Historical Setting

The relationship of the book of Jeremiah to historical events in the seventh and sixth centuries BCE (and beyond) has been a central question of much of the last century of scholarship. The book presents itself as relating to the final years of Judah's existence and to the immediate aftermath of its fall and destruction. Whether this setting derives from the actual historical location of its author(s) or is merely a literary device, it is useful to have some sense of the events of this period, in order to better understand the way that the book engages with and is shaped by these events.

The grand stage on which Judah's demise was to play out in the latter part of the seventh and early part of the sixth centuries was one dominated by struggles for power among the major ancient Near Eastern empires.[1]

1. All dates are BCE unless noted otherwise. Accessible overviews of ancient Near Eastern history which include this period are Marc Van De Mieroop, *A History of the Ancient Near East: ca. 3000–323 BC* (2nd ed.,

For much of the previous century, the southern Levant had been overshadowed by the Neo-Assyrian empire, whose imperial ambitions had brought its armies to the west in the middle of the eighth century, under Tiglath-pileser III. Though the latter part of the century was marked by various Levantine efforts to repulse or throw off Assyrian dominance, the advent of the seventh century saw the widespread realization that political and military resistance to the Assyrian behemoth was largely futile. The phrase *pax Assyriaca* is often applied to this period, intended as a description of the relative stabilization in the relationships between Assyria and its western vassals and the overall reduction in the political and military tumult of the region. Biblical writers turn this period of calm to their theological and ideological advantage: the chronicles of this period in 2 Kings maintain a nearly complete silence concerning the presence of foreign powers in the region, bolstering an illusion of an autonomous and isolated Judah.

In the last third of the seventh century, however, the hitherto unshakeable Assyrian its empire started to wobble. Although the exact reasons for its collapse remain opaque, it is widely suspected that it was a result of two main factors. On the one hand, the empire was plagued in its last years by a succession of ineffective kings, whose personal weaknesses were exacerbated by their relatively brief tenure (the accession of any new king was widely seen an opportunity for the empire's subordinate territories to rebel). On the other hand, the empire over which these kings were meant to wield their authority had probably finally overstretched itself, not least in its determination to exert control over Egypt. In theory, the mighty Assyrian empire sprawled outward from its Mesopotamian heartland—around Nineveh, Assur, and Kalhu—in all directions: eastward to Media, southward to Elam and Babylonia, northward to Urartu, westward to the Levant, and to Egypt in the far southwest. In reality, Assyria's grip on the outer reaches of this empire had always been tenuous. Egypt's submission to Assyria, for example, lasted less than two decades in the middle of the seventh century. This renewed autonomy was accompanied by renewed interest and involvement in the affairs of the southern Levant; Egypt had

Oxford: Blackwell, 2007), and Amélie Kuhrt, *The Ancient Near East: c.3000–330 B.C., Volume 2* (2nd ed., Routledge History of the Ancient World; London: Routledge, 1997). For a guide to the kings of Judah, Assyria, Babylonia, and Egypt, see Appendix B.

been Judah's intermittent ally in the preceding century and, relieved of Assyrian authority, it would it become a regular player in Judahite affairs at the end of the seventh and beginning of the sixth centuries. The temptation to an Egyptian alliance would ultimately play a fatal role in Judah's downfall.

Nearer to home, Babylonia constituted a long-standing thorn in Assyria's southern flank.[2] With the empire overstretched and lacking in leadership, it became increasingly vulnerable to Babylonian efforts to resist its authority. In contrast to previous Babylonian rebellions, which had been emphatically quashed, the late seventh century ultimately saw the resurgence of an autonomous Babylonia—the fledgling Neo-Babylonian empire. In the face of this challenge to its authority Assyria was forced to consolidate its defenses in Mesopotamia, abandoning its western ambitions and withdrawing from the southern Levant.

The traditional narrative of this period has portrayed the Assyrians' departure as resulting in a power vacuum, into which the Judahite king Josiah stepped boldly, purging the temple of Assyrian elements and campaigning into the former northern kingdom in an attempt to reestablish a grand, Davidic kingdom. More recent analysis, however, has suggested a more or less seamless handover of regional control from the Assyrians to the Egyptians, with whom they had allied against the Babylonians.[3] Although the details remain vague, it appears that the Egyptians had established a successor state—collecting tithes and tributes and dictating regional policy—by at least 610.

Somewhere in the midst of this transition Josiah lost his life. Traditionally, this has been attributed to a failed attempt on Josiah's part to prevent the Egyptians from supporting the Assyrians against

2. The situation was further complicated by Esarhaddon's decision to put his two sons on the thrones of Assyria and Babylonia, respectively; the middle part of the seventh century was marked by an ugly war between the two brothers. The ambiguity of Assyria's attitude to Babylonia is reflected in its extensive assimilation of Babylonian culture, such as the acquisition and pride of place given to major literary works—most notably, *Enuma elish*—in the royal libraries. For more on this relationship, see Grant Frame, *Babylonia 689–627 B.C.: A Political History* (Istanbul: Nederlands Historisch-Archaeologisch Instituut te İstanbul, 1992).

3. Bernd U. Schipper, "Egypt and the Kingdom of Judah under Josiah and Jehoiakim," *Tel Aviv* 37 (2010): 200–26.

the Babylonians, with the meeting between Josiah and Pharaoh Necho
II at Megiddo (recounted, very briefly, in 2 Kgs 23:29) interpreted
as a military confrontation. More recently, it has been suggested
that Josiah was at Megiddo to register the transfer of his allegiance
from Assyria to Egypt, but that he was suspected of disloyalty and
executed.[4] Whatever the reason for Josiah's death, the degree of Egypt's
involvement in Judahite politics at this turbulent time is clear from its
subsequent interference in the succession of Judah's kingship. Though
one of Josiah's sons, Jehoahaz, succeeded Josiah on the throne, he
was almost immediately deposed by Necho in favor of his brother
Eliakim, who took Jehoiakim as his throne name.

As for the Assyrians, their retrenchment would be to no avail.
Nineveh fell to Babylonian troops in 612 and by 609 the Babylonian
army had defeated the remaining coalition of Assyrians and Egyptians.
In due course the Babylonian empire would assume control of all of
Assyria's territories, claiming for itself the riches and rewards of its
far-flung provinces and vassal kingdoms and using them as stepping
stones to even wider powers. From a Judahite perspective, however,
the eventual success of the Babylonians in gaining control over the
whole of the ancient Near East was by no means obvious. Indeed, the
chaos of the final decades of the kingdom of Judah and its ultimate
demise at the hands of the Babylonian king, Nebuchadnezzar, may
be understood as the result of a series of ill-fated decisions by Judah's
leaders concerning the strengths and objectives of the three major
ancient Near Eastern powers on the scene: Assyria, Babylonia, and
Egypt.

After successfully taking the Mesopotamian heartland, the
Babylonians sought to gain control of all of Assyria's former territories,
including the southern Levant. As the southern Levant had passed
into Egyptian hands upon the Assyrians' withdrawal from the area, it
became a point of conflict between Egypt and Babylonia. This began
in the last decade of the seventh century—once the Babylonians had
firmly established their base in Mesopotamia—and continued into the

4. Richard D. Nelson, "Realpolitik in Judah (687–609 BCE)," in *Scripture
in Context II: More Essays on the Comparative Method,* ed. William W. Hallo,
James C. Moyer, and Leo G. Perdue (Winona Lake, IN, Eisenbrauns, 1983),
177–89; Nadav Na'aman, "The Kingdom of Judah," in *Ancient Israel and Its
Neighbors: Interaction and Counteraction,* vol. 1 of *Collected Essays* (Winona
Lake, IN: Eisenbrauns, 2005), 329–98.

first decade of the sixth century. Evidence about who had control over the southern Levant (and in what sense) at any given moment during this period is not very clear. However, this uncertainty is probably a fair reflection of the era's atmosphere of upheaval and confusion. With Egypt and Babylonia fighting for dominance, the small states of the southern Levant would have found themselves between a rock and a hard place; Judah, along with its neighbors, would have been trying to guess which side would eventually triumph so that it might throw in its lot with the winning side.

In hindsight, the turning point was a major battle at Carchemish, which took place in 605. In this battle the Babylonian army, led by Nebuchadnezzar II, defeated the Egyptian army under the leadership of Necho. As a result, the Levant came under Babylonian control for the first time. In practice, this meant that all of the kings of the area—including the king of Judah, Jehoiakim—paid tribute and swore loyalty to the Babylonian king. In Jehoiakim's case, this entailed a shift of allegiance away from the very Egyptians who had put him on the throne in the first place.

At the time, however, the battle at Carchemish hardly appeared so decisive; just a few years later, the failure of a Babylonian campaign to Egypt prompted Jehoiakim and several others of these new vassals to throw in their lots with the Egyptians, effectively rebelling against their Babylonian overlord by ceasing to pay tribute. In 598/7, the Babylonian army invaded Judah. Prior to their arrival Jehoiakim died, leaving his throne to son Jehoiachin. Almost immediately Jerusalem fell to the Babylonians. The novice king was deposed and he and his family were deported to Babylonia, along with other members of the royal court. This group constituted the first group of deportees from Judah. Nebuchadnezzar's chronicles report:

> The seventh year (598/7): In the month Kislev (November/ December) the king of Akkad mustered his army and marched to Hattu (Syria). He encamped against the city of Judah and on the second day of the month Adar (16 March 597) he captured the city and seized (its) king. A king of his own choice he appointed in the city (and) taking the vast tribute he brought it into Babylon.[5]

5. A. K. Grayson, *Assyrian and Babylonian Chronicles* (Winona Lake, IN: Eisenbrauns, 2000), no. 5 11'–13'.

The next decade, between 597 and 587, would be the last of Judah's independent existence. At the time, however, Judah and Jerusalem's ultimate fate was unknown. Parts of the books of Jeremiah and Ezekiel reflect an intense argument over whether 597 already represented YHWH's final judgment, or if there was more destruction still to come. Because this was Judah's first rebellion, the Babylonians elected not to completely destroy either Judah or Jerusalem. Nor did they take it under direct control; rather they allowed it to continue as a vassal state. To ensure a more compliant local monarchy, however, they chose to install another member of the royal family as a puppet king: Jehoiachin's uncle, Mattaniah, who took the throne name Zedekiah.[6] In either case, the expectation that Zedekiah, as a Babylonian appointee, would remain loyal to the Babylonians turned out to be ill-founded. In 589 he too rebelled. Though the reasons for this are unclear, they are probably related to perceived changes in the balance between Babylonia and Egypt; though there was no direct confrontation between the two armies during this period, the balance appears to have shifted enough that the latest pharaoh, Psammetichus, was able to undertake a royal procession through the region in 590, unopposed by the Babylonians. The next year Zedekiah rebelled, and the Babylonians responded by again laying siege to Jerusalem. Finally, in 587, Jerusalem fell for a second time. This time the Babylonians meted out their punishment unreservedly: the city was sacked, the temple was burnt, and Zedekiah was deported to Babylon with the rest of the city's remaining leadership.

From this point onward, Judah was no longer an independent, semiautonomous state but a province of foreign empires: first the Babylonian, then later the Persian, the Greek, and the Roman. This is also the point from which historical details become hazy—in no small part because the Babylonian sources have broken off by this point, leaving the book of Jeremiah, with all its complexity, as one of the only sources of information about what happened.

According to Jeremiah (mostly in chs. 40–44), the Babylonians appointed Gedaliah ben Ahikam ben Shaphan to a gubernatorial role of some kind. This government was not based in Jerusalem but in the town of Mizpah in the region of Benjamin. After some unknown length of time, however, Gedaliah was assassinated

---

6. A dispute over whether Zedekiah should be considered the legitimate king of Judah is especially apparent in the book of Ezekiel.

by Ishmael ben Nethaniah. Fearing Babylonian reprisals for the death of their appointee, the remaining inhabitants fled to Egypt. Perhaps connected to these events was a third deportation in 582, which is reported only in the book of Jeremiah (52:30).

After this there is almost complete silence. Apart from the claim that the exiled king Jehoiachin found favor in the Babylonian court (2 Kgs 25:27-30 // Jer. 52:31-34), there is no biblical material concerning the fate of the inhabitants of Judah between 582 and the prophetic material in Isaiah 40–55, usually dated to the late 540s. Outside the biblical texts, there is some significant archival material from the Mesopotamian town of Al-Yahudu ("the City of Judah") and from the region of Nippur (the Murashu archive), recording aspects of everyday life among some of the descendants of Judah's deportees. The Babylonian chronicles break off after 594 and the other surviving Babylonian inscriptions are primarily building inscriptions, rather than campaign accounts of the kind that provide scholars with extensive information about the Assyrian period.

Whether the book of Jeremiah's information about life in Judah after 586 may be considered historically reliable is part of a wider debate over the nature and purpose of the biblical texts. In the immediate context, it is important to observe that the events recounted by the book create the appearance of a land devoid of inhabitants, insofar as everyone is either deported to Babylonia or flees to Egypt. Archaeological evidence, however, indicates that the area continued to be inhabited; this would have been consistent with Assyrian and Babylonian deportation policies, which focused on the ruling classes who might foment further rebellions, rather than the general population.[7] The books of Jeremiah and Ezekiel both suggest that there were significant disputes about the interpretation of the destruction of the Judahite state and the desecration of the Jerusalem temple in the aftermath of the deportations of 597 and 586 (and perhaps also 582, if that report is reliable). What was the purpose of this destruction and the consequent division of the population of Judah? Both those left in exile and those in the land saw themselves as the preferred of Yʜwʜ—those left in the land because they had been spared deportation and those in Babylonia because they

7. Hans M. Barstad, *The Myth of the Empty Land: A Study in the History and Archaeology of Judah during the "Exilic" Period* (Oslo: Scandinavian University Press, 1996); Oded Lipschits and Joseph Blenkinsopp (eds.), *Judah and the Judeans in the Neo-Babylonian Period* (Winona Lake, IN: Eisenbrauns, 2006).

had been extracted from Jerusalem prior to its complete destruction. These arguments resurface in the accounts of the early Persian period, especially in the books of Ezra, Nehemiah, and Chronicles. The biblical texts indicate that it was the community in Babylon—those who had been deported and their descendants, who viewed the destruction and subsequent exile as a form of purifying judgment—who ultimately prevailed, successfully laying claim to the land, its traditions, and its god while rejecting the legitimacy of those in the land and their later descendants. An important part of this argument, however, was to deny that there had been any ongoing Judahite existence in the land during the deportees' absence in Babylonia; like the deportees, the land was also undergoing a period of purification (sometimes articulated in terms of sabbatical rest, as in Lev. 26:34-35). The theological, political, and practical exigencies of this mean that the book of Jeremiah's account of the complete desertion of the land—especially the (purportedly) voluntary flight of Judah's remaining inhabitants to Egypt—may be viewed as a means of clearing the land, so that it will be empty and waiting when the time comes for the deportees to return. It is therefore difficult to know just how seriously to take this material as an historical source. As we shall see, this has been one of the most vexed questions in the study of the book of Jeremiah.

Chapter 2

THE BOOK(S) CALLED JEREMIAH

The majority of this *Introduction* will focus on a handful of specific passages, observing what happens when they are approached with a variety of different methodologies. Before we investigate these passages in detail, however, it is useful to gain a sense of the contents of the book as a whole, noting points which have attracted particular scholarly attention as well as just how problematic it can be to refer to "the book of Jeremiah" at all. This is the task of this chapter.

Chapter 1

Chapter 1 begins with a heading, the first of several. This heading identifies what follows as "the words of Jeremiah," thus beginning the book's emphasis on the word of the prophet (and the word of Yhwh, which the words of the prophet are meant to reflect) from the very first verse.[1] The chapter goes on to recount the prophet's call and to provide a summary statement of the message which the prophet is commissioned to deliver. This is full of language and images reminiscent of other call accounts, including those of Moses, Samuel, Isaiah, and Ezekiel. Unusually, this prophet is said to be "a prophet to the nations" (v. 5), in a statement that looks ahead to the oracles against the nations (OANs) in chs. 46–51.[2] Because of the different location of these oracles in the

---

1. Following the Jewish tradition of not pronouncing the divine name, Yhwh is rendered by most English translations as "the Lord."

2. As most English Bibles follow the Hebrew chapter and verse order, rather than those of the Greek text, the references in this *Introduction* follow the Hebrew/English numbering unless otherwise noted. Where the English and Hebrew differ, the English is given first, followed by the Hebrew in square brackets.

Greek text (where they come after 25:13, instead of after ch. 45), this declaration has been the focus of discussions about whether the OANs were spoken by a historical Jeremiah, or added to the book at a later stage. Of similar interest is the summary of the prophetic message which appears in v. 10: the prophet has been appointed "to pluck up and to pull down, to destroy and to overthrow, to build and to plant." These words, in varying combinations, are echoed at key points in the rest of the book and thus serve as an important literary motif linking together its different parts (12:14-17; 18:7-9; 24:6; 31:28, 38–40; 42:10; 45:4). A significant feature of the list is that it includes two positive elements ("to build and to plant"), even as it places more emphasis on the negative ("to pluck up and to pull down, to destroy and to overthrow"). The appearance of words of hope in what purports to be a summary of Jeremiah's message has contributed to debates over whether only the words of judgment contained in the book reflect the message of the prophet, or if the prophet also offered an element of hope. More recently, the study of this chapter has focused on its role as an introduction to the book. We will return to this and other recent issues in the chapter's interpretation in more detail in Chapter 5.

Verses 11–19 contain a pair of visions, the first of an almond branch (a play on the Hebrew word for almond branch, *shaqed*, and the word for watching, *shoqed*) and the second of a boiling pot, oriented in relation to the north, whence judgment and disaster come. These visions are similar in form to the visions in Amos 7–9; Yhwh asks the prophet what he sees, the prophet responds with a description of some kind, and then Yhwh provides an explanation. In the book of Jeremiah, these visions are paralleled only by ch. 24, which recounts a vision of good and bad figs. Together, these visions form an *inclusio* (a literary form of parentheses) for the first half of the book. In their immediate context, they also provide a transition to the oracles of judgment in chs. 2–6, especially in their reference to an enemy which will come from the north, which will be a key image in chs. 4–6. The vision report also alludes to opposition to and rejection of the prophetic message, which is a significant theme throughout the book.

Chapters 2–6

Chapters 2–6 are the first major poetic section, though short sections of prose do appear intermittently and the section as a whole has clearly been composed by linking together a number of smaller poetic pieces. Much of this material refers to its audience as Israel, with Judah sometimes appearing alongside or in contrast to this Israel. This variation in terms has piqued the interest of many readers, not least because the book only ever identifies Jeremiah's audience as the inhabitants of the kingdom of Judah. Whether these Israel passages were originally addressed to the northern kingdom and only later adapted (by Jeremiah?) to address the southern kingdom, or if their Israel always referred to a constituency in the south, remains uncertain. At this point in the book, the possibility of repenting and thereby avoiding punishment remains open to Israel; these chapters are littered with multiple forms of the Hebrew root *šûb* (to turn, return, or repent), though this is not always obvious in English translations.

These chapters are also characterized by the powerful images they invoke as they try to persuade their audience to return to an exclusive relationship with YHWH. Many of these images are drawn from the natural and agricultural spheres—cracked cisterns (2:13), roaring and ravening lions (2:15, 30; 4:7; 5:6), vineyards (2:21; 5:10; 6:9), a camel in heat (2:23-24), shepherds (3:15; 6:2-3), and so on. The chapters also draw heavily on traditions about Israel's origins, including the exodus from Egypt (2:6), the period of wandering in the wilderness (2:2, 6, 31), and the Israelites' eventual entry into the Promised Land (2:7; 3:19).

The most persistent of the images in these chapters, however, and also the most disturbing, is that of Israel as YHWH's wife. These chapters refer to the audience as YHWH's bride (2:2), liken her to a camel and an ass in heat (2:23-25), call her a faithless wife (3:20), and accuse even her children of adultery (5:7-8). Both Israel and Judah are condemned together as promiscuous sluts (3:6-10). These passages make extensive use of the stereotype of an uncontrollably promiscuous woman, whose licentiousness represents a threat to society (or, more accurately, to patriarchal society, in which sexuality is carefully controlled by men, especially fathers and husbands). The metaphor relies on social assumptions about the shame of sexual infidelity; to call a woman a whore or an adulteress is to publicly humiliate the woman, but also to humiliate her husband who, the accusation implies, is unable to control her behavior. The sexualization of the relationship between YHWH and Israel also effects the rhetorical emasculation of the audience to whom these words are directed: in the frame of the metaphor, the Israelite men are placed in the role of the (adulterous) female. In a social world in which power is, at least on the face of it, in the hands of men, for these men to be called women—and adulterous women at that—would have been the height of insult.

The theological point of this explicit language is to describe Israel's and Judah's worship of other gods in terms of unfaithfulness, with religious infidelity to Yʜwʜ analogized to the sexual unfaithfulness of an adulterous wife. Though readers have tended to focus on the metaphor's claims that Yʜwʜ's actions were motivated by his love for Israel—a husband driven to extreme by the force of his passionate, exclusive love for his wife—this obscures the fact that Yʜwʜ's response to Israel is described in alarmingly violent terms. Interspersed among these accusations of adultery are references to the murder of Israel's children (2:30), her exile at the hands of foreign powers (2:37), punitive drought followed by famine and starvation (3:3), and military destruction with all its attendant horrors (e.g., 4:5-18). The depiction of the object of Yʜwʜ's judgment as female is also reiterated in the devastation which awaits "Daughter Zion" (4:31; 6:2, 23) and "Daughter (of) My People" (4:11; 6:26; 8:11, 19, 21, 22, 23; 9:7 [9:6]).[3] Similar imagery appears intermittently elsewhere in the book—the coming defeat by the enemy from the north, for example, is described in 13:22 as sexual humiliation or rape.

While the depiction of divine violence presents a theological challenge whatever its target, the particular focus on violence against women has made this metaphor especially difficult in the twentieth and twenty-first centuries. By describing Israel as Yʜwʜ's wife and describing Yʜwʜ's punishment of Israel's religious infidelity as though it were punishment for sexual infidelity, these chapters depict Yʜwʜ's actions as divine domestic violence: a male God wreaking violence against the female body of Israel. The major theological issues raised by this metaphor and the power of such images to shape contemporary ideas about sexuality, gender, and personal relationships have attracted especially close attention from feminist scholars, who have rightly challenged many of the traditional theological formulations and developed new approaches to these disturbing texts.

Chapter 7

Chapter 7 (more properly, 7:1–8:3) is the first of two accounts of Jeremiah's so-called "Temple Sermon." The other appears in ch. 26. This is also the first major prose passage in the book. As its nickname

---

3. Sometimes this is obscured by English translations, such as the NRSV's "poor people" for "daughter of my people."

suggests, it takes the form of an extended speech to the people of Judah, placed in the mouth of Jeremiah as he stands before the temple in Jerusalem. It repeats in prose form many of the complaints lodged by the preceding and following poetry, but its special emphasis is to decry the trust which the people have placed in the temple to save them from the consequences of their behavior. In making this complaint, it seems to target a particular kind of "Zion theology." This theological outlook probably arose in response to the preservation of Jerusalem and its temple from destruction by Sennacherib a century before: the idea that Jerusalem, as the city of Yhwh, was invulnerable to enemy attack. Wherever the idea came from, ch. 7 is at pains to deny that the presence of the temple, even though it is Yhwh's own abode, will save Jerusalem from its sins.

This chapter uses a great deal of language familiar from the book of Deuteronomy, such as "going after other gods," oppression of "the alien, the orphan, and the widow," and the idea that the land had been promised to the ancestors (vv. 6–7, 14, etc.). This language and theology is commonly described as "deuteronomistic," reflecting its derivation from Deuteronomy, and this chapter forms an important part of discussions about the extent and nature of deuteronomistic influence on the book as a whole. A major theme of this argument has been whether such language stems from Jeremiah himself, or if it derives from the interests of deuteronomistic scribes who received, edited, and transmitted the Jeremiah traditions at a later date. More about this may be found in Chapter 3.

Chapter 7 also appears to make reference, in v. 8, to some of the Ten Commandments (also known as the Decalogue)—"steal, murder, commit adultery, swear falsely, make offerings to Baal, and go after other gods"—and therefore has appeared in debates about whether or in what form the prophets (or the editors of the books attributed to them) might have known the legal material preserved in the Pentateuch. For the most part the prophetic books do not seem to be familiar with the Pentateuchal legal traditions, at least not in the form in which we now have them; this passage in Jeremiah is quite unusual in this respect.

The chapter also marks the first appearance of a prohibition against Jeremiah praying on the people's behalf to Yhwh. The normal role of a prophet was to act as a mediator (a go-between) between Yhwh and the people, conveying the people's pleas to Yhwh in the form of prayers and Yhwh's responses in the form of oracles. For Yhwh to prohibit Jeremiah from interceding for the people marks a significant departure from the expected prophetic task. It also raises the specter of inevitable judgment: YHWH will no longer listen to the people's pleas for mercy because he has already determined to punish them. Thus there is no reason for Jeremiah to intercede.

Chapters 8–10

Chapter 7 (7:1–8:3) now acts as a hinge for the poetic material preceding (chs. 2–6) and following it (8:4–10:25). The second half of this diptych (8:4–10:25) is much more sustained in its negativity, with the call for repentance which characterized chs. 2–6 nearly absent in chs. 8–10. The expansive use of metaphor which dominated the earlier chapters is also much less prominent here. It is replaced by repeated statements attributing the cause of the coming downfall to the people's disloyalty to YHWH and by descriptions of the downfall itself, ranging from the piling up of corpses (9:22 [9:23]) and the summons of the women whose role was to mourn over the dead (9:17-21 [9:18-22]) to the siege (10:17) and devastation of Jerusalem (9:11 [9:12]; 10:22) and the conquest of Israel's women and its land (8:10).

Of theological note is the near interchangeability of the prophetic and divine voices throughout these chapters. Thus the grief and weeping expressed at the end of ch. 8 ("My joy is gone, grief is upon me, my heart is sick," v. 18) and beginning of ch. 9 ("O that my head were a spring of water, and my eyes a fountain of tears, so that I might weep day and night for the slain of my poor people," v. 1 [8:23]) are attributed by some interpreters to the prophet—yet the words may equally be attributed to YHWH, agonizing over the suffering of the people. The close identification of YHWH and his prophetic messenger is a recurring theme of the book, often linked to its effort to present the prophet's message as authoritative. It is implied in much of the poetry, in which the identity of the speaker is often indeterminate, and it is argued more explicitly in the prose passages, in which the rejection of Jeremiah (and his word) is depicted as tantamount to the rejection of YHWH (and his).

Chapter 10, beyond the more usual condemnation of the worship of other gods, focuses on these gods' corporeal form, in language redolent of the idol polemics of Second Isaiah, especially Isa. 44. The Aramaic of v. 11 is an exceptional departure from the Hebrew of the rest of the book. It is probably related to the implied international audience of the sentence; Aramaic was the lingua franca of the ancient Near East from the middle of the Assyrian period until the arrival of the Greeks.

Chapters 11–20

Following these often-overlooked chapters is one of the most attended-to sections of the book: the "confessions" or "lamentations" of Jeremiah, which are scattered across chs. 11–20. These are presented as the personal words of the prophet, agonizing over the private doubts and public abuse he has suffered as a result of his commission. Using a lament form familiar from the psalms, this material challenges the justice of YHWH; it contends that the suffering endured by the speaker is unjustified and demands that YHWH remedy the situation. The extent of the fury lodged against the deity is widely recognized as locating these passages among the most extreme variants of the form: the speaker describes himself as "a gentle lamb led to the slaughter" (11:19), reminds YHWH that "on your account I suffer insult" (15:15), and curses the day of his birth (20:14, cf. 15:10). He even accuses YHWH of having taken him into prophetic service against his will, under false pretenses (20:7).

Material in these chapters recalls imagery familiar from the earlier poetic chapters, including the sexual and marital metaphor in which religious infidelity is depicted as adultery and its punishment as sexual humiliation (e.g., "I myself will lift up your skirts over your face," 14:26). It also depicts the people, Jerusalem, and Zion in sexualized female terms, again echoing the language of chs. 2–6: the people are called "virgin daughter" (14:17) and "virgin Israel" (18:13), while the coming devastation will be borne by Jerusalem's women as wives and mothers (15:8-9; 18:21) and inspire agonies like those of a woman in labor (13:21). References to the natural world are again common.

Traditionally these passages have been ascribed to the prophet himself. However, there have also been arguments for seeing them as expressions of communal distress; the laments in the psalms come in both individual and communal forms and at times an apparently singular "I" may be interpreted as a communal voice, or as an individual speaking on behalf of the group. The distinction between an individual and a communal voice in these passages was perhaps more significant in an era in which the words of the historical prophet comprised the ultimate goal of research; in more recent studies the interest in whether these passages are "Jeremianic" or not has given way to an interest in the way that these passages provide a voice for the sufferings of the people as a whole. This will be discussed in further detail in Chapter 5.

These poetic laments are interspersed among a series of prose passages. Like the Temple Sermon in ch. 7, several of these passages (parts of chs. 11, 17, and 19) condemn the population for their disobedience and worship of other gods, using language strongly reminiscent of the book of Deuteronomy. Chapter 11, for example, invokes the exodus from Egypt (vv. 4, 7), declares to the audience that "you will be my people, and I will be your God" (v. 4), and makes repeated references to the ancestors (vv. 5, 7, 10). Other prose sections focus on a kind of prophetic activity called "sign-acts" or "symbolic actions," in which a prophet undertakes activities with symbolic significance. Chapter 13 describes Jeremiah's purchase, wearing, burial, and excavation of a loincloth, with the ruined loincloth shown to be a symbol of the people's ruination; ch. 18 shows the people's fate as like that of a clay pot in its maker's hands, precarious and easily crushed—a theme continued in ch. 19. Perhaps the most striking of these actions is the injunction in ch. 16 that Jeremiah remain unmarried and childless (commentators often refer to this as a command to celibacy, but this is not strictly correct). This prohibition is explicitly linked to the fate of the people, whose spouses and children will die as a result of the judgment wrought by Yhwh for the parents' sins, and represents a key component in the book's presentation of Jeremiah's life, as much as his words, as having prophetic significance. These chapters also contain further reiterations of ch. 7's prohibition against intercession. Often these are accompanied by an explanation that such prayers are already futile: "do not pray for this people, or lift up a cry or prayer on their behalf, for I will not listen" (11:14), "do not pray for the welfare of this people ... I do not hear their cry" (14:11), "though Moses and Samuel stood before me, yet my heart would not turn" (15:1). That the book—at least in its canonical form—does not see all hope as lost is nevertheless apparent from a few passages, such as 17:24 and 18:8-11.

An important function of these prose passages is to identify more explicitly the anonymous enemies of the poetic laments. The laments, like much of the rest of the book's poetry, contain little concrete detail about their context or significance. Much of this is supplied by the surrounding prose material. Of particular note in these chapters are the "false" prophets whose words of hope and salvation are, in contrast to Jeremiah's warnings of judgment and calls to repentance, deemed

responsible for the people's continued wayward behavior.⁴ This focus
on specifically prophetic opposition is a repeated theme in the book—
though it is also only one example of a wider rejection of Jeremiah's
words by the people and their other leaders. Whether these prose
passages preserve accurate historical information about the origins
of the poetic material—for example, whether Jeremiah spoke these
laments in response to his experience at the hands of his relatives from
Anathoth (11:21-23) or his suffering at the hands of Pashur the priest
(20:1-6)—is not agreed.

Chapters 21–23

Chapters 21–23 contain two shorter poetic collections, directed toward
kings and prophets in turn. These are bracketed by and interspersed
with further prose material. We have already caught sight of the
tumultuous relationship between Jeremiah and other prophets in the
prose sections of chs. 11–20; this conflict is reiterated in the second of
these collections, while the first introduces the relationship between
Jeremiah and the kings of Judah, a prominent theme in the latter half of
the book. Jehoahaz (a.k.a. Shallum), Jehoiakim, and Jehoiachin (a.k.a.
Coniah) are addressed by the poetry alongside the Davidic dynasty
as a whole, while Zedekiah is on the receiving end of the divine word
conveyed through the section's opening prose. Zedekiah's appearance
at the beginning highlights one of the puzzling features of the book's
organization: though it sometimes seems to follow a chronological
logic, it does so without a great deal of consistency.

Perhaps significantly, there is no mention here of Josiah, other than
as Jehoiakim's father; although 1:2-3 says that Jeremiah was active in
Josiah's reign, there is no material in the book which is directed to him.
This silence has prompted some scholars to search for passages which
ought to be associated with Josiah, even if only implicitly, while others
have concluded that the heading in ch. 1 is simply wrong, perhaps

---

4. The phrase "false prophets" does not occur in the Hebrew, but
derives from the Septuagint's intermittent identification of such persons as
pseudoprophetes (LXX 6:13; 33:8, 11, 16; 34:7; 36:1, 8). The Hebrew simply calls
them *nevi'im*, "prophets", using the same title which is given to Jeremiah, and
locates the problem in their message, describing it as "lies" or "deceit."

intentionally, in order to associate Jeremiah with the deuteronomistic reforms attributed to Josiah, or to give him a forty-year ministry, akin to that of Moses.

Whatever the explanation of ch. 1, the attention of chs. 21–23 is on the last four kings of Judah prior to its final destruction by the Babylonians in 587: Jehoahaz (22:11-12), Jehoiakim (22:18-19), Jehoiachin (22:24-30), and Zedekiah (21:1-10). The poetic sections of these chapters echo the moral concerns of First Isaiah and Amos, criticizing Judah's kings for their failure to execute justice (21:12), to deliver the oppressed (21:12, 22:3; cf. 23:17), to protect the socially marginal (22:3), and to pay proper wages (22:13-15). This emphasis on royal injustice strikes a different tone than the condemnations of these kings elsewhere in the book, which focus more strongly on their disloyalty to YHWH through the worship of other gods and their failure to trust in YHWH's word as communicated through his prophet.

Also notable is that none of the final four kings of Judah is excused from this roll call. This attracts attention to one of the book's unresolved points of theological contention: which, if either, of Judah's last two kings—Jehoiachin in exile in Babylon or Zedekiah in Judah—retained any legitimacy after the defeat of Jerusalem and which, if either, of the remnant communities—the exiles in Babylonia or the remnant in the land—might represent a legitimate focus of future hope. This section, unlike passages which seem to favor Jehoiachin and his fellow exiles (e.g., chs. 24; 29; 52), describes him (as Coniah) as a humiliated vassal, a personal and political failure (22:28-30). If the future is not with Jehoiachin, however, neither is it with Zedekiah—who will be swept up in the Babylonian devastation of Jerusalem (21:3-7). That some of the rest of those in Judah might yet survive—if they surrender to the Babylonians—is suggested by 21:8-10.

This message to Zedekiah introduces the dominant note of the following chapters: judgment is now inevitable and the only chance of survival is for the people to accept their fate and surrender to the Babylonian king. Nebuchadrezzar has been sent by YHWH to exact divine punishment.[5] As a consequence of his divine commission,

---

5. Most of the book of Jeremiah spells the Babylonian king's name as Nebuchadrezzar, though otherwise this spelling appears only in the book of Ezekiel. Chapters 27–29 use the more common form, Nebuchadnezzar.

surrendering to Nebuchadrezzar's authority is tantamount to surrendering to Yhwh's authority. Over and over again, Jeremiah's words in the subsequent chapters will convey a similar message: surrender to the Babylonians and thereby seize the possibility of survival.

The following complaints about prophets focus on their failure to lead the people properly, paying particular attention to their encouragement of the worship of other gods and their perpetuation of false messages of hope. In the context of the book's other complaints about prophets, this is usually understood to be referring to prophets who were claiming that all would be well, despite the Babylonians' looming presence; there was no need to worry about, let alone submit to, that pesky Babylonian king and his army. The passage is thus connected to the question of the book's vision for the future: is there a possible future in the land, as surrender to Babylonian authority and the implied permission to continue living in Judah suggests, or is future hope only located with the exile community in Babylonia? It is also connected to the book's interest in the importance of the (true) prophetic word and its alignment of the word of the prophet with the word of Yhwh.

Chapter 24

Chapter 24 unequivocally declares that hope resides with the Babylonian remnant, as it recounts a vision of good and bad figs in which the "good figs" are explicitly identified as the exiles in Babylonia. These are the Yahwists on whom the divine blessing will come to rest, complete with an assurance of their eventual return to the land. As already noted, this vision account mirrors the vision account in ch. 1. It also repeats certain key words from that chapter, with the positive elements used to reverse the negative: "I will build them up, and not tear them down; I will plant them, and not pluck them up" (v. 6). Together these features help to frame the contents of the first half of the book. The motif of the new or changed heart appears here for the first time (v. 7); the image of the new covenant to be written on the people's hearts at the time of restoration (31:33; 32:40) is one of the most influential images of the book. The fate of Zedekiah and the remnant in the land evoke the curses of Deut. 28.

Chapter 25[6]

This frame is continued in the first half of ch. 25, which echoes the formulae and chronological notice of 1:2-3. Verses 1–13 recapitulate key themes from the intervening chapters, including the people's failure to attend to the prophetic word (although, given that they have been apparently quite happy to attend to hopeful prophetic messages, the offense would be more correctly described as a failure to attend to the right prophets), the worship of other gods, the punishing foe which will come from the north, and the presentation of Jeremiah as a prophet to the nations.

At this stage the Greek Septuagint text turns to the oracles against the nations, which are located in chs. 46–51 of the Hebrew Masoretic text and in most English Bibles. In addition to being in a different place, the OANs also occur in a different order; perhaps the most notable difference is that the oracles against Babylon, which occur third in the Septuagint (after the oracles against Elam and Egypt), are at the end in the Masoretic text. After the OANs, the Septuagint continues with the material which in the Masoretic text is found between 25:15 and 45:5. The implications of these differences for interpretation will be discussed in more detail below and in Chapter 5.

Chapter 25 concludes with an extended description of the cup of YHWH's wrath, which is proffered first to Judah but then to all the rest of the known world. It is not only Judah which stands under divine judgment, but all people. Though not explicit, the image of eventual universal destruction suggests that the apparent success and power of these other nations while Judah undergoes its punishment is temporary; their power is illusory and they too will eventually fall.

Chapters 26–29

Chapter 26 again recounts Jeremiah speaking judgment in the temple precincts. Unlike ch. 7, however, the underlying issue in this and the following three chapters (chs. 26–29) is the legitimacy of Jeremiah's prophetic word, especially in contrast to the illegitimacy of his contemporaries. The first episode (ch. 26) focuses on the potentially

---

6. From the middle of ch. 25, the Hebrew and Greek chapter numbers diverge. The following uses the Hebrew numbering; to locate the corresponding material in the Greek, consult Appendix A.

lethal consequences of Jeremiah's doom-laden message. Fortunately for Jeremiah, he is spared on precedent: similarly grim words of Micah of Moresheth are cited in support of allowing Jeremiah and his message to stand, in the only explicit citation of another prophet's words in any prophetic book (26:18, cf. Micah 3:12). The closeness of the escape is highlighted by a report about another prophet who was not so lucky. The chapter ends with the book's first reference to the family of Shaphan, an extended family group of some apparent power in Jerusalem. Said to include a number of scribes, including Baruch, the family has been the focus of a number of proposals concerning the book's origins, transmission, and purposes. These will be discussed in further detail in Chapter 5.

Chapters 27–28 contain one of the more memorable episodes in Jeremiah's struggles with other prophets. Still prophesying submission to Babylon, Jeremiah dons a yoke to symbolize Judah and its neighbors' subordinate status—only to have it torn off by another prophet, Hananiah. Set between the first siege of Jerusalem in 597 and the second siege in 587, at stake is the question of how long Babylonian domination is expected to last. Rejecting Hananiah's and other prophets' claims that it will be temporary—that "the vessels of the LORD's house will soon be brought back from Babylon" (27:16) along with the exiled king and part of the population (28:4)— Jeremiah insists that the destruction of 597 was merely a preview of what is yet to come. Similar optimism is said to be circulating among the exiles in Babylon (ch. 29). Jeremiah again disputes the authority of such assertions; not only are the prophets, diviners, and dreamers conveying these words of imminent return condemned, but the exiles are instructed to settle down in Babylon—even to pray for its welfare. These instructions are presented using language which echoes that used to describe life in the Promised Land: the exiles are to build houses, plant gardens and harvest them, marry and reproduce (compare Deut. 6; Josh. 24).

Explicit to varying degrees in these chapters are questions about how true and false prophets are to be distinguished. Thus the death of Hananiah (28:17) is presented as the fulfillment of a divine word against him, pronounced by Jeremiah in judgment for the delivery of false optimism in YHWH's name. The deaths of Ahab and Zedekiah (not to be confused with the kings of the same names) (29:21-23) and the punishment of Shemaiah (29:31-32) in Babylon are likewise pronounced in response to their "lying words" and deceit of the people. The declaration that "as for the prophet who prophesies peace, when the word of that prophet comes true, then it will be known that Yʜwʜ has truly sent the prophet" (28:9) echoes Deut. 18:21: "If what a prophet proclaims in the name of the Lord does not take place or come true, that is a message Yʜwʜ has not spoken." The discernment of true and false prophecy is a particular concern of the book of Jeremiah. Although ultimately the words of judgment which are associated with Jeremiah were perceived have been fulfilled the destruction of Jerusalem in 587, the delay between these word of judgment and their fulfillment would have been seen as problematic for the prophet's legitimacy as a spokesman of Yʜwʜ; this perhaps explains the prominence of this issue in the traditions associated with him.

Of final note regarding ch. 29 is the fact that the narrative presupposes the possibility of written communication between those exiled to Babylon and those remaining in Judah. Whether or not the chapter preserves the actual content of such letters, it refers to at least three, and the final third of the chapter is narratively dependent on the plausibility of such an exchange.

Chapters 30–31

Though reiterating the justice of divine judgment, chs. 30–31 offer a rare positive interlude. This "Little Book of Consolation" promises that the period of judgment will come to an end, the fortunes of Yʜwʜ's people will be restored, and those who are in exile will be returned to the land. Family imagery is prominent in these chapters; one of the most poignant is that of the matriarch Rachel, weeping for her lost children—children who are now to be returned to her and to the homeland, brought back from distant lands (31:15-17). The "pluck up," "break down," "build," "plant" language in 31:28 recalls ch. 1. Here it invokes the authority of Yʜwʜ, both to destroy and to create, in defense of the justice of the divine course of action vis-à-vis the people, rebutting a saying apparently in circulation among the deportees: "The parents have eaten sour grapes, and the children's teeth are set on edge" (31:29, compare Ezek. 18:2). The restored relationship between Yʜwʜ and his people is described as a "new covenant" (31:31), different from and replacing the earlier covenant, now broken, which Yʜwʜ had made with the ancestors on their way out of Egypt. Like 16:14-15 and 23:7-8, this contributes to a strand of thought in the book of Jeremiah which sees, in a future restoration, a significant break with the past. No longer will the narrative of Israel's origins begin with the exodus from Egypt and the covenant with the ancestors, but with a new exodus and a new covenant. This covenant will be written directly on the hearts of the people and give them direct knowledge of Yhwh. This "new covenant" later inspired the name of the Christian scriptures.

Much of this material, like the poetry of chs. 4–6, speaks to its audience as "Israel." As with those chapters of judgment, some have proposed that these chapters of hope were originally directed at the former northern kingdom, before being reapplied to the south. Others, seeing in them an audience already in exile, view them as added to the Jeremiah material at a later date, in order to assuage an unrelenting message of doom. This debate over the place of chs. 30–31 in the book of Jeremiah is part of a wider discussion about whether the prophets of ancient Israel and Judah spoke words of hope, or if they only spoke words of judgment. If a prophet such as Jeremiah could speak only words of judgment, then any words of hope or salvation which appear in the book cannot derive from him but must be later additions. If the prophet was thought to have held out some degree of hope to his audience, however, then such passages might be allowed to stand. There is an element—or at least a strong risk—of circularity here: if Jeremiah is supposed to have spoken only judgment, words of hope are excised from the text as later interpolations and the picture of Jeremiah which results is unremittingly doom-laden. Although the idea that prophets only spoke judgment—and that hopeful elements of the prophetic books were later, ameliorating additions—was dominant through much of the twentieth century, more recent work has suggested that hope, or the possibility of hope, is likely to have comprised at least a part of prophetic efforts to motivate behavioral change. This does not, of course, mean that all expressions of hope in the prophetic books should be attributed to the prophets for whom these books are named.

Chapters 32–39

The following two chapters, chs. 32–33, have sometimes been combined with chs. 30–31 on account of their similarly positive content. In most terms, however, they go more sensibly with the several chapters which follow (chs. 32–39). Thus, for example, they are written in a similar prose style, attend to events in and surrounding the life of the prophet, and are literarily linked forward—the recurring motif of Jeremiah imprisoned, for example—rather than to what has preceded. With the exception of the narrative about the two scrolls in ch. 36, which jumps backwards to the reign of Jehoiakim, this group of chapters are also all set in the reign of Zedekiah, the last king of Judah—and mostly in the last year and a half of Judah's existence, when Nebuchadrezzar has arrived to execute YHWH's judgment as well as to exact his own punishment for Zedekiah's rebellion. The section culminates with the fall of Jerusalem in ch. 39.

Chapter 32 contains a lengthy account of Jeremiah's acquisition of a field in his ancestral home in Anathoth. Only in the final section is this explained as a response to Zedekiah's demand (vv. 3–5) for an explanation of Jeremiah's negativity about the king's fate.[7] Though the act does little to address Zedekiah's personal fears, it is interpreted as a sign that—despite the coming Babylonian conquest—the land will eventually be re-inhabited by a restored people (32:15, 42–43). The heart-covenant imagery which appeared in ch. 31 reappears in 32:38-40 in slightly different terms; here it is the fear of YHWH that will be in the heart(s) of the people. This message of restoration is continued in ch. 33, in which previous announcements of judgment are reworked or further developed in order to articulate a message of hope (compare, for example, vv. 10–11 with 7:34; 16:9; 25:10). The second half—the single longest passage present in the Hebrew text but lacking in the Greek—pays particular attention to the restoration and perpetuity of the Davidic dynasty (vv. 14–26). References to YHWH's covenant with David are interspersed with references to a covenant with the Levites and an emphasis on their role in this vision of a restored future.

After an oracle promising defeat and deportation—but not (violent) death—for Zedekiah, judgment regains the dominant note from ch. 34 onwards. The focus is on the people's disobedience and refusal to attend to the divine command as the principle cause of the coming judgment. This disobedience takes various forms, including reneging on an agreement (a "covenant") to free the slaves of Jerusalem. Of special interest is that this is based on a principle of the seventh-year manumission of slaves, known also from the laws in Leviticus and Deuteronomy. Chapter 35 contrasts this disobedience with the obedience of a group called the Rechabites, who steadfastly obey the command of their ancestral leader, Jonadab son of Rechab, not to consume wine. Nothing is known of this group other than what is said in this chapter.

---

7. Though note that the words concerning Zedekiah's fate in 32:3-5 are not as dire as the fate promised or reported for him elsewhere; compare 21:7; 24:8-19; 27:15; 52:8-11.

Chapter 36 jumps back to the reign of Jehoiakim in order to recount a curious story concerning the production of two scrolls. Both are said to record the words of Jeremiah/Yнwн, though their contents are not specified. The second scroll is created after Jehoiakim has personally destroyed the first; it repeats the words of the first, as well as adding further material. Theologically, the narrative serves to depict the complete failure of the king to hear the divine word. Although some of the royal officials react more positively, even going so far as to protect Jeremiah and Baruch from the king, the king's willful refusal is portrayed as symptomatic of a wider problem. It is also worth noting that, unlike other passages which locate future hope with Jehoiachin and the exiles, the judgment pronounced on his father in vv. 30–31 implicitly precludes this. "He [Jehoiakim] shall have no one to sit upon the throne of David … I will punish him and his offspring and his servants for their iniquity." That is, Jeremiah warns Jehoiakim that no son of his will succeed him on the throne; instead, he and everyone associated with him will suffer for his unwillingness to pay attention to the prophetic word. The dynastic component of this proclamation turns out to be false, because Jehoiachin does become king, even if not for very long. It is one of the passages in the book of Jeremiah which appears to preserve oracular material which did not come to pass. Historically, the chapter has been the focus of intense scrutiny because it has been thought to recount the origins of the Jeremiah tradition at the hand of Baruch and from the mouth of Jeremiah. (See Chapter 5 for a detailed discussion.)

Chapter 37 returns to the reign of Zedekiah. The declaration that Jeremiah is not yet in prison (v. 4) seems to suggest a setting prior to the narratives of chs. 32–35, though the section's logic seems to be driven more by its literary structure than by a sense of clear chronological progression. In any case, at this point of the narrative the final stage of the siege of Jerusalem has not yet begun. The Babylonian army has withdrawn to deal with a challenge from the Egyptian army (v. 5) but, despite this temporary respite, Jeremiah insists that this is not the end of the matter; judgment is still coming and remains inevitable. With this treasonous and demoralizing talk, it is little surprise to see Jeremiah arrested, accused of attempting to leave the city and defect to the Babylonian side. Though he maintains that he was only going out to Anathoth to deal with a property matter (perhaps something related to the account in ch. 32), he is thrown into prison, apparently to remain there until the fall of the city: note the recurring phrase throughout this section that "Jeremiah remained in the court of the guard." Chapter 38 recounts his imprisonment on another pretext. Both of these episodes seem in part designed to emphasize the impotence of Zedekiah. In ch. 37, he is so afraid of his courtiers that he sees Jeremiah in secret; in ch. 38, he surrenders Jeremiah to the same courtiers, de facto condemning him to die in an old well. It takes a foreigner, Ebed-melech the Cushite, to save the prophet from certain death. His intervention earns him one of only two individual oracles of salvation in the book (39:16-18; the other is the oracle for Baruch in ch. 45). Though Zedekiah is shown repeatedly attempting to see Jeremiah and receive the divine word, he is also depicted as unwilling, or unable, to follow his advice. Over and over throughout these chapters, Jeremiah reiterates that judgment is coming at the hand of the Babylonians, advocating voluntary surrender as the best of an already bad situation. Politically, surrender would have rendered the physical survival of the city and its inhabitants more likely; though Zedekiah and the city's other leading figures would probably have been deported, as punishment for their original rebellion, the city itself would probably have been allowed to stand. Many of its people would have been allowed to remain in the city and far fewer would have died in the course of defending it. Theologically, Jeremiah advocates voluntary surrender to Nebuchadrezzar because it represents surrender to the divine will: the Babylonian king is the agent of YHWH's punishment. Acquiescence to the punishment meted out by his hand represents, by extension, acquiescence to YHWH. The failure of the king to heed Jeremiah's warnings culminates in ch. 39 and its depiction of the final fall of the city and the exile of all its inhabitants. Jeremiah, whose imprisonment has been a recurring theme of chs. 32–39, is finally released—not by Zedekiah, but by the Babylonians.

Chapters 40–44

Chapters 40–44 transition to the aftermath of the city's fall. Much of this material is implicitly or explicitly concerned with the locus of the community's future hope: is the future with the Babylonian exiles, with those in the land, both, or neither? In ch. 40, Jeremiah is given the choice of staying in the land or going to Babylon. The words in which the Babylonian captain offers this choice echo Jeremiah's own earlier oracles, explaining Babylonian victory as YHWH's punishment of Judah's sins. His words, at least on the surface, present an open-ended choice. Jeremiah's decision to remain—specifically with Gedaliah, a nonroyal member of the family of Shaphan, whom the Babylonians have appointed governor—suggests that those left in the land represent a legitimate possibility for the future. This contrasts with other passages, such as the vision of good and bad figs in ch. 24, in which the future lies only with the Babylonian exiles.

Although Jeremiah's choice holds out this possibility, its reality is rapidly denied. Almost as soon as the remnant community is constituted around Gedaliah at Mizpah, the peace and prosperity promised by this arrangement ("gather wine and summer fruits and oil…," 40:10) is disrupted by an assassination plot, apparently engineered by the king of Ammon (40:14) but carried out by Ishmael, said to be a member of the royal family (41:1). A civil war (or civil skirmish) ensues. Among the more intriguing elements of the narrative is the appearance of a group of pilgrims from Shechem, Shiloh, and Samaria, apparently intent on going to the temple to lament; though the members of the group are all killed or co-opted, their mention has raised questions about the state of the temple after the fall of the city and the continuation of some form of liturgical activities at the site prior to its reconstruction in the Persian period. Ishmael is eventually seen off but the remaining population, under the leadership of Johanan, is prepared to flee to Egypt—afraid of reprisals from the Babylonians. For most of chs. 40–41, Jeremiah is absent. Then comes the critical moment: the people and their leaders enquire of Jeremiah as to the divine will and are told—at length—that their future is in the land and that there is no future for them in Egypt, but then flee to Egypt anyway (chs. 42–43). Jeremiah and Baruch—who is accused of deliberate treachery in 43:3—are said to be among "all the remnant of Judah" (43:5) who go to Egypt. With the whole of the population now either in Babylon or in Egypt, the opportunity for continued life in the land is extinguished. Given the negativity with which first the decision to go to Egypt (ch. 42) and then the fate of those who do so (ch. 43) are presented, it is often suspected that a major purpose of this section is to deny the legitimacy of any Yahwistic community other than the one in Babylon. The land is empty and the Egyptian remnant is a group of disobedient apostates. The Babylonian deportees are the chosen ones by default.

Chapter 44 is the icing on this cake of condemnation. Not only have the remaining people disobeyed the direct orders of YHWH in going to Egypt, they have failed to heed the lessons of Judah's destruction. Jerusalem was destroyed and its people exiled as punishment for their worship of other gods and their failure to listen to the voice of

Y{\sc hwh} through the prophets, yet these disobedient people in Egypt are once more worshiping other gods. In various permutations, the complete destruction of this remnant is announced by Jeremiah. Though there is little direct reference to the exiles in Babylon, the implication of the condemnation of those who had been left in Judah and have now gone in their entirety to Egypt is plain: there is no one else left to claim the divine blessing.

Chapter 45

Chapter 45 offers a curious sort of appendix: a personal oracle of salvation for Baruch, linked to his work as Jeremiah's scribe and apparently in connection with the episode of the two scrolls in ch. 36. Its location at the end of the Septuagint ordering of the text has been cited in support of the idea that Baruch was himself directly involved in the formation of the written Jeremiah tradition. It offers a sliver of hope—at least one person will survive the preceding wreckage—while at the same time its echo of the verbs from ch. 1 ("break down," "build," "pluck up," "plant") suggests the deliberate creation of a frame for a form of the book involving material between these two chapters, with the use of these same verbs in ch. 25 providing a middle support for this structural arc.

Chapters 46–51

After this the Masoretic text (chs. 46–51) turns to the oracles against the nations, which the Septuagint places in a different order after 25:13. In the Masoretic text the opening oracle against Egypt (ch. 46) provides a link to the preceding narratives, before the following chapters turn to address Philistia (ch. 47), Moab (ch. 48), Ammon, Edom, Damascus, Kedar and Hazor, and Elam (ch. 49) in turn. The Masoretic series culminates with Babylon (chs. 50–51). Throughout these chapters the language is vivid, often echoing the chaos of battle in the way that it piles up images in short, staccato phrases. Implicit in the structure of the section, and often explicit in the oracles, is that the destroyer of the other nations is Babylon, whose own destruction thus forms the final stage of the Masoretic version of the OANs cycle. The consequences of this destruction for Israel and Judah are addressed intermittently, with the destruction of the nations presented as a prerequisite for Israel's and Judah's restoration (46:27-28 and 49:2). Implicitly or explicitly, the nations which have contributed to Israel's sins or been the agents of YHWH's punishment must be cleared away to make room for Israel's restoration. This is especially pronounced in the oracle(s) against Babylon, which has expanded in proportion to the special place of this particular nation in Judah's history and Israel's psyche; note the frequent shifts between poetry and prose and these chapters' composite character, with numerous short passages strung together. Chapter 51 ends with a short account of a scroll of anti-Babylonian oracles, entrusted to Seraiah ben Neriah —apparently Baruch's brother—and taken to Babylon during a visit by Zedekiah (vv. 59–64). Seraiah is instructed to read out the oracles, then to weight them and throw them into the river Euphrates, where their sinking symbolizes the eventual descent of Babylon's power. The chapter concludes with the declaration that "thus far are the words of Jeremiah" (v. 64), echoing the emphasis on the word of Jeremiah and the word of YHWH which appeared first in ch. 1.

Chapter 52

The note of YHWH's ultimate vengeance on Babylon—with its corollary of restoration for Israel—is tempered in the final form of the book by the addition of ch. 52. Widely viewed as an historical appendix tacked onto the end of the Jeremiah traditions and often omitted from considerations of the book's structure and meaning, it closely parallels, though does not quite replicate, the contents of 2 Kings 25. Here, for example, is the only account of a third round of deportations (52:30). The chapter renews the book's emphasis on judgment and exile, ameliorated only by an ambiguous final notice of Jehoiachin's establishment in the Babylonian king's good graces, in which he ultimately dies.

The Two Books of Jeremiah

The preceding has noted the existence of the Jeremiah traditions in not one but two forms: the Hebrew Masoretic tradition, which in translation will be the version familiar to most English readers, and the Greek Septuagint version. Because of the importance of this double tradition for interpretations of the book of Jeremiah, it is worth attending to it in some detail before proceeding further.

The Masoretic text (MT) is so called because of the Jewish scribes and scholars, the Masoretes, who preserved this Hebrew text through the latter half of the first millennium CE. The earliest complete Masoretic manuscripts date to the end of this period and one of these, *Codex Leningradensis*, is the basis for the critical edition of the Hebrew text used by most biblical scholars, *Biblia Hebraica*.[8] The Masoretes produced extensive notes on the text, known as the *masora magna* and the *masora parva*; these notes appear in a form of abbreviated Aramaic in the margins and at the foot of the page in *BHS*. In addition to various statistical information (e.g., "this phrase appears eight times elsewhere, all in Deuteronomy"), they include occasions on which the scribes thought there was a mistake in the text they were copying and wanted to signal to readers that they should read something (usually only slightly) different from what was written in the text. These are referred to as *ketiv* ("what is written") and *qere* ("what is read").[9] The Masoretic text is the basis for most English Bible translations.

The name of the Septuagint (LXX) alludes to the tradition that the original Greek translation of the Pentateuch was produced by a group of seventy (or seventy-two) translators, all of whom miraculously produced the same Greek text. Strictly speaking, "the Septuagint" refers only to the oldest Greek translation of the Pentateuch. However, it is often used more generally to refer to the various ancient Greek translations of the Hebrew Bible, even though these were undertaken by different translators in different places at different times. A close look at the translation habits of different books confirms that the Greek texts which comprise the Septuagint do not represent a systematic translation effort by one (or seventy) translator(s). Rather, these translations were made over the last few centuries BCE, with some texts, including Jeremiah, subsequently revised or retranslated. Though it is impossible to know for sure, it has been suggested that the translation into Greek of sacred Hebrew texts was motivated by the existence of a large number of Greek-speaking Jews, for whom the Hebrew was increasingly inaccessible; by a need for such texts in the classroom or for exegesis; and by a desire to be able to communicate and defend

---

8. In its one volume fourth edition, *Biblia Hebraica* is called *Biblia Hebraica Stuttgartensia*, or *BHS*, and in its still incomplete fifth edition is called *Biblia Hebraica Quinta*, or *BHQ*.

9. For more on the collection of manuscripts which comprise the Masoretic tradition, see Emanuel Tov, *Textual Criticism of the Bible* (3rd ed.; Minneapolis, MN: Fortress, 2012), 24–74.

the Jewish scriptures to a wider Greek-speaking audience. Though originally produced for Greek-speaking Jews, the LXX was later adopted by early Christians, many of whom could not speak or read Hebrew.[10] The principal critical edition of the LXX texts is the so-called Göttingen Septuagint; this is a multivolume, eclectic text, which uses many different manuscripts in order to try to reconstruct the most accurate and most reliable version of the text.[11] The most recent translation of the LXX into English is the *New English Translation of the Septuagint* (NETS).[12]

Unlike most of the biblical books, the MT and the LXX of Jeremiah preserve markedly different versions of the Jeremiah traditions. Many of these differences are substantial enough to be apparent even to the lay reader and even in translation. Perhaps the most obvious is their respective running orders: whereas the LXX has the oracles against the nations in the middle of the book, the MT has them at the end. Another is their notable difference in size: depending on who is counting and how, the MT is between one-eighth and one-seventh longer than the LXX, with about 2700 words of the MT having no counterparts in the LXX. There are also about 100 words of the LXX absent from the MT. In many cases these extra words come from the MT's tendency to fill out titles and descriptions in full: Jeremiah becomes "Jeremiah the prophet," Baruch is "Baruch the scribe," Nebuchadrezzar is "Nebuchadrezzar, the king of Babylon," and so on. There is also some duplication in MT. For example, a passage condemning false promises of peace appears only at 6:14-15 in the LXX, whereas in the MT it appears at 6:14-15 but also at 8:11-12. The MT also has some material which is absent from the LXX entirely; the longest such passage is 33:14-26.

10. For more on the Septuagint's origins, later use, and influence, see Timothy M. Law, *When God Spoke Greek: The Septuagint and the Making of the Christian Bible* (Oxford: Oxford University Press, 2013), and Karen H. Jobes and Moisés Silva, *Invitation to the Septuagint* (Grand Rapids, MI: Baker Academic, 2000); for a book by book introduction, see James Aitken (ed.), *The T&T Clark Companion to the Septuagint* (London: Bloomsbury, 2013).

11. The volume containing the book of Jeremiah is Joseph Ziegler (ed.), *Jeremias—Baruch—Threni—Epistula Jeremiae* (Septuaginta: Vetus Testamentum Graecum 15; Göttingen: Vandenhoeck & Ruprecht, 1957).

12. Albert Pietersma and Benjamin G. Wright (eds.), *A New English Translation of the Septuagint and the Other Greek Translations Traditionally Included under That Title* (Oxford: Oxford University Press, 2007).

Some of these differences are quite obvious and do not require a very close comparison of the two traditions in order to identify. Many of the smaller variations, however, depend on scholars' ability to compare the Hebrew text which is preserved in the MT tradition with the Hebrew text which the LXX was translating. This text is referred to as the Hebrew *Vorlage* ("antecedent") of the LXX of Jeremiah. As this Hebrew *Vorlage* no longer exists, however, scholars working on the relationship between the MT and LXX texts have to use the Greek text to try to recreate it. This process is called retroversion. For these purposes, it is important that the majority of the Greek text of the LXX correlates to the Hebrew text of the MT very closely.[13] This is true of the relationship of the LXX and the MT in their entireties, but especially so of the book of Jeremiah, which is generally recognized as one of the most literal translations of the LXX. This means that scholars are usually able to make a reasonable guess about the Hebrew that the LXX was translating. This reconstructed Hebrew text may then be compared to the Hebrew of the MT and, where the two texts diverge, scholars may enquire as to the reason. Has the Greek translator misunderstood the Hebrew—the result of a rare word or difficult syntax? Might the translator have deliberately changed the text—because the Hebrew syntax didn't work in Greek, for example, or to make sense out of a text which had some sort of error in it already, or for theological reasons? Or does the Greek reflect something different in its Hebrew *Vorlage*—a different Hebrew text than that which has been preserved by MT?

As these questions suggest, there are a variety of ways to explain the differences between the LXX and the MT traditions. Once of the most popular explanations down the centuries was to attribute the shorter LXX text to a translator who was attempting to streamline the text and therefore tended to abridge and eliminate repetition, or to a translator who was sloppy and made frequent mistakes. More recent investigation, however, has largely abandoned this as a general explanation. The overall similarities of the MT and the LXX suggest that—most of the time, at least—the LXX translator was employing a translation technique in which one of the priorities was to have the Greek text reflect its Hebrew

---

13. A sense of this may be gained by comparing the NRSV, which is based on the MT, and NETS, which is based on the LXX but deliberately tries to convey this effect by triangulating its English to the NRSV.

source very closely.[14] The Greek text was not created just to convey the general idea of the Hebrew, or as a paraphrase of it, but was designed to mirror it as nearly as possible. The care taken in the passages which do parallel MT therefore weighs against a picture of a sloppy or free translation and in favor of a translator who rendered his Hebrew text into Greek to the best of his ability. This suggests that the main reason that the LXX and the MT differ is because the LXX's Hebrew *Vorlage* differed from the MT. In other words, the LXX is shorter than the MT not because it has omitted material but because the translator was working from a shorter Hebrew text. In fact, concrete evidence of such a shorter Hebrew text exists in fragments of the book of Jeremiah preserved at Qumran.[15] The Greek text is thus now widely recognized to be a translation of a Hebrew *Vorlage* which was different from MT in a number of important respects, including overall length and structure; it is therefore seen as an important witness to an alternative version of the Jeremiah tradition.[16]

The next question is how these two traditions relate to each other. One possibility is that the shorter LXX (and its *Vorlage*) represent an early stage in the book's development, while the longer MT represents a later stage. In this scenario, the relationship between the

---

14. One of the curious features of the LXX translation of the book of Jeremiah is that chs. 1–28 (MT 1:1–25:13; 46; 50–51) and chs. 29–52 (MT 25:15–45:5; 47; 48; 49; 52, though not in that order) exhibit a number of differences in translation style. The most notable of these differences is the phrasing used to render the so-called messenger formula, "thus says the LORD": chs. 1–28 render it with "this is what the Lord says", whereas chs. 29–52 render it with "thus did the Lord say". There is a long-running discussion over whether these differences reflect the existence of two translators or the existence of a translator and then a reviser whose work, for some unknown reason, is preserved only in the latter half of the book. This is an area in which there is not yet a consensus.

15. Though no complete manuscript of the book of Jeremiah has survived at Qumran, there are also fragments which attest to a longer Hebrew text, very similar to that which appears in the MT. Both versions of the Jeremiah traditions, in other words, appear to have been in use by the Qumran community.

16. See especially J. Gerald Janzen, *Studies in the Text of Jeremiah* (HSM 6; Cambridge, MA: Harvard University Press, 1973); Emanuel Tov, "Exegetical Notes on the Hebrew Vorlage of the LXX of Jeremiah 27 (34)," *ZAW* 91 (1979): 73–93.

texts is viewed as a direct line of descent; it is as though the LXX is a childhood snapshot of the text, which later grew up to become the MT. The second option is that the two texts are like different branches on a tree; they have the same roots and trunk, but at some point they grew apart and developed their own distinctive shapes. In this case, the LXX's *Vorlage* is usually thought to have stopped growing earlier than the text which would go on to become the MT, because it has fewer additions to the common core material than does the MT. Probably both of these models are right to some degree; some features of the LXX text suggest that its *Vorlage* did continue to grow after the MT branched off, but the relatively limited extent of this growth means that it probably looks very similar to an earlier stage of the text which became MT.

One of the consequences of this is that textual criticism of the MT has to use the evidence of the LXX very carefully. *Textual criticism* is an approach concerned with the integrity of the text; it usually focuses on the micro-level of the text, concentrating on words or phrases which make little or no sense in the preserved Hebrew text and attempting to restore them to comprehensibility. Usually one of the major resources for text critical work is the Greek version of the book, insofar as the Greek version is normally understood to be a close translation of a Hebrew text older than that which is preserved by the medieval Masoretic manuscripts. For the book of Jeremiah, however, this usual scenario is challenged by the extent of the differences between the two texts. Scholars wanting to turn to the Greek for insight into a "better" or clearer version of the Hebrew text are obliged to consider whether the comparison is a meaningful one in the particular case at hand. The texts might differ because an aspect of their shared tradition was lost or changed accidentally—the ancient equivalent of a typo—but they might differ because of a deliberate decision to add, subtract, or alter the text by the editor(s) of the MT, by the editor(s) of the LXX *Vorlage*, or by the translator(s) of the LXX. To undo such a change would be to undo a deliberate editorial or translational decision. It is important to distinguish between use of the two texts in attempts to correct transmission errors and their use in attempts to trace the editorial development of the book. As ultimately this requires an interpretation of the nature of the overall relationship between the Hebrew and Greek texts, text critical work on the book of Jeremiah has often blended into discussions of the book's formation.

Depending on the kinds of questions a scholar is trying to answer, his or her use of the MT and LXX texts will also vary. Someone doing *canonical criticism*, for example, will probably make little use of the LXX other than perhaps an occasional text-critical reference, because he or she is primarily interested in the canonical form of the text.[17] Enquiries into the formation of the book through progressive stages of editing (*redaction criticism*), on the other hand, will usually refer to both texts extensively. In this respect, the book of Jeremiah presents an unusual opportunity. Most of the LXX translations of other biblical books are translating from Hebrew texts very similar to MT and therefore offer a window into only the very latest stages of the tradition's development and the earliest stages of its interpretation. The differences between the LXX and MT of the book of Jeremiah, by contrast, are extensive enough to form the basis for discussions about the formation of biblical books over longer periods.

At the same time, these differences have been one of the causes of the especially acute methodological concerns which have characterized the study of the book of Jeremiah over the last few decades. The traditions associated with Isaiah or the traditions associated with Amos have been preserved in an essentially monolithic form—all the versions of the text look, for the most part, extremely similar. Though there will be attempts to distinguish between older and newer levels of these traditions and there may be questions about how old their various parts are, the antiquity of the core material and the historical reality of the prophet are often taken for granted. The traditions associated with Jeremiah, by virtue of their remarkable divergence, demand that scholars pay attention to the fact that this prophetic tradition continued to change for a very long time after the time in which Jeremiah is supposed to have lived and worked. To these challenges and their scholarly response we will turn in the next chapter.

---

17. Although it would be possible to do a canonical reading of the LXX—in which case there would be relatively little attention paid to the MT—this particular approach tends to prefer the MT.

Chapter 3

JEREMIAH IN THE TWENTIETH CENTURY

The next two chapters will be devoted to recent developments in the study of the book of Jeremiah. As these evolved from and in many respects are a direct response to the methods applied in the several previous decades of Jeremiah research, it will be useful first to sketch the outlines of these methods and their objectives.

Origins

The agenda for twentieth-century research on the book of Jeremiah was set, first and foremost, by the work of Bernhard Duhm.[1] Working in an era dominated by *source criticism*, in which a major goal of research was to identify and separate the originally independent sources which had been brought together to form the extant biblical books, Duhm's work did for the book of Jeremiah what Julius Wellhausen had done for the Pentateuch. That is, in the same way that Wellhausen identified four documents (Yahwist, Elohist, Deuteronomic, and Priestly) as the major sources of the Pentateuch, Duhm identified three major sources behind the book of Jeremiah: the prophet's own poetry, a collection of prose biography about the prophet, and a series of prose sermons placed in his mouth.

Duhm identified these three sources by first distinguishing between the book's poetic material and its prose material, then dividing the prose material into two types: biographical material focused on the life of the prophet and a collection of prose sermons attributed to him. While the poetic material is mostly contained in chs. 1–25, the biographical material is mostly concentrated in the second half of the (Hebrew version of the) book (chs. 26–45). The latter includes narratives

---

1. Bernhard Duhm, *Das Buch Jeremia* (Kurzer Hand-Commentar zum Alten Testament; Leipzig: Mohr, 1901).

about Jeremiah's encounters with Zedekiah and Jehoiakim, Jeremiah's various incarcerations at the hands of his political adversaries and his eventual liberation by the Babylonians, and his ultimate departure for Egypt with a group of Judahites afraid of Babylonian reprisals for the death of Gedaliah. Most of the prose sermons, by contrast, are interspersed among the poetic passages in chs. 1–25. These passages are characterized by language and theology closely related to the books of Deuteronomy and Kings. Duhm considered the poetic material the most likely to derive from the historical prophet Jeremiah, on the assumption that prophetic proclamations were most likely to have been poetic in character. However, on the basis of his belief that the prophet only spoke using a specific genre (the lament), he limited the authentic words of Jeremiah to poetry appearing in that form. This poetry, he argued, had been gathered together and supplemented with biographical narratives by Jeremiah's amanuensis and friend, the scribe Baruch. Finally, this collection of the words of and narratives about the prophet Jeremiah was expanded through the addition of the prose sermons.

Duhm's threefold schema was reinforced and further developed by Sigmund Mowinckel.[2] Mowinckel recognized Duhm's three sources, dubbing them sources A (poetry), B (biographical prose), and C (prose sermons). In addition, he identified a fourth source, source D, which was made up of the poetic material in chs. 30–31. He separated this from the rest of the poetry because it exudes a much more positive and hopeful note when compared to the book's dominant message of judgment. The oracles against the nations (chs. 46–51) and the appendix (ch. 52) were excluded from consideration entirely.

A significant influence on the research to follow was the relative value Duhm and Mowinckel placed on each of the three principal types of material they identified. The poetry stemming from the prophet was seen as the most sophisticated, appropriately reflecting the theological sophistication of the prophet. The true message of Jeremiah was contained in this material. Then, though not the words of the prophet himself, the biographical narratives were of value because they offered important insights into Jeremiah's life and into the relationship between his life and his prophetic message. They were thus useful for the correct interpretation of the poetry. The prose sermons, however, were

---

2. Sigmund Mowinckel, *Zur Komposition des Buches Jeremia* (Kristiania: J. Dybwad, 1914).

perceived to be theologically crude, simplifying the complex and vivid theology of the poetry into stereotyped and repetitive prose. Rather than contributing to a theology of Jeremiah, this material only served to obscure it.

Consequences

Three major features of the twentieth-century research agenda may consequently be traced to Duhm's and Mowinckel's work: the origins of the biographical prose, the extent of the deuteronomistic prose, and the quest for the historical Jeremiah. The first and second of these were largely subservient to the third.

Origins of the Biographical Prose

The first line of research concerned the origins of the biographical narratives, or B source. Baruch the scribe has played a central role in these discussions. He makes intermittent appearances in these narratives and, in ch. 36, is involved in the production of two scrolls containing the words of Jeremiah; there is also an entire oracle addressed to him personally (ch. 45), which concludes the LXX version of the book. Given the perceived prominence of Baruch in the narrative, Duhm thought this material was likely to have stemmed from Baruch's own hand. Mowinckel initially held back from making this identification, but later agreed that Baruch was the most likely candidate for the author of these chapters. Many scholars, though by no means all, followed their lead.

In addition to the relevance of the Baruch–Jeremiah model for theories about the involvement of scribes in the formation of prophetic books, an immediate issue at stake in this discussion concerned the dating of the book and its constituent parts. If this biographical material could be traced to an immediate contemporary of Jeremiah—a close friend, even—then the stories contained in them could be taken as accurate, eyewitness accounts of significant events in the life of the prophet. As such, they offered important insights into the context of Jeremiah's mission and message, as well as a reliable biographical and historical framework on which the poetic material could be hung. If these narratives are not attributed to Baruch, however, their reliability vis-à-vis the life of the prophet is less certain; the greater the distance between the man Jeremiah and the text which tells of him, the greater the scope for literary and artistic alterations and the higher the likelihood that they include legendary and apocryphal elements. In a scholarly context prioritizing the words of the prophet himself, the importance of correctly identifying the historical context in which the prophet's words were uttered should not be underestimated. Assessing the likelihood that these narratives stemmed from the hand of Baruch or another of Jeremiah's immediate contemporaries was therefore critical to assessing their credibility and usefulness for the interpretation of Jeremiah's message.

The Extent of the Deuteronomistic Prose

A second major focus of research which arose from Duhm and Mowinckel's work concerned the extent of the prose sermons (the C source) and the process by which this material had been incorporated into the book. Here, too, the primary motivation was a desire correctly to identify the words of the prophet. Though some discussions considered the possibility that the gist of prophetic sermons or other public proclamations by Jeremiah might be preserved in this material, most analyses assumed that it was the work of later editors and sought ultimately to set it to one side, to reveal the words of the prophet as preserved in the poetry . This kind of effort to identify the work of editors ("redactors") is known as *redaction criticism*. During this period relatively little of this work was interested in editorial activity for its own sake. Rather, it had one eye on the formation of the book and the other on the possibility that the editorial process might be reversed, enabling an unobstructed view of the prophet and his message. Only toward the end of the twentieth century did discussions of this material begin to consider its significance in its own right.

A major feature of these discussions concerned the nature and extent of the relationship between this material and theologically and stylistically similar prose material elsewhere. This material is commonly described as "deuteronomistic," referring to its close connection to the book of Deuteronomy. Its main theological features are its stress on the exclusive worship of YHWH and on the concentration of this worship at a single cult site. The language with which these concerns are expressed is often very stereotyped, using phrases such as "go after other gods," "the land which YHWH swore to the ancestors," "YHWH who brought you out of the land of Egypt," and "statutes and ordinances." Just how much variation on these themes and this language that a text may exhibit and still be considered "deuteronomistic" has been an important element in of more recent discussions, but it is most universally recognized in the framework to Deuteronomy and in the books of Kings, where criteria laid out in Deuteronomy are used to evaluate the successes and failures of the kings of Judah and Israel, with their failures in particular blamed for the eventual destruction of these kingdoms.[3] It appears also in the other books of the "Deuteronomistic History" (Joshua, Judges, 1 and 2 Samuel), although less comprehensively, and to a much lesser extent in some of the prophetic books.

As the book of Jeremiah exhibits the most extensive and most comprehensive connections to this material outside the Deuteronomistic History, it has stood at the center of a complex of questions about the existence of a group of deuteronomistic(ally-minded) scribes in the late preexilic, exilic, and postexilic periods and about the involvement of such scribes in the production and transmission of the prophetic books, in addition to questions about deuteronomistic involvement in the transmission of the biblical literature more generally. In the midst of this, the nature and extent of the deuteronomistic features of the Jeremiah tradition have been highly contested. Some have perceived clearly deuteronomistic characteristics in this material and concluded that it points to extensive deuteronomistic involvement in the process of the book's development, even to the point of attributing the book in its entirety to deuteronomistic editors. However, given that the deuteronomistic material in the book of Jeremiah and the deuteronomistic material in Deuteronomy–Kings are theologically and stylistically similar, but not identical, there has also been disagreement about whether the deuteronomistic prose in the book of Jeremiah ought to be differentiated from the rest of the book's prose material on this basis. Some have argued that the "deuteronomistic" prose in the book of Jeremiah is neither more nor less than the ordinary theology, style,

3. As with other biblical books, most scholars understand Deuteronomy to have developed in stages over the course of several centuries. The oldest part is preserved in the center (chs. 12–26), with significant additions over time to the introductory and concluding material (and, to a lesser degree, within the core). Most scholars use the adjective "deuteronomic" to refer to the language, theology, and contents of the core material and the adjective "deuteronomistic" to refer to the language, theology, and contents of the later additions and to related material elsewhere.

and language of the late seventh and sixth centuries; its affinity to other books of the biblical canon is simply a result of their common origins in this period.

Much of the discussion about the deuteronomistic character of the book of Jeremiah is related to whether—or to what extent—the prophet was involved in, supported, or opposed the cult reforms propagated by Josiah. As reported by 2 Kings 22–23, these reforms had a strongly deuteronomistic flavor and were motivated by the discovery of a "book of the law," which is clearly meant to be understood as Deuteronomy. According to the superscription to the book of Jeremiah (1:1-3), the prophet was active during Josiah's reign (640–609) and therefore while he was undertaking these reforms. Given the significance of the reforms as presented in 2 Kings, one might reasonably expect a prophet active at the time to have had an opinion about it—especially when the book bearing that prophet's name contains a number of similar sentiments, such as the condemnation of the worship of gods other than Yнwн. Surprisingly, however, there are no passages in the book which are addressed to Josiah, nor are there any explicit statements revealing the prophet's opinion about Josiah's activities. A wide variety of explanations for this silence have been proposed. Some have assumed that Jeremiah must have said something during and about these events and have therefore sought to identify passages which might be plausibly dated to this period and plausibly understood to refer to Josiah's reforming activities. Others have suggested that Jeremiah's silence indicates either his tacit support or his implied disapproval of these reforms. Still others have interpreted the call narrative (ch. 1) in a way which sees him "called" at birth but not "commissioned" until a later date. This interpretation grants the veracity of the reference to Josiah in 1:2, by dating the prophet's birth to the reign of Josiah, but gets around the apparent absence of any oracles from that period by suggesting that Jeremiah's prophetic activity began only later. Another option is to conclude that the reference to Josiah in 1:2 is incorrect: the result either of a mistake or of a deliberate addition—perhaps in order to link Jeremiah's message to the famous king or to round off Jeremiah's activities into a Mosaic forty years.

Underlying these discussions is an assumption, implicitly or explicitly stated, that the deuteronomistic editors whose stamp is now on the book must have been attracted to the Jeremiah traditions for a reason—and that this reason was that Jeremiah's message was in line with their own theological ideals. In other words, the belief that Jeremiah must have said something about Josiah's reforms is very much rooted in the idea that Josiah's reforms were essentially deuteronomistic in character, that Jeremiah was active during this period, and that the deuteronomistic tradition latched on to the Jeremiah tradition for such extensive development because the prophet had been supportive of Josiah's reform program. However, both the existence and the specifically deuteronomistic character of Josiah's reforms as recounted in 2 Kings have been called into question by recent investigations into the theological and ideological purposes of the account. Furthermore, the details of Jeremiah's life—even basic information about when he lived and worked—are now considered to be much less accessible than they once were. Last but not least, the extent to which the final form of the book has maintained, rather than subverted, the message of an historical seventh–sixth century prophet has been increasingly called into question. Thus, though the relationship of Jeremiah to Josiah's reform was once a major point of contention, it is now largely abandoned as a scholarly line of enquiry.

The Quest for the Historical Jeremiah

Before turning to more recent discussions, one further feature of twentieth-century research on the book must be mentioned: the chase for the original words (*ipsissima verba*) of Jeremiah himself. Combined with and contributing to a widespread prioritization of the lives of the prophets as of the utmost importance for the interpretation of the works bearing their names—a "great men of history" approach dominant in the intellectual world of the nineteenth century— this research sought to reconstruct, as thoroughly as possible, the life and words of the prophet. Commentators sought to narrate the events of Jeremiah's life—from his birth to his disappearance into Egypt—in their correct historical order, rather than in the erratically chronological order that these events appear in the book, and to understand how Jeremiah's message was connected and responded to the various events of his life.

This intense focus on the prophet Jeremiah and his words was closely connected to the two research areas already noted, insofar as investigations into the authorship of the biographical narratives and the extent and origins of the deuteronomistic(?) prose were often undertaken for their potential contribution to investigations of the poetic material attributed to Jeremiah. Discussion of the deuteronomistic material asked whether any of it might reflect the sense of Jeremiah's original teaching or (more usually) sought to correctly identify its extent, in order to extract these later additions and correctly to delimit the parts of the poetry which could be attributed to Jeremiah. Discussion of the biographical material was focused on its usefulness in providing a background of specific episodes in the life of the prophet against which the poetry might be properly understood.

The exceptional level of scholarly attention given to Jeremiah as a person—compared, for example, to the personal lives of Isaiah, Ezekiel, or Amos (let alone Micah, Malachi, or Nahum)—was motivated in part by the driving historical interests of the discipline as a whole, but was also provoked by the contents of the book itself. Unlike any other prophetic book, the book of Jeremiah contains extensive material purporting to recount the life and times of the prophet. We hear of his call (ch. 1) and of his visions (chs. 1; 24); accounts of his preaching in the temple (chs. 7; 26) and of his symbolic acts (chs. 13; 16; 19; 27); stories of his struggles with other prophets (chs. 14; 23; 26–29) and of his encounters with kings (chs. 32–39).

This material also draws a direct link between Jeremiah's life and Jeremiah's message. This is evident in two parallels which the book makes: a parallel between Jeremiah and Yhwh and a parallel between Jeremiah and the people. In the former, the message of Yhwh and the message of Jeremiah are presented as essentially coterminous. The scroll of ch. 36 for example, is described as both the "word of Yhwh" and the "word of Jeremiah". The people's rejection of the prophet and his message is therefore tantamount to (and reflects) their rejection of Yhwh. This is presented most extensively in the laments or "confessions" of chs. 11–20, in which Jeremiah's frustration at the people's stubborn refusal to hear his message arises from and reflects the people's refusal to listen to Yhwh. It is also visible in the narratives in the latter half of the book, in which the final destruction of the king and the people of Judah is correlated to their rejection of Jeremiah and his prophetic word. The agonies of Jeremiah at the hands of the people who reject his message are perhaps also paralleled to the agonies of Yhwh, both full of frustration and grief as a result of the people's rejection. At the same time, the life of Jeremiah is paralleled to that of the people to whom he speaks. Although he is set apart from the people by his relationship with Yhwh and his role as Yhwh's representative, Jeremiah is among the people who experience the siege and fall of Jerusalem, as well as the exile which follows. Whereas the prophet's status as Yhwh's messenger makes him an outsider, his participation in the suffering of the people keeps him within the community and its experience. The focus on Jeremiah's personal suffering thus mirrors the suffering of the people as a whole. The book of Jeremiah, by giving such prominence and significance to the life of Jeremiah, thus does its part to encourage its interpretation in personal terms.

Cracks

Though the source-critical paradigm did substantially dictate the parameters of discussion on the book of Jeremiah for most of a century, challenges began to come with increasing frequency and intensity in the third quarter of the twentieth century. These came from a variety of angles, which collectively served both to blur the boundaries of the materials conventionally designated A, B, and C (and D) and to dissolve the uniformity within each of those blocs. The result of these efforts has been a substantially revised interpretive landscape, in which old assumptions about the existence—let alone the origins or intentions—of a small number of clearly defined sources are no longer a matter of widely held consensus. A few of the more prominent of these are worth note, before we turn to some of the most recent efforts to interpret the book.

Among the most influential of the investigations to challenge the source-critical paradigm was the work of Ernest Nicholson, who argued that the distinction between the B and C sources is not nearly as pronounced as Duhm and Mowinckel had made it out to be and drew attention to the theological and social purpose of both types of material in an exilic context.[4] Both the "biographical" material and the prose sermon material, he suggested, originated among deuteronomistic writers in Babylonia after 587, who sought to reuse and reinterpret a collection of Jeremiah traditions for a community of deportees. These writers were more than merely editors concerned with collecting and preserving the past words of the prophet (which Nicholson did see as substantially preserved in the extant book). Rather, they were interested in the interpretation and application of these words and ideas for their community, developing an inherited tradition to speak to their current circumstances. They therefore ought to be considered creative authors in their own right.

---

4. Ernest Nicholson, *Preaching to the Exiles: A Study of the Prose Tradition in the Book of Jeremiah* (Oxford: Basil Blackwell, 1970).

While Nicholson was busy blurring the distinction between B and C, Helga Weippert took aim at the differentiation between the A material traditionally associated with Jeremiah himself and the C material ascribed to later editors.[5] To do so, she first argued against the characterization of the prose sermons as "deuteronomistic." This style, she contended, was simply the common language and theological outlook of the seventh and sixth centuries. Its similarity to certain material in the book of Deuteronomy and the Deuteronomistic History was a coincidence of their shared historical origins and had no greater significance for the interpretation of Jeremiah. Having weakened the association between the prose sermons and the deuteronomistic literature outside of the book of Jeremiah, Weippert then sought to prove that the prose sermons could derive from Jeremiah. Going beyond other attempts to connect these sermons to Jeremiah (which tended to suggest that they might contain the gist of something the prophet had said but that this had been subsequently been worked over and developed by deuteronomistic editors), Weippert pointed out that many of the thematic interests of the prose sermons occur also in the poetry. Furthermore, much of the prose material exhibits an elevated, artistic style which, while not full-on poetry, is nonetheless somewhat poetic. She dubbed this style *Kunstprosa*, "artistic prose." Although Weippert's decision to associate the prose material more directly with the prophet has not been widely followed, her work substantially softened the strict prose–poetry distinction which provided the foundations of the A-B-C schema.

Challenges to Duhm and Mowinkel's source-critical approach to the book were also under way from the opposite extreme, as a number of works began to question the internal coherence of these blocs of material. Gunther Wanke, for example, argued that the chapters attributed by Duhm and Mowinckel to the B source (chs. 26–45) actually derive from at least three separate sources: 19:1–20:6, which

---

5. Helga Weippert, *Die Prosareden des Jeremiabuches* (BZAW 132; Berlin: de Gruyer, 1973). After a number of decades of continual expansion, the reach of "deuteronomistic" style and theology in the biblical texts has come in for skepticism and heightened scrutiny (see, for example, the essays in Linda S. Schearing and Steven L. McKenzie [eds.], *Those Elusive Deuteronomists: The Phenomenon of Pan-Deuteronomism* [LHBOTS 268; Sheffield: Sheffield Academic, 1999]). The book of Jeremiah, however, remains one of the few texts outside of the Deuteronomistic History in which deuteronomistic phraseology and theology is widely recognized.

is linked to chs. 26–29; chs. 37–44; and ch. 45, which is of a piece with 51:59-64.[6] Wanke suspected that these three sources had been broken up and expanded by other material in the course of their incorporation into the book. Herbert Migsch similarly argued against the original uniformity of these chapters, suggesting that their origins lay in an earlier collection comprising parts of chs. 34, 32, and 37, preceded by chs. 26 and 36 and followed by parts of chs. 38–43.[7] As the enumeration suggests, Migsch argued that original material was quite severely disordered in the process of its inclusion in the present text. Although Migsch's reconstruction contained more of the traditional B material in a single collection than did Wanke's, both excluded significant sections of the text and reordered what remained. This breakdown of the B source is also evident in a number of other studies that appeared around the same time, ranging from Karl-Friedrich Pohlmann's redactional analysis of chs. 37–44 to Christopher Seitz's analysis of a "scribal chronicle" in chs. 37–43.[8]

As theories of the book's formation became ever more complex, the nature and extent of deuteronomistic involvement in this process came more and more to the fore of scholarly interests. In no small part this attention reflected efforts to formulate a semblance of order out of the book's apparent chaos; if the rhyme and reason driving the book's deuteronomistic editors could be discerned, it might not only reveal a logic to the book's structure but also a clearer sense of the origins of the book's contents and their development. Nicholson's argument for a significant contribution by deuteronomistic authors during the exile has already been noted; Winfried Thiel's two-volume redactional analysis took a completely different approach, but reflected a similar focus on the role of deuteronomistic editors in the formation of the book.[9] Undoubtedly the crowning glory of redactional studies of

6. Gunther Wanke, *Untersuchungen zur sogenannten Baruchschrift* (BZAW 122; Berlin: de Gruyter, 1971).

7. Herbert Migsch, *Gottes Wort über das Ende Jerusalems: Eine literar-, stil- und gattungs-kritische Untersuchung des Berichtes Jeremia 34,1-7; 32,2-5; 37,3-38,28* (Österreichische biblische Studien 2; Klosterneuburg: Verlag Österreiches Katholisches Bibelwerk, 1981).

8. Karl-Friedrich Pohlmann, *Studien zum Jeremiabuches: Ein Beitrag zur Frage nach der Entstehung des Jeremiabuches* (FRLANT 118; Göttingen: Vandenhoeck & Ruprecht, 1978); Christopher R. Seitz, *Theology in Conflict: Reactions to the Exile in the Book of Jeremiah* (BZAW 176; Berlin: de Gruyter, 1989).

the deuteronomistic prose in the book of Jeremiah, Thiel's volumes describe in detail the deuteronomistic contribution to the book and argue that these efforts were comprehensive and intentional, resulting in an edition of the book which contained chs. 1–45. The question of intentionality—and the viability of its discernment by modern scholars—would be of critical importance in the next stage of research.

Tipping Point

It was the midst of this fragmenting consensus that three major commentaries appeared in 1986, authored by William Holladay, Robert Carroll, and William McKane.[10] Though wildly diverse in their results, these works have formed the background of and the basis for scholarship of the subsequent three decades.

Holladay's work represented in many ways the culmination of a redaction-critical approach to the book of Jeremiah, which sought as its ultimate aim to identify the original words of an historical prophet, through the identification and removal of progressive layers of editorial additions to these words, and to locate them correctly in their proper historical context.[11] This enabled a contextualized analysis of Jeremiah's oracles and message as well as a discussion of the development of the prophetic message over time, first within the life of

9. Winfried Thiel, *Die deuteronomistische Redaktion von Jeremia 1–25* (WMANT 41; Neukirchen-Vluyn: Neukirchener Verlag, 1973); Winfried Thiel, *Die deuteronomistische Redaktion von Jeremia 26-45: mit einer Gesamtbeurteilung der deuteronomistischen Redaktion des Buches Jeremia* (WMANT 52; Neukirchen-Vluyn: Neukirchener Verlag, 1981).

10. William L. Holladay, *Jeremiah 1: A Commentary on the Book of the Prophet Jeremiah (1–25)* (Hermeneia; Philadelphia, PA: Fortress, 1986), followed in due course by William L. Holladay, *Jeremiah 2: A Commentary on the Book of the Prophet Jeremiah (26–52)* (Hermeneia; Philadelphia, PA: Fortress, 1989); Robert P. Carroll, *Jeremiah: A Commentary* (OTL; London: SCM, 1986); William McKane, *Introduction and Commentary on Jeremiah I–XXV*, vol. 1 of *A Critical and Exegetical Commentary on Jeremiah* (ICC; Edinburgh: T&T Clark, 1986), followed eventually by William McKane, *Commentary on Jeremiah XXVI–LII*, vol. 2 of *A Critical and Exegetical Commentary on Jeremiah* (ICC; Edinburgh: T&T Clark, 1996).

11. Though the commentary reflects some changes in opinion in the interim, the method is the same as that behind William L. Holladay, *Jeremiah: Spokesman out of Time* (Philadelphia, PA: United Church Press, 1974).

the prophet and second (and secondarily) at the hands of the prophet's later compilers and editors. Identification of the secondary material is an objective directly subordinate to the desire to identify the words of Jeremiah. An essential premise of Holladay's reconstruction of the life of Jeremiah and his attribution of the prophetic words to specific events within that life concerns the injunction in Deut. 31:9-13 to recite the deuteronomic law every seven years and the apparent fulfillment of this injunction during the reform of Josiah in 622 (2 Kgs 22–23). A series of subsequent readings of Deuteronomy (in 615, 608, 601, 594, and 587) provided Holladay with a basic chronological structure for Jeremiah's career. In addition to the usual attribution of the poetry to Jeremiah, it allowed Holladay to attribute much of the deuteronomistic prose to him as well, because Jeremiah's activity is seen as arising from and focused on the essentially deuteronomistic reforms of Josiah. Each passage in the book is carefully dated in relation to these recitations. Though his prose is littered with "if" statements, Holladay thus felt himself ultimately able to declare that the book of Jeremiah reflects "a prophetic career which we can come to know in unparalleled detail."[12]

Though in many respects very characteristic of the methods and results deployed up to that time, Holladay's methods came under indirect but immediate fire from the commentaries of Carroll and McKane. Crucial to the turn represented by these works was the emphasis which they placed on the extent and the significance of the involvement of deuteronomistic editors in the formation of the book. Unlike Holladay, neither Carroll nor McKane could view this material as simply the deuteronomistically-flavored prose of Jeremiah. Though they were by no means the first to attend to this material, the extent of the influence which Carroll and McKane saw the deuteronomistic editors as having had on the Jeremiah traditions went well beyond their predecessors.

Carroll, for many, still represents the epitome of extreme opinions regarding the extent of editorial activity in the book of Jeremiah and its consequences for our knowledge of an historical Jeremiah.[13] Although

12. Holladay, *Jeremiah 2*, 35.
13. In addition to the commentary, see Robert P. Carroll, *From Chaos to Covenant: Prophecy in the Book of Jeremiah* (London: SCM, 1981). There he still retains, a priori, the assumption that the core of the poetic oracles is the work of an historical Jeremiah. However, he categorically rejects attempts to attribute the prose material—even its gist—to the prophet and consequently already concludes that scholars' ability to reconstruct Jeremiah's life and thought is extremely limited.

Carroll believed that there may well have been an historical prophet called Jeremiah and that some of the words of this man may yet be preserved in the book which bears his name, the extent of the editorial involvement in the preservation, transmission, and reformulation of this Jeremiah tradition means that it is now impossible to identify those words within the extant text.

This profoundly altered the nature of the investigation which Carroll saw himself as undertaking. Instead of seeking out the words of the historical Jeremiah by peeling back layers of subsequent tradition, Carroll shifted his attention to the use made by these later editors of the Jeremiah traditions they had inherited. Carroll first observed that the poetic material—the material most usually identified as the words of Jeremiah—consistently fails to identify its prophetic speaker as a man called Jeremiah. Read within its own frame of reference, the poetry is anonymous. Its link to a prophet called Jeremiah comes only from its placement alongside and within the book's extensive prose material. Even in the prose, however, the prophet called Jeremiah is not a consistent character; he is full of contradictions. To Carroll this suggested that the "Jeremiah" of the book of Jeremiah is a composite figure and essentially a literary creation of the editors of the book, who used numerous and originally independent traditions—some of which mentioned or may have been traditionally associated with a prophet called Jeremiah, but not necessarily all—to create a prophet who never existed in any historical reality.

Having declared that the Jeremiah of history is so buried under the tradition accrued to his name that he can no longer be found, Carroll focused his attention on the subsequent tradition. His intention was to discern the ways in which deuteronomistic editors used a prophetic tradition to convey their own ideas, especially regarding the culpability of those who worshipped other gods in bringing about the destruction of Jerusalem and the deportation of its inhabitants. In his analysis Carroll deliberately spoke in terms of the "ideological" aspects of the deuteronomistic efforts vis-à-vis the Jeremiah traditions. Though his use of the term approximates what many scholars mean when they refer to the theology of the deuteronomists, Carroll wished to emphasize that these efforts, though expressed in theological terms, were very much caught up in the social and political struggles of the deuteronomists' exilic and postexilic contexts. The point he was trying to make with this language was that the deuteronomistic material was not abstract theology, but theology grounded in and motivated by the deuteronomists' social and political contexts.

It is critical to note—for a significant trend in what follows is a reaction to this point—that Carroll did not see or seek out coherence or consistency in the materials preserved as part of the Jeremiah tradition. To the contrary, he drew attention to instances in which the book of Jeremiah has preserved multiple and not always compatible traditions and perspectives. He suggested, for example, that the book preserves two different views of prophecy: one in which Jeremiah is shown "in conflict with the other prophets, whose false behaviour is held responsible for the disasters befalling the community (e.g., Jer. 23.9-32; 27–29)" and another reflecting "the deuteronomistic ideology of prophecy as the sending of Yahweh's servants throughout history to the nation and their rejection by that stubborn nation (e.g., Jer. 7.25f; 25.4; 26.5)."[14]

Carroll abandoned both the search for an historical Jeremiah and the expectation that the extensive deuteronomistic activity in the book should exhibit a common theological or ideological intention. His interests, however, remained essentially historical; instead of an interest in the words and work of an historical prophet in the late seventh and early sixth centuries, Carroll was interested in the words and work of historical editors and authors in the mid- to late sixth century. History was not abandoned; the focus was merely moved forward by several decades. Nevertheless, the shadow he threw over the scholarly pursuit of an historical Jeremiah cast a pall which persists to the present; though historical work continues to be done on the book, even on the man, it reflects a caution and uncertainty which is directly traceable to Carroll and to McKane.

Though he does not deny the theoretical possibility that we might say something about an historical Jeremiah, McKane despaired of our ability to do so in practice. Like Carroll, he placed considerable emphasis on the book's development by deuteronomistic editors. In direct opposition to the overarching structure and intent discerned

---

14. Carroll, *From Chaos to Covenant*, 26–27. He also discusses this issue in Robert P. Carroll, "Halfway through a Dark Wood: Reflections on Jeremiah 25," in *Troubling Jeremiah*, ed. A. R. Pete Diamond, Kathleen M. O'Connor, and Louis Stulman (JSOTSup 260; Sheffield: Sheffield Academic, 1999), 73–86, where he suggests that the book of Jeremiah's internal logic rules Jeremiah himself a false prophet.

by Thiel, however, McKane argued that there was no comprehensive or purposeful effort involved in this deuteronomistic material. Where Thiel saw order and cohesion, McKane saw dissonance and an untidy aggregation of disparate material. In lieu of an ordered and intentional process of formation in the hands of a small number of conscientious editors, the book of Jeremiah came to its present shape through a long history of growth involving many minor additions. McKane coined the phrase "rolling corpus" to describe this process, envisioning the progressive expansion of individual passages through a series of small accretions. Extant material would inspire a comment or an addition by a later copyist; this in time would prompt its own additions. Thus, for example, a short piece of poetry now preserved in 7:29a attracted the explanation in v. 29b that YHWH has rejected his people, then a speech by YHWH in vv. 30–34 describing their sins. In support of this theory, McKane drew attention to the relationship of the MT to the LXX, arguing that the differences between the two versions reflect a practice of making minor, localized exegetical additions rather than systematic and comprehensive revisions. Such a gradual accumulation of material does not reflect any more sustained or more ordered intention regarding the whole. Especially significant was his argument that material added to the book in the later stages of its development should naturally be expected to resemble material already present at the time of addition. Such continuity makes it very difficult to distinguish multiple and specific layers of the text's development; as a result, the finely tuned differentiations on which the more ambitious redactional studies rely as evidence are difficult if not impossible to sustain. If the prophet's words remain in the text at all—and if they do, they are still mostly likely in the poetry—then they are buried deep, under many strata of editorial deposits. Furthermore, whereas earlier scholars tended to assume that passages derived from the historical Jeremiah unless they had reason to conclude otherwise, McKane concluded that in the majority of cases there is little, if anything, to support one particular historical context—that of an historical Jeremiah or otherwise—over another.

Carroll's and McKane's efforts have profoundly affected subsequent work on the book of Jeremiah. Undoubtedly the most fundamental effect of their work has been to throw into doubt scholars' ability to discern the words or message of an historical Jeremiah. Whereas previous generations had assumed a Jeremianic core and a coherent and deliberate process by which this core was expanded into its present form—even if our ability to discern this process and its coherence might be hindered by later editors' muddling in the text and own ignorance—McKane and Carroll cast these most fundamental assumptions about the nature and origins of the text into doubt. Subsequent attention to and perceptions of the coherence of the book continue to be dictated in large part by these two scholars' assertions that there is little, if any, to be found. Similarly, their suspicion of the viability of historical criticism, at a deep and fundamental level, continues to resonate. Though a deeply felt uncertainty in the legitimacy and prospects of the historical enterprise are characteristic of most of biblical scholarship of the last three decades, the particular acuity with which these doubts were expressed by Carroll and McKane with regard to the book of Jeremiah has profoundly affected subsequent scholars' confidence in pursuing historical work on this book in particular. Yet, though these scholars' damning judgment on the legitimacy of the search for an historical Jeremiah posed a major challenge to the field, it also introduced the space for a wide range of other interpretive methodologies—the most recent of which, as we shall see, have begun to return, cautiously and differently, to historical questions. To these various approaches the next two chapters are devoted.

Chapter 4

CONTEMPORARY APPROACHES

There are a number of axes on which current approaches to the book of Jeremiah may be charted. Perhaps the most obvious, in light of the recent history of the discipline, is the degree of interest a particular approach exhibits in history. Until the mid-1980s, *historical criticism* enjoyed undisputed dominance over other methods of approaching biblical texts, including the book of Jeremiah. Though now less dominant, it remains a significant voice in attempts to understand the book. Alongside historical criticism, however, a number of other approaches are making significant contributions to our understanding of and engagement with this complex text.

Historical Criticism and Its Servants

Historical approaches are driven by a desire to understand the biblical texts by understanding their historical origins and contextualizing their contents in a particular historical epoch. Historical-critical analysis argues that by understanding the historical context of the man and prophet Jeremiah, as well as the historical context of his immediate interpreters, we will be better able to understand and interpret the meaning of the words attributed to him, because we will have a clearer sense of the society from which they arose, the people to which they were directed, and the people by whom they were preserved and further developed. Among the strengths of historical criticism is the recognition of the potential of knowledge about a historical context to improve our understanding of texts and their interpretation, as well as the recognition of the long and complex process by which the texts as we now have them came to be.

At least in theory, this means that it is not only the historical context of the prophet Jeremiah himself but also the historical contexts of his later interpreters which shed light on the extant text. However, historical-critical approaches have often been associated with the quest for the historical Jeremiah, in which the life and words of the prophet were considered the ultimate object of study. In practice, the discovery of the original words of the prophet has often been given greater attention than the elucidation of later editorial interventions. Among historical criticism's weaknesses, therefore, has been a tendency to focus its attention on the oldest form of the text and its earliest historical context, with little attention to spare for later stages of the process or the final form of the text. Frustration with this perceived disregard for the shape and significance of the final form of the text—especially among those for whom the book has an ongoing religious significance—has been a major motivation behind recent gains in canonical and theological approaches. To these we will return in a moment.

Whichever stage of the prophetic tradition is of interest to the historical critic, the texts themselves pose an immediate difficulty: the prophetic books represent not (or not only) the direct speech of the prophets with whom they are associated but—like their nonprophetic counterparts, albeit perhaps more obviously so—a long history of the interpretation and re-interpretation of the traditions associated with these figures. This means that historical criticism is not a simple matter of interpreting the words of the prophet against his particular historical backdrop; it is necessary first to determine which parts of the preserved text should be associated with the prophet and with his particular context and which parts should be associated with other periods of history. A variety of methods have been developed in order to facilitate this process, as means by which the history of the book might be elucidated and its parts correctly associated with specific historical periods.

Source Criticism

As noted in the previous chapter, the principal methodological approach used by Duhm and Mowinckel was *source criticism*. The ultimate goal of this approach was to put all of the various parts of the biblical text into their correct chronological sequence, so that they might be used as the basis for a comprehensive history of the religion of Israel.[1] The deployment of source criticism as a method

1. This wide-angle focus is apparent even in the title of Wellhausen's famous work on the Pentateuch; his investigation into the Pentateuch's sources

for analyzing the book of Jeremiah was a direct consequence of the discipline's historical orientation. As the bold identification of a small number of sources suggests, source criticism is oriented toward the identification of large, homogenous blocs of text. It tends to imagine these sources as discrete documents that led independent textual lives prior to being incorporated into the text now in hand. This mind-set is reflected in the common name for Wellhausen's source theory of the Pentateuch, which is widely known as "the Documentary Hypothesis" because it envisions each of its four sources as originally independent documents. As far as the book of Jeremiah is concerned, the A material was one source, the B material was a second, and the C material was a third. These three separate sources were put together by an editor to form the extant book of Jeremiah.

As some of the discussion in Chapter 3 has already implied, however, this kind of broad-brush approach only gets the scholar interested in the origins and development of the book—either for its own sake or for the sake of identifying the original words of the prophet Jeremiah—so far. Part of the problem is that source criticism is not a particularly delicate analytical tool; it is focused on broad differences, such as

---

is merely a *Prolegomena to the History of Israel* (transl. J. Sutherland Black and Allan Menzies [Gloucester, MA: Peter Smith, 1973], from *Prolegomena zur Geschichte Israels* [2nd ed.; Berlin: G. Dreimer, 1883]). This interest in narrating a complete history of Israelite religion was driven by the belief that the "ethical monotheism" of the eighth-century prophets marked the height of Israelite religion, which over the following centuries had deteriorated into a petty legalism dominated by priests. Both anti-Semitism and anti-Catholicism, whether conscious or simply absorbed from the dominant cultural norms of nineteenth-century northern Europe, played a part in the creation of this narrative. While many of these scholars' observations about the characteristics of biblical texts—differences in language, theology, outlook—represent foundational work, it is important to remember the assumptions underlying their evaluation of this material. On the various cultural influences on Jeremiah research in the nineteenth and twentieth centuries, see Joe Henderson, "Duhm and Skinner's Invention of Jeremiah," in *Jeremiah Invented: Constructions and Deconstructions of Jeremiah*, ed. Else K. Holt and Carolyn J. Sharp (LHBOTS 595; London: Bloomsbury, 2015), 1–15, and Mary C. Callaway, "Seduced by Method: History and Jeremiah 20," in *Jeremiah Invented: Constructions and Deconstructions of Jeremiah*, ed. Else K. Holt and Carolyn J. Sharp (LHBOTS 595; London: Bloomsbury, 2015), 16–33.

poetry and prose, and is limited in practical terms by its assumptions about originally independent documents. In the case of the book of Jeremiah, for example, the appearance of the deuteronomistic prose sermons in the midst of the poetry in chs. 1–25 is hard to explain if the poetry and the prose originated in two separate documents, as it implies that two whole and self-sufficient sources were broken up for parts. Furthermore, though a large percentage of the deuteronomistic material does appear in long sermonic prose passages such as ch. 7, a significant amount of this material appears in short bursts, interspersed with the poetry. The extent of the interweaving of the poetry and prose in these chapters has prompted significant arguments about which passages belong to which source, or whether it is right to think of these passages as belonging to "sources" at all. With such small fragments scattered throughout the chapters, it begins to look as though at least some of this material might have been composed with its present location in mind, rather than broken out of an extant text. In other words, much of the C material suggests editorial activity within the text, rather than a preexisting source incorporated from outside of it.

Form Criticism

Another weakness of source criticism is that it fails to pay much attention to how its source materials came to exist in written form. Certain features of the prophetic literature have led scholars to the conclusion that the characteristic mode of prophetic expression in the ancient world was oral, short and poetic. This is suggested by the dominance of poetry in the prophetic material overall, by narrative indications that prophetic oracles were delivered primarily in public contexts, and by the brevity of other ancient Near Eastern prophetic texts. While there are some possible exceptions—the lengthy prose sections in the book of Ezekiel are one example—most scholarship on the prophets and the prophetic books has accepted the origins of this material in short, poetic proclamations as a basic premise. However, to assume that the prophetic word was originally oral entails the recognition of some sort of gap between the prophet's initial proclamation and the eventual written form of his or her words. This raises significant questions about the relationship between speech and text, especially with regard to the length of time thought to have elapsed between the two events. Were prophetic proclamations written down relatively soon after their pronouncement, either by the prophet or by a close associate? Or did they circulate orally for some period of time, only to be written down later? The interpreter must reckon with the fallibilities of human memory if the period of oral transmission is anything more than a few moments. The significance of this period is difficult to underestimate—especially if the object of investigation is the identification and explication of the unadulterated, original words of the prophet.[2]

Form criticism was designed to elucidate the relationship between the words of the prophet as originally uttered and the words of the prophet as preserved on the page. Underlying this approach was the idea that the oral speech of the prophets took the form of a relatively small number of established speech patterns or forms, such as laments, disputations, and oracles of judgment. Form criticism assumes that these textual forms are closely related to and reflective of earlier oral forms and that these oral forms originated in particular historical contexts (which are referred to as their *Sitz im Leben*, "setting in life"). Laments, for example, could be best understood as a form used in the temple (hence there are many such laments in the Psalms), while disputations had their origins in the law court. Form criticism has a particular interest in how the extant written words reflect and reveal these presumed oral predecessors.

Underlying this method are two important assumptions: first, that the prophet's spoken utterances would have followed certain fixed patterns of speech and, second, that these fixed patterns may still be discerned in the written form of the text. Where an individual example does something different than what is expected on the basis of the pattern, scholars ask why this has occurred. One possibility is that the change was made for a specific rhetorical effect—as, for example, when Deutero-Isaiah uses a legal disputation which expects a response from

2. One suggestion has been to observe that though many of the short poetic passages seem to jump from topic to topic, many of these jumps involve catchwords, in which a word (or more than one word) at the end of one oracle is repeated at the beginning of the next. In ch. 2, for example, a verb which appears in v. 2 (Hebrew *hlk*, translated as "followed" in NRSV) appears three more times in vv. 4–8 (the second "went" in v. 5, "led" in v. 6, "went" in v. 8) and three more times in vv. 14–25. This kind of repetition, it has been suggested, resulted from the way in which these oracles were recalled in the oral stage of transmission: a key word or words at the end of one oracle provided a reminder of key words occurring in the next.

the defendant, but then omits this response because the "defendants" in question are gods other than Y<small>HWH</small>. The point Deutero-Isaiah is trying to make is that these other gods are powerless to speak, to hear, or to act on behalf of their worshippers; the deviation from the standard form is a device which emphasizes this point. In the case of the book of Jeremiah, form criticism has been particularly prominent in analyses of the so-called "laments" or "confessions" which appear in chs. 11–20, because of the similarities between this material and laments in the Psalms. As determined especially from the Psalms, the standard version of this form is thought to include an invocation of the deity, a complaint (a reference to the speech or offenses of the speaker's enemies), a declaration or affirmation of the speaker's innocence, and a petition (a request for vengeance or appeal for justice). The recognition of this common pattern helps to locate the laments theologically in ideas about divine justice, as well as to provide a comparative frame of reference for the vehemence with which the speaker calls down judgment on his enemies.

A comparison of the laments in Jeremiah and the laments of the Psalms, however, draws attention to the variability with which the various individual instantiations of the lament form adhere to the abstracted form constructed from the collection as a whole. For example, some of the Jeremiah laments are followed by or include a divine response, an element which never appears in the Psalms. One interpretation of this difference is to see it as a reflection of a slightly different *Sitz im Leben*—the personal lamentations of an individual prophet in direct communication with the deity, as compared to the more generalized and mediated context of the Psalms laments. Another possibility, however, is to see such differences as evidence of editorial tampering with an originally pristine form. The divine responses, in such an interpretation, might represent an editorial attempt to soften the audacious fury of the lamenting prophet. This use of form criticism might also occur on a more detailed level: by focusing on the characteristic meter of the laments (a 3–2 pattern called the *qinah*), for example, Duhm argued that no material which deviated from this pattern could be attributed to Jeremiah. On this basis, he concluded that only 280 verses could be attributed to the prophet.

Underlying his argument was the assumption that Jeremiah's oracles invariably took the form of the *qinah* and that the *qinah* invariably used the 3–2 pattern. Unfortunately, form criticism has suffered from doubts regarding the extent to which we may confidently delineate the precise outlines and contents of specific ancient speech patterns. Particularly problematic are assumptions about the rigidity of particular forms and the extent to which deviation from the established norms should be interpreted as later editorial alteration, as opposed to deliberate alterations on the part of the speaker (or writer) in order to make a rhetorical point. More recent discussions of the formal aspects of the book of Jeremiah have thus tended to exhibit less of an interest in the minute details of a form and its variants, in favor of an interest in the way in which the use of conventional forms may respond to a particular need, such as—in the case of the lament—providing space for the articulation of acute distress and a means of processing the traumatic experiences which gave rise to that distress.

Redaction Criticism

In the identification of variations between the assumed forms of prophetic speech and the actual forms of prophetic text—the gap between theory and practice—form criticism intersects most significantly with the objectives and application of *redaction criticism*. If scholars could identify the characteristic forms of prophetic expression, this could be used to identify where and to what extent these forms had been supplemented or altered by later editors. This, in turn, could be used to reveal the original words of the prophet. Redaction criticism is undoubtedly the most prominent method deployed in the service of the historical project. As the name suggests, this approach is concerned with the process by which the text was progressively redacted—that is, edited—into its canonical form. It begins from the belief that the text shows signs of having undergone such a process: an abrupt change of subject in the middle of a passage, inconsistencies in the use of specific words, apparently incompatible theological viewpoints within the same book, and so on. These rough edges reveal the points in the text where later editors added, deleted, or changed their existing material for some particular purpose. By finding patterns in these changes, it becomes possible to discover the progressive layers of editorial activity which, one on top of the other, eventually produced the book in its current form.

The idea that editors or redactors have contributed to the shape of the book of Jeremiah as it now stands is based in part on evidence about the formation of the biblical books more generally, but also on evidence from within the book of Jeremiah. There is, for example, a general movement of the book from material exhorting its audience to repentance (chs. 2–6) to material which presupposes the inevitability of judgment (chs. 8–10) and material which is therefore concerned with the respective fates of those deported, those left in the land, and those who fled to Egypt (chs. 24; 26–45). This suggests a more thoughtful arrangement and a greater sequential logic than a mere hodgepodge of texts strung together at random. The book would convey quite a different message if chs. 2–6 appeared at the end of the book rather than the beginning; the degree of logic with which it proceeds suggests some degree of editorial intention in its arrangement. Similarly, the twofold location of the oracles against the nations—after ch. 45 in the Hebrew but halfway through ch. 25 in the Greek—is a very prominent reminder that the shape of the book could be altered to suit an editor's interpretation of its overall purpose until quite a late stage. The structure of the book of Jeremiah—as baffling as at times it may seem—appears to have been shaped in some way by editorial interventions, beginning when the Jeremiah traditions were put into written form for the first time and continuing over many subsequent revisions.

This raises questions about how these editorial activities might be identified and how they might shed light on the intentions of the editors who preserved and transmitted the book.[3] There is also a working assumption—visible in the perceived relationship of the *Vorlage* of the LXX to the MT—that editors were more likely to add material than delete it. Although it is likely that some editorial activity involved the removal of words and verses, or even entire passages, evidence of such deletion is by its very nature obscure. Much easier to identify are redactional activities involving the addition of new material to the text—to explain, nuance, or even alter the message of a particular verse or passage. Ironically, this is easiest to identify when it is done somewhat clumsily—when there is a sudden, incongruous change or modification in theology or writing style. Where an editor has been particularly skillful, the seams of the

---

3. Like the historical criticism which is its methodological master, a redaction-critical approach is theoretically interested in all stages of this process. In practice, however, it has often prioritized the earliest layer(s) of the text, with later layers identified in order to be peeled away so that the oldest, "original" form of the book might be revealed. Only in the final third of the twentieth century did the significance and sophistication of these editorial activities begin to be considered in their own right.

text may now be invisible. In ch. 5, for example, a long section of poetry suddenly jolts in v. 18 into prose, stays in prose for two verses, then reverts to the poetry in v. 20. The poetry up to v. 17 describes the complete destruction of Israel; everything will perish, including its children, its livestock, its agricultural produce, and its cities. This categorical proclamation of destruction is suddenly tempered by v. 18, which jumps in with the promise that "even in those days, says YHWH, I will not make a full end." This seems to speak from the perspective of one who has already lived through this destruction and therefore knows that there are some survivors. The change in message, combined with the change from poetry to prose, leads most scholars to understand vv. 18–19 as later commentary on an earlier poetic text, explaining that, even though the earlier words had appeared to condemn the whole of Israel, a remnant was ultimately permitted to survive. It also speaks from a theological perspective typical of deuteronomistic texts, in which blame for the disaster is placed on the shoulders of the people for having persistently worshipped other gods. By distinguishing between an oracle and its subsequent interpretation, the chronological antennae of redaction criticism begin to address both the general challenge of the formation and shape of the book as well as the specific challenge posed by the interweaving of the deuteronomistic prose material and the poetry, by interpreting the deuteronomistic material as prose insertions designed to interpret the poetry for later generations.

As a general principle, such alterations and additions have a thrust of contemporaneity; each time the scroll containing "the words of Jeremiah" was copied out—when the scroll had worn out or someone needed a copy at another location—the scribe doing the copying had the opportunity to clarify, for his contemporary audience, the ongoing significance of the words of a long-dead prophet.[4] Such passages have attracted attention from scholars trying to identify the original words of the prophet—digging through these various accretions in order to identify what lies beneath—as well as from scholars interested in understanding the editorial processes of the book's formation,

---

4. How long scribes were able to incorporate significant editorial interventions in the process of copying out manuscripts is not wholly clear. Indeed, the book of Jeremiah is a particularly prominent witness in this discussion, as its two substantially different versions reflect the ability of scribes to move an entire section of text—and to make significant alterations to the text in order to do so—even at a stage when the substantial majority of the

observing the thematic or theological interests of the text as clues that this passage or that verse was added to address the concerns of a particular audience at a particular time.

In its more extreme manifestations, however, redaction criticism raises the specter of interpretive overconfidence. Dissections down to the verse, half verse, or even word begin to raise questions about the certainty with which such dissections and reconstructions may be undertaken, especially when the resulting conclusions find little agreement. The confidence with which we may locate the layers thus determined in particular historical circumstances—these words are from Jeremiah, these passages from Baruch, this explanation from an editor working in Babylon early in the exile, that phrase from a later editor in Persian Yehud, and so on—comes in for similar doubt. While the different forms and interests of various parts of the book of Jeremiah are all but universally agreed to reflect its lengthy and complex process of development, opinions diverge on the nature of this process and how deep into its details we may reasonably expect to be able to go given the information currently available.

The End of History?

Uncertainty about in the ultimately historical goals of source, form, and redaction-critical approaches with regard to the book of Jeremiah reflects a widespread loss of confidence in historical investigations among biblical scholars working at the end of the twentieth century, as the relationship between the biblical texts and the historical events they purport to relate were recognized to be far more complicated than had previously been appreciated. One contributor to this realization was the increasing availability of other sources from the ancient world.

book was nearing its final form. The fragments of Jeremiah found at Qumran also suggest that the existence of manuscript variants, even within a single community, could still be tolerated at that time (compare also the extensive "rewritten Bible" literature, found alongside and in dialogue with the more familiar canonical—or what would eventually become canonical—forms of books such as Genesis). Eventually this process shifted outside the text, instead of taking place within it—into the Jewish *pesher* and Christian commentary traditions, the Mishnah, the New Testament, and beyond, all the way to the efforts of Jewish and Christian leaders to explain to their communities the significance of these texts today.

Though sometimes these confirmed the occurrence of specific events (Sennacherib's annals report on his campaign against Judah in 701 BCE, for instance) or the existence of named individuals (Judah's king, Hezekiah, who appears in those reports), these other sources also led to the realization that the biblical accounts were not engaged in writing what modern academics would recognize as "history," in the sense of a critical account of events and their terrestrial causes.

The consequences of these observations for the discipline as a whole have been substantial and, in the context of the book of Jeremiah, they have contributed to a growing uncertainty about studying the book in historical terms. Much of the work on the book of Jeremiah which has occurred since these wider developments accordingly locates itself on a spectrum relative to the author's level of confidence in his or her ability to locate the text in an appropriate and accurate historical context. Though there remain scholars working on the book of Jeremiah from an historical-critical perspective, they tend overall to be much less confident in their conclusions than their predecessors. Where Holladay felt able to assign each individual oracle and sermon to a specific time in Jeremiah's life or to a specific event in the community life and history of Judah, most current work will make such claims only cautiously, if it makes them at all. Historical suggestions tend rather to be ventured with broad brush strokes—this passage seems to reflect the circumstances of a group of exiles in Babylon, for example, while that passage seems to reflect the concerns of the early postexilic community in Yehud.

Beyond History

One positive result of the weakening of the hitherto unquestioned dominance of historical approaches to the biblical texts is that it has opened up significant and productive space for other approaches to the text. Though historically oriented discussion of the book of Jeremiah is by no means dead, much of the work on the book done in the last three decades reflects the rise of these other approaches.

Structure and Meaning

One of the first harbingers of such changes was an increase in the attention paid to the text as a literary entity. Literary approaches operate on a sliding scale between those which are primarily interested in the text's mechanics—how they create meaning—and those which are primarily interested in the meaning thus created.

Rhetorical criticism, for example, tends to focus on the mechanical side of this equation. Drawing on the results of form criticism, it may pay attention to the occasions on which a particular passage deviates from the standard form in the service of making a rhetorical point. It is especially characterized, however, by an interest in structural elements, such as *inclusio* (the repetition at the end of words or a theme introduced at the beginning) and *chiasmus* (in which elements in the first half of the work approach a central climax and the same or similar elements are repeated, in reverse order, en route to the conclusion). It will also attend to devices such as rhetorical questions and the repetition of key words or phrases. It may also notice the way in which a text uses metaphors and similes in order to achieve a particular rhetorical effect. In certain manifestations this too is historically oriented—a consideration of the means by which a historical Jeremiah used his rhetorical skills to persuade his audience of his message (albeit apparently without a great deal of success), for example, but this is not of itself a necessary element of the approach. Rather its emphasis is on the technical mechanics of the text. This may be undertaken on a very small scale, within the confines of a few verses or a chapter, or it may be undertaken on a much larger scale, considering how the design of a book in its entirety constructs and/or contributes to its overall meaning.

At this wide-angle end of rhetorical criticism, this interest may merge into approaches known as *canonical criticism* and *final form criticism*. In both of these the goal is to understand the meaning of the book as a whole. Whereas final form criticism tends to focus on the interpretation of the book at hand, canonical criticism may also refer more widely to the—usually Christian—canon in which the book is found. In Jewish scholarship, this type of approach may be referred to as *holistic*. These investigations may focus on the way in which the structure of the book as a whole contributes to its meaning or message, or they may place a greater emphasis on the meaning thus created. Within the context of the book of Jeremiah, such readings tend to integrate these two elements—the mechanics, on the one hand, and their results, on the other—more than most. This is because the differences between the Hebrew and Greek texts provide an unusual opportunity to examine the way that mechanics contribute to the creation of meaning. In the case of the LXX, for example, the location of the OANs in the middle of the book is often seen as contributing to an overall structure which presents judgment on the nations as a prerequisite to salvation or restoration for Israel. The location of the OANs at the end of the book in MT, by contrast, combined with their rearrangement so that they culminate with the oracle(s) against Babylon, places a much greater significance on the role of Babylon in Judah's judgment. In other words, the different structural decisions made by the editors of MT and LXX make a significant contribution to these books' distinctive theological emphases. The two versions highlight the way in which form and structure can contribute to meaning and accordingly give structural mechanics a significant role in form and canonical critical discussions of the book.

Though not strictly requisite, canonical approaches also tend to be more explicitly theological in orientation than many of the other approaches used in the interpretation of the book. This push toward *theological interpretation* may be especially traced to the frustration of many late twentieth-century interpreters with the fragmentation of the book brought about by redaction-critical approaches. In some cases, the fragmentation of the book in pursuit of the historical Jeremiah had resulted in commentaries on a substantially rearranged or amended text. This was perceived to be achieved at the cost of any attempt to make sense of the final shape of the text, even though this final form was what had been received, preserved, and used by Jewish and Christian communities. As the resulting text little resembled the book of Jeremiah used among contemporary faith communities, the rewards of these approaches were felt to have come at the cost of results which might be of use for these communities. Especially in light of the challenges which redaction criticism and related historical approaches were facing by the last third of the twentieth century, many scholars felt that the gains of these approaches were not sufficient to warrant their abuse of the canonical text.

Assumptions

Another major change in approaches to the book of Jeremiah has been the development of approaches explicitly intending to identify and to question the assumptions made by the authors, editors, and readers of the text. One of the first and most prominent of these was *feminist criticism*. Often employing the tools of rhetorical criticism, feminist approaches attend specifically to the way in which the construction of the book's message depends on certain social assumptions about the role and function of women. Particularly close attention has been paid to the poetic material in chs. 2–6 from this perspective, because of the explicit usage there of sexual and marital metaphors which depict a female Israel in a subordinate position to a male Yhwh. The violence which these metaphors describe male Yhwh inflicting on female Israel poses significant theological questions about the character of the God thus depicted, as well as major pastoral issues for contemporary communities dealing with real violence against women. Feminist criticism asks about the assumptions which the text makes about women and about how these assumptions relate to real women, as well as to "women" as imagined by the text's (presumed) male authors. With regard to the former, feminist approaches tend to be especially attentive to the effects of these texts on their modern audiences and the way in which they underline or undermine the patriarchal structures of contemporary societies.

Although the analysis of biblical texts from a feminist perspective is now a well-established methodological voice within the discipline, the significance of its introduction into the guild should not be underestimated. Feminist analyses of the book of Jeremiah (and other biblical texts) were among the first attempts to deliberately and explicitly question the underlying assumptions of these texts—to approach the texts with a "hermeneutic of suspicion," which sought to expose and examine the patriarchal foundations on which the biblical edifice had been built, then perpetuated by the subsequent two millennia of interpretation. It thus opened the door to a wide range of other approaches seeking to identify and interrogate the implied or assumed ideologies of the text.[5] As an approach, *ideological criticism*

---

5. The word "ideology" may be used in one of two ways. The first reflects its use in the Marxist tradition to refer to a system of beliefs which obscures reality and prevents a person from seeing the true nature of things; it is in this sense that it tends to be used in everyday parlance in North America especially. Thus, a politician might be said to have made an "ideological" decision, implying that his or her beliefs obscured the real nature of the situation and prevented him or her from taking a logical decision based on the facts. A less pejorative use of "ideology" uses it to talk about a person's overall worldview—a system of ideas and beliefs according to which he or she makes sense of the world and its workings (this meaning is associated especially with the work of the sociologist Clifford Geertz). It is in this sense that it is usually (albeit not always) used in scholarly discourse: as a way of referring to the overall system of beliefs by which a person's relationship with the world is organized. It is in this sense that it overlaps with "theology," insofar as a theological system is also a system of ideas and beliefs which organizes the world and a person's place in it.

emphasizes the social location of the text's theological assumptions and interests. It attends especially to the construction and assertion of power within and by the text, as well as highlighting the ways in which the text may—either inadvertently or deliberately—undermine itself in this respect. These concerns have been taken up by various methods, including several which may be loosely gathered under the umbrella of *postmodern approaches*, which emphasize the instability of meaning within the text, and by a number of approaches attending to the power structures within and behind the text.[6] Among the most prominent of these at present are approaches working from the perspective of *gender* or *queer theory* and *postcolonial criticism*. Attending to power relations from a specifically political perspective, postcolonial criticism suggests that the relationship between the colonized and the colonizer—which has been especially well theorized with respect to modern European and global history—offers a productive analogy for understanding the relationship between the population of Judah and politically dominant Babylonia. It draws on the insights of twentieth and twenty-first century postcolonial theorists to examine the way in which the relationship between Judah and Babylonia is depicted in the book of Jeremiah, with particular attention to the way in which the book both constructs and deconstructs the power dynamics of this relationship. Gender or queer theory builds on the work of feminist criticism to interrogate the text's use (and abuse) of binary gender categories, often with particular attention to the way in which the text inadvertently(?) undermines those categories. Thus, for example, a gendered critique of the depiction of Israel as the wayward wife of YHWH might observe that it plays on socially situated tropes about the sexually promiscuous woman while, at the same time, undermining Israel's masculinity by placing it in the role of the female.

These approaches to the text are often motivated by the significant gap between the ancient origins of the text and the modern world in which its contemporary readers reside. Characteristic of all of them is an interest in and willingness to question the received interpretation(s) of a given text. In light of the more or less concurrent development of several explicitly theological approaches to the text, such as canonical criticism, it is worth noting that these ideological approaches are not anti-theological. To the contrary, they are frequently interested in complicating, and thereby

6. As many of these feature in the most recent work on the book of Jeremiah, they will be discussed in greater detail in Chapter 5.

enhancing, nterpreters' understanding of the theological interests
and theological significance of the text.

Author and Audience

Another way of thinking about approaches to the study of the book
of Jeremiah is to locate their users relative to their ultimate interests
vis-à-vis the text. Are they ultimately interested in authorship—that
is, in what lies behind the text? Or are they interested in audience
—what lies in front of the text? Scholars interested in authorship are
ultimately asking, "How did we get this text?" This may, in its most
traditional guise, take the form of a search for the historical man
Jeremiah, working from the implicit or explicit assumption that some
core of the current book may be traced to such a person and attempting
to determine the extent and content of the material which might be
attributed to him. Questions of authorship may also focus on later
stages of the book's development—asking after process, purpose, and
context at various stages of its formation. One of the most prominent
such stages, as we have seen, concerns the book's relationship to
deuteronomistic language and theology and to other biblical texts
exhibiting similar language and theology, especially Deuteronomy
and Kings. Investigations of the deuteronomistic features of the book
of Jeremiah notice the unusual extent of such features compared to
other prophetic books and are interested in why someone (or multiple
someones) with deuteronomistic interests developed the Jeremiah
tradition so extensively. He or she might also look for signs in the
text of how these deuteronomistic interests have (re)shaped older
traditions, changing the form of the book and the message it conveys.
Scholarship interested in the book's formation and authorship may also
pay particular attention to the different forms which the book takes in
its Greek and its Hebrew versions, asking why, as well as how, two such
divergent forms of the Jeremiah tradition developed and then survived.

    Scholars whose interests are broadly authorial are thus interested in
understanding how the text developed into its current form and who
might have been responsible for different stages in this process. This
is often closely related to an interest in why the text developed in this
way. This might be mechanical and small scale—the text looks like this
because a scribe made the ancient equivalent of a typo, or this section
was added to that section because it shared key vocabulary—but author-

oriented scholarship is equally likely to be interested in the thought processes of the human beings responsible for these developments. Depending on the scholar, the motives of these authors and editors might be described as ideological or theological, but both terms reflect an interest in understanding the formation of the book in terms of the message and meaning its authors were trying to convey.

Attending to the reception of these intentions are scholars whose main interests in the book concern its audience. Audience-oriented approaches tend to be asking one of two related questions: "How does the text work on its audience?" OR, "How does the audience relate to the text?" The audience in question may be located in one of an almost infinite variety of times and places, but there is a consistent attention in these discussions to the potential of the text to act on (and with) its audience; it is a live entity of significant scope and power.

Like author-oriented approaches, audience-oriented approaches may include an interest in the mechanics of the text, as they investigate how the text creates meaning. Rather than focusing exclusively on the text or on authorial intention, however, an audience-oriented approach will extend its enquiries into the makeup and expectations of the audience, recognizing the role of human experience in coloring audiences' responses to particular ideas, images, and language. These efforts may focus on the ancient audience—so, for example, studies which discuss the rhetorical features of the text in terms of Jeremiah's efforts to persuade a seventh- or sixth-century audience in Judah to submit to Babylonian authority—but audience-oriented approaches may also be interested in the book's modern audiences, such as in feminist discussions of the way in which the sexualized imagery of women in the book might be read, either positively or negatively, by women in the twenty-first century. (Sometimes this is referred to as a *reader-response* approach.) Up to and including the modern period, the latter may sometimes be very broadly referred to as *reception history*, an approach which attends to the reception of the biblical text by successive audiences over the last two and a half millennia.

It is also not unusual to find audience-oriented investigations in which the ancient and the modern audiences are brought to bear on each other. Sometimes this is because the difficulty of the text for modern audiences prompts a turn to the ancient audience, in an attempt to gain a better sense of how or why the text was conceived in a certain way. The book's use of sexualized images of women, for example, might prompt an investigation into the assumptions of the ancient audience concerning gender categories, in order to shed light on the function of these images as part of the book's overall message. Conversely, insights drawn from modern audiences may be used to shed light on the meaning of the book in its ancient context, as when the forms of resistance used by modern colonized populations against modern colonial powers are brought to bear on the book's presentation of Jeremiah's relationship with Babylonia, or when the methods by which survivors of natural or human disasters process trauma offer a way of making sense of the book's disorganized and chaotic structure.

Audience-oriented work thus focuses on how the text is, or may be, received by particular audiences. It varies from discussions which focus on the production of meaning in specific contexts—the response of a survivor of domestic violence to the depiction of YHWH as a violent husband in chs. 2–6, for example—to discussions which seek meaning in the most abstract, universalizing sense—the meaning of the text as perceived to be constant across all audiences, times, and places. Though hardly exclusively, the latter tend to emanate from those in traditional positions of power (by virtue of gender, race/ethnicity, or religion), whereas the former tend to be championed by those at the margins. The former are also especially likely to ask how an audience might read the text in a way not intended by the author(s) (insofar as authorial intention is knowable). This means paying attention to ways in which the text allows for multiple, even contradictory, interpretations, as well as to ways in which the experience of the audience can affect the perspective from which the text is received—especially in terms of how this can affect which parts of the text resonate, jar with, or attract particular attention as a result of particular experiences.

A Multiplicity of Methods

Whereas author-oriented study of the book of Jeremiah is interested in whence the book came, audience-oriented study is interested in where the book goes: how we got it, compared to what happened to it once it arrived. What has become increasingly apparent in the most recent work on the book of Jeremiah, however, is that these different perspectives are not mutually exclusive concerns. There were ancient audiences as well as modern ones, so an interest in how a text works on its audience may work back and forth between its effect on modern audiences and its effects on ancient ones. Similarly, thinking about how modern audiences respond to and react to the text highlights aspects of the text's function and rhetorical effect on certain types of experiences in a way which can help to make sense of why the text might have developed the way it did. Conversely, investigations into the lengthy and complex process by which the book of Jeremiah came to its current form(s) may highlight sites of theological and ideological conflict, many of which are as contested today as they were at the time the book was forming. Recognizing the text's historical complexity can open a door to engagement with the complexity of the modern world, as well as the complexity of the book of Jeremiah as it is now situated in that world.

It may thus come as little surprise that much of the most recent work on the book of Jeremiah works across multiple approaches and methods, bringing the insights of various perspectives to bear on a persistently multivalent text. Such cooperativeness, it should be noted, has been hard won—the last two decades of the twentieth century were witness to a heated battle between the traditional chase for the historical Jeremiah and alternative approaches interested in the text as literature and as a text read and engaged by modern audiences—reflecting a wider disciplinary struggle over the purpose and methods of biblical research in a particularly intensified, gladiatorial form. The dust seems now somewhat to have settled, however, and a truce of sorts reached. Certainly the halcyon days in which this verse or that passage might be confidently attributed to a seventh–sixth century prophet proclaiming judgment in the last days of Judah and Jerusalem are long gone; the significance of the tradition's subsequent development is much more fully recognized and the implications of this for the understanding and interpretation of the text are widely acknowledged. Rather than beating a full retreat into ahistorical treatments of the text in the abstract, attending to its final form divorced from any kind of context, however, most recent approaches are working in pursuit of a balance, somewhere between a recognition, on the one hand, of the very real limitations on our knowledge of the book's textual development and of the historical contexts in which this took place and, on the other, that the book's theological interests and significance came out of a particular historical milieu and are now situated in another particular historical milieu. The acknowledgment of the significance of history for theology, as well as the significance of theology for history, can lead to a much richer understanding of both.

Chapter 5

RECENT APPROACHES IN ACTION

The diversity of approaches currently in use in the interpretation of the book of Jeremiah, together with the enormity of the book itself, means that a systematic treatment of the current state of scholarship on its many and complex parts and subparts is well beyond the scope of a mere introduction. Rather than skimming over the surface in pursuit of comprehensiveness, the following takes five chapters or groups of chapters from the book and investigates the interpretive consequences of approaching these particular texts using certain methodological frameworks. How does our understanding of a text differ, for example, if we approach it from a redaction-critical perspective as compared to a postcolonial one? How might approaching the text from multiple perspectives help us to see elements of its meaning—intended or otherwise—which might have remained hidden had we only looked at it from one angle?

The passages selected for attention in this chapter include the call and vision material in ch. 1, the laments and their surrounding prose in chs. 11–20, the juxtaposition of Judah with the nations in ch. 25 (MT) and chs. 25 and 32 (LXX), the episode involving the field in Anathoth in ch. 32, and the drama surrounding the production of an oracular scroll(s) in ch. 36. Each is introduced by a close reading of the primary text, highlighting points which have proved to be of particular interest or challenge in the history of scholarship. This is followed by a sampling of recent scholarship on the chapter, demonstrating the variety of interpretive emphases achieved through the application of different methodologies. Other chapters might have been chosen; these are hardly the only—or arguably even the most—significant passages in the book. They do, however, happen to be passages which have borne the scrutiny of a particularly diverse array of methods in recent scholarship and thus serve our current methodological enquiries well.

Chapter 1

Jeremiah's Call Begins the Book

The Text

The first verse of the first chapter identifies this book as "the words of Jeremiah." Though large portions of the following fifty-two chapters, especially the poetic oracles, will pass with no mention of the prophet whose name the book bears, the interpretation of the entirety as relating to and part of a Jeremiah tradition is determined from the first moment by these words. That these are *words* is equally noteworthy; unlike other prophetic books which speak of the visions which came to the prophet, the book of Jeremiah is explicitly and determinedly a book of words. Throughout the many chapters to come, the legitimacy of these words will be questioned and defended and the response to them by Judah's kings and people will determine their ultimate fate.

That Jeremiah is said to be of a family of priests and from a town called Anathoth has been the source of much speculation. The location of Anathoth, for example, is often cited as an explanation for Jeremiah's apparent knowledge and use of "northern Israelite" traditions (the references to Jacob and Ephraim, for example) as well as his apparent interest in the northern kingdom—"Israel"—in chs. 2–6 and chs. 30–31 especially. A rural priestly heritage, in combination with a Josianic reform which dismantled the rural sanctuaries in favor of a centralized Jerusalem cult (per 2 Kgs 22–23), is sometimes proposed as an explanation both for Jeremiah's familiarity with and access to priestly traditions and the temple, as well as his dissatisfaction with the Jerusalem sanctuary in particular.[1]

More of a challenge are the chronological parameters laid out in vv. 2–3. According to v. 2, Jeremiah was already active as a prophet—or at least already in receipt of the divine word—in the reign of Josiah, from about 627 (the beginning of Josiah's reign is usually dated to 640). Although Josiah is mentioned at other places in the book (3:6; 25:3; 36:2, in addition to several appearances as father of Jehoiakim and Zedekiah), none of these passages contain oracles explicitly addressed to him, unlike the oracles addressed to Jehoiakim and Zedekiah

---

1. Rural priests would have been put out of work as a result of these reforms, though offered the option of transferring to Jerusalem; Jeremiah's origins in Anathoth, followed by work in Jerusalem, is thought to reflect this shift.

(21:3-7; 22:18-19; 27:12-15; 34:2-6; 36:29-31; 37:17; 38:14-23). Nor is there anything for which a clear case for a Josianic context may be made elsewhere, either among the oracles addressed to unnamed kings or among those accusing the people of particular moral and cultic failings. Although certain oracles may be located in the period of Josiah's reign, none must be located there. Given the momentousness of the reform attributed to Josiah by 2 Kings 22–23, this is odd; one would expect that if Jeremiah were alive and working during that period he would have said something about it. Jeremiah's apparent silence on the subject has prompted a variety of solutions. These range from proposals that Jeremiah's attitude to Josiah's reform was ambiguous or even antagonistic to the rejection of the dating given in v. 2, as being motivated by later theological interests and factually inaccurate.[2] As for the reference in v. 3 to Jehoiakim and Zedekiah, the book itself describes Jeremiah interacting at a distance with Jehoiakim (ch. 36) and offers headings locating various oracles during his reign, but only depicts him in direct engagement with Zedekiah.

Less noted is that v. 3 apparently concludes Jeremiah's activities with the siege of Jerusalem, though the book as it stands contains material in chs. 40–44 which explicitly discusses Jeremiah and his activities after the fall of the city. The effect of the heading is to introduce the reader into exile; the dating of the end of Jeremiah's prophetic career to the "captivity of Jerusalem" means that there is no ambiguity about where the following pronouncements are ultimately headed. This also mirrors the end of the book (ch. 52), in which the reader is—at least in the final form of the book—likewise left in exile.[3] There is no reassuringly happy ending; the book begins in exile and will end in exile.

2. As noted in Chapter 3, the relationship between Jeremiah and Josiah was previously the focus of intense discussion, but has more recently fallen out of scholarly fashion. For a brief review of the points of contention concerning the association between Jeremiah and Josiah, see Leo G. Perdue, "Jeremiah in Modern Research," in *A Prophet to the Nations: Essays in Jeremiah Studies*, ed. Leo G. Perdue and Brian W. Kovacs (Winona Lake, IN: Eisenbrauns, 1984), 2–6.

3. On the suspension of the reader in exile as a metaphor addressing the indefinite postponement of restoration for the book's postexilic readers, see John Hill, " 'Your Exile Will Be Long': The Book of Jeremiah and the Unended Exile," in *Reading the Book of Jeremiah: A Search for Coherence*, ed. Martin Kessler (Winona Lake, IN: Eisenbrauns, 2004), 149–61.

An immediate consequence of 1:1 is that the reader automatically interprets the "me" of vv. 4, 9 and the "I" of v. 6 as Jeremiah. The speech of Yhwh (the "I" of vv. 5, 7–10, as indicated by vv. 4, 9) is of a type generally known as a "call narrative," although in this case it is a narrative in only the lightest sense. Other examples of this genre include the call of Moses in Exodus 3–4, the call of Samuel in 1 Samuel 3, and the call of Isaiah in Isaiah 6, with each of which this text has particular connections.[4] The protest about ineloquence in v. 6, for example, echoes Moses's protestations in Exod. 4:10, while the touching of the mouth as a crucial moment in the commissioning is akin to Isa. 6:6. A similar gesture appears in Ezek. 3:1-3, in which Ezekiel is told to eat a scroll containing the words he is to speak (compare Jer. 15:16, "Your words were found, and I ate them"). 1 Samuel 3 consistently refers to Samuel's youth, in a way which Jer. 1:6-7 seems to echo in its use of the term "boy."[5] The effect of these multiple intertextual allusions is to locate Jeremiah in an esteemed lineage of prophets and imbue him and the words associated with him with the weight of their authority. Perhaps the warning of v. 8, "Do not be afraid," foreshadows the resistance which these words will face in the chapters to follow.

Both the beginning (v. 5) and concluding (v. 10) sections of the call and commissioning refer to the nations. This notion of Jeremiah as the bearer of the divine word to a wider audience than just Israel or Judah is a significant element of the final form of the book, in which the oracles against the nations (OANs) play a prominent role—especially in the MT, which climaxes with the oracles against Babylon (chs. 50–51). The fact that the OANs are located in two different places in the LXX and the MT traditions draws particular attention to the description of Jeremiah as "a prophet to the nations" in ch. 1, because the apparent flexibility of the OANs' location in the book seems to suggest that they may not have been an originally integral part of the Jeremiah traditions. (This will be addressed in greater detail in the discussion of ch. 25.) Closely associated with the global commission in v. 10 is a

---

4. The seminal discussion of the depiction of Jeremiah in Mosaic terms is Christopher R. Seitz, "The Prophet Moses and the Canonical Shape of Jeremiah," *ZAW* 101 (1989): 3–27.

5. Hebrew *na'ar*, which may refer to a child but also to a young man. For a discussion of other call narratives in the Hebrew Bible and their relationship to or use by ch. 1, see Robert P. Carroll, *From Chaos to Covenant: Prophecy in the Book of Jeremiah* (London: SCM, 1981), 30–51.

sextet of verbs describing the purpose for which Jeremiah is appointed: "to pluck up and to pull down, to destroy and to overthrow, to build and to plant." Various combinations of these verbs appear elsewhere in the book (12:14-17; 18:7-9; 24:6; 31:28, 38–40; 42:10; 45:4) and have been especially discussed in relation to the inclusion of any optimism or hope in the proclamations of an historical Jeremiah.

The latter half of ch. 1 consists of two visions. As initially visual rather than verbal messages, these are very unusual for the book of Jeremiah. Only the extended vision and interpretation of the baskets of good and bad figs in ch. 24 offer an obvious counterpart; though a brief reference to a vision of the royal women leaving the defeated city appears in 38:21-23, the symbolic aspect which characterizes chs. 1 and 24 is absent. Indeed, even the visions in ch. 1 are described as "the word of Yhwh" (v. 11). The significance of the first vision depends on a wordplay, with the image of an almond branch (*shaqed*) interpreted as a symbol for the certainty of the divine word: Yhwh is watching (*shoqed*) over the word in order to ensure that it is fulfilled. The second vision, of a pot turned away from the north, merits a much longer interpretation relating the orientation of the pot to the agents of Yhwh's punishment who will come from that direction. The reason for the punishment—disloyalty to Yhwh through the worship of other gods—acts as a summary of and as a lens through which the following material will be read. The final verses implore the prophet in martial language, warning that the delivery of the divine word to these people will be a battle but reassuring the prophet that Yhwh will equip and support him appropriately.

Approaches to Interpretation

For obvious reasons, much of the work on ch. 1 focuses on the figure of the prophet. This has been the case for many years, with earlier studies attempting to determine how much of the material might be traceable to an historical Jeremiah. Despite the aforementioned difficulties posed by 1:1-3, the editorial nature of the verses themselves is not at issue; the crux of the matter commences with v. 4. Here the first-person speech produces a strong predilection for viewing this material as the voice of the prophet. Already, however, the poetic form of vv. 4–10 and the prose format of vv. 11–19 challenge the unity of the material (recall the dominance of the expectation that prophetic utterances appear in poetry rather than prose); the visions as such are atypical of the majority of the material associated with the Jeremiah tradition; and the enumeration appears confused (the "second time" in v. 13 is, in the extant text, the third time that "the word of Yʜwʜ came to me," not the second).[6] There is also the vexed issue of the characterization of "you"—nothing in vv. 4–10 identifies the addressee by name, though the preceding and the following predispose the reader to identify him as Jeremiah—as "a prophet to the nations," an epithet which makes sense only in the context of a book which contains the OANs, a section of the book whose origins with a historical prophet have been consistently doubted. These various issues, plus the use of the verbs of v. 10 as a leitmotif at key points later in the book, have suggested that a focus on the literary function of ch. 1 offers greater insights into the chapter's origins, preservation, and purpose than an assumption of its roots in the personal experience of Jeremiah the prophet.[7]

Combined with the wider crisis of historiography and the increasing recognition of not only the redactional complexity but also the literary artistry of the book of Jeremiah, the overwhelming majority of analyses of ch. 1 now approach it in literary rather than historical terms. Essential groundwork for such investigations was laid by the work of Timothy Polk, who deliberately bracketed historical questions about the man Jeremiah in favor of questions about the

6. Though largely now forgotten, the identification of the "foe from the north" also poses a difficulty for attempts to read the whole of vv. 4–19 as a single episode in 627 (per 1:2) at the beginning of the prophet's career, because the Babylonians were not a threat at that early date. (The idea that prophets were predictors of distant future events is not native to the biblical category of prophecy; in biblical texts, this idea begins to appear only with the development of more apocalyptic works, such as the book of Daniel.) As a "foe from the north" could not at that time have referred to the Babylonians, scholars wishing to see the whole of ch. 1 as originating with Jeremiah around 627 were obliged to rely on a supposed threat from Scythian tribes (on the basis of a passage in Herodotus's *History*), or to allow that at least the final vision stemmed from some later date, when the Babylonians could be in view. For more on the history of this debate, see David J. Reimer, "The 'Foe' and the 'North' in Jeremiah," *ZAW* 101 (1989): 223–32, and Perdue, "Jeremiah in Modern Research," 6–10.

7. On the transformation of these verbs throughout the book, see Saul M. Olyan, "To Uproot and to Pull Down, to Build and to Plant: Jer 1:10 and Its Earliest Interpreters," in *Hesed Ve-Emet: Studies in Honor of Ernest S. Frerichs*, ed. Jodi Magness and Seymour Gitin (Atlanta, GA: Scholars, 1998), 63–72.

Jeremiah created within and by the text.[8] Although Polk's work does not deal directly with ch. 1, it marked a key point in the changing tide of scholarly approaches to the book of Jeremiah, away from attempts to identify the words and actions of an historical person and toward the interpretation of the figure, or *persona*, of Jeremiah the prophet that is created in and by the book as it now stands. This kind of approach to the text is essentially *synchronic*, which means that it proceeds by analyzing the text in its entirety, rather than analyzing its constituent parts or layers individually (a kind of approach which is described as *diachronic*).

Very much in this vein are recent works by Kathleen Rochester and by Carol Dempsey, who explicitly set aside historical questions about the life and career of the prophet and textual questions about the stages by which the text reached its present form in favor of treating the text as a whole.[9] It is worth drawing attention to the fact that this "as a whole" is twofold. First, the text is analyzed synchronically, without attempting to discern the process of its development or bring this to bear on the interpretation of the text. In the case of ch. 1, this means that any differences in the origins of the poetic material of vv. 4–10 and the prose vision accounts of vv. 11–19 are disregarded in favor of a reading of their current conjoined location in the book. (Sometimes this approach is referred to as a "final form" reading.) Second, the text is read in its wider canonical context. This may mean reading the particular passage under discussion in light of the rest of the book in which it appears, or a scholar may also attend to material elsewhere in the (usually Christian) canon. A canonical reading of ch. 1, for example, will attend to its place in the book of Jeremiah as a whole and interpret its statements in light of that whole; it may also interpret these statements in light of material elsewhere in the canon.

A notable feature of these and other works approaching the book of Jeremiah from a synchronic perspective—whether focused on the presentation of the prophet specifically or on other figures and themes which appear repeatedly—is the particularly close attention which they pay to theological issues. This collocation of synchronic approaches

8. Timothy Polk, *The Prophetic Persona: Jeremiah and the Language of the Self* (JSOTSup 32; London: T&T Clark, 1984).

9. Kathleen M. Rochester, *Prophetic Ministry in Jeremiah and Ezekiel* (Contributions to Biblical Exegesis and Theology 65; Leuven: Peeters, 2012); Carol Dempsey, *Jeremiah: Preacher of Grace, Poet of Truth* (Interfaces; Collegeville, MN: Liturgical, 2007).

with theological exegesis often reflects a particular sense of frustration with other approaches to the text (redaction criticism in particular). The accusation leveled against such approaches is that they have focused on the historical questions—usually the search for the historical prophet and questions about the formation of the book—to such an extent that the book of Jeremiah as it now stands has been largely ignored. That is, the diachronic interpretation of the book's manifold parts is said to have obscured the artistry and significance of the whole. Often this appears in conjunction with concerns about the accessibility of the more technical scholarly analyses for untrained nonspecialists, especially members of the faith communities for whom the book of Jeremiah remains a living text rather than an object of analytical abstraction (hence a near-equivalence of synchronic and canonical in methodological discussions).

Rochester and Dempsey treat ch. 1 as part of their wider considerations of the figure of the prophet. Though ch. 1 plays a key role in framing the parameters of this figure as subsequently developed in the following fifty-one chapters, it is only one part of the picture; other passages may be introduced in order to interpret the text most immediately at hand.[10] Appealing to Polk, Rochester argues that the historical prophet is in any case "impossible to access...we can only access the texts' portrayal or characterization of each prophet."[11] With historical investigation ultimately impossible, the only sensible recourse is to canonical interpretation. Rochester's discussion of ch. 1 therefore appears as part of a synchronic analysis of prophetic ministry in the books of Ezekiel and Jeremiah.

---

10. A consistent complaint in reviews of these and related studies is the inability of such work to take the full breadth of the entire book into account in the discussion. Almost inevitably, the depth of analysis required by individual passages makes the inclusion of all relevant material impossible. Although most synchronic studies are theoretically justified on the basis of the book's canonical form, therefore, they usually struggle to include the whole of that form in the discussion. As two immediate examples: Polk concentrates his analysis on 4:19; 8:18–9:25; 10:19-25; 14:1–15:4; 17:12-18; and 20:7-18, while Rochester's discussion of Jeremiah is limited to 1:1-19; 6:27-30; 7:1-15; 18:1-12; and 23:9-32. Though practically necessary, such selectivity runs the risk of creating an overly systematic analysis, emphasizing passages which fit with the portrait being sketched while ignoring or minimizing those that do not.

11. Rochester, *Prophetic Ministry*, 7.

The detailed exegesis of ch. 1 draws attention to a number of elements of the text. One that is particularly essential to her comparison of the figure of Jeremiah to the figure of Ezekiel is the focus on the prophetic word, which dominates the book of Jeremiah in the way that image and vision dominate the book of Ezekiel. Rochester suggests that this emphasis on the word is reflected also in the heavily dialogical character of the relationship between YHWH and Jeremiah, both in ch. 1 and in subsequent chapters (especially chs. 11–20). That is, Jeremiah is portrayed as conversing with YHWH in a way in which Ezekiel is not. In ch. 1 this takes the form of YHWH's address to Jeremiah, Jeremiah's protestation, and YHWH's response (vv. 4–10), as well as their conversation about the almond branch and the pot (vv. 11–13). The major purpose of the call, Rochester suggests, is to establish Jeremiah's prophetic legitimacy, with YHWH's choice of Jeremiah antedating his existence (v. 5) and something which Jeremiah is unable to resist (vv. 6–7, 9). It is structured as a fivefold response to Jeremiah's objections regarding his lack of authority and his inability to speak, as voiced in v. 6. In wider canonical terms, Rochester's approach draws attention to the relationship of certain features of ch. 1 to other parts of the book, including the bookend effect created by the references to exile in 1:1-3 and 52:27b-34; the recurrence of the womb image (15:10 and 20:14-18), the motif of "watching" (5:6; 44:27), and the verbs in v. 10; and the conflict over the prophetic word which is anticipated by vv. 17–19.

Rochester's overall objective is explicitly theological rather than historical; it is on this basis that she justifies the synchronic reading of the canonical form of the text (the MT, in this case). Nevertheless, the comparative element of Rochester's investigation highlights differences between the persona of Jeremiah and the persona of Ezekiel. Her attempts to explain these differences prompt a cautious attention to history—if not to actual events, at least to the setting in which these books portray their protagonists as working. That is, elements of Jeremiah's *persona* are tied to his depiction in the context of the final decade(s) before the fall of Jerusalem, from the perspective of those left in the land after the first deportation in 597, whereas Ezekiel's *persona* is affected by his depiction among the deportees in Babylonia at that time. Rochester walks a careful line between an abstracted literary and synchronic analysis of the persona of the prophet as portrayed by the book and an attempt to recognize that the book, whatever the relationship of the people and events it portrays to actual historical events, nonetheless portrays the prophet within a specific historical setting.

Dempsey's discussion is also literarily and theologically oriented, relying especially on the rhetorical critical work of Jack Lundbom.[12] Treating Jeremiah as a literary character, Dempsey examines how this character evolves through speech, action, experience, and interaction with other human characters, with God (who may equally be considered a character in the book), and with the social, political, and religious situation of the late seventh and early sixth centuries. Like Rochester, Dempsey tries to balance this literary and synchronic reading with a historical perspective "that takes into account those events that shaped the life, mission, ministry, and preaching of Jeremiah the character as reflected by the biblical text."[13] The entire study is grounded especially on 1:4-10, which Dempsey sees as Jeremiah's self-introduction. This emphasizes the relationship between Jeremiah and Yнwн, focusing on the communicative process by which Yнwн calls Jeremiah to prophecy and installs him in a long line of divine intimates. Dempsey suggests that this presents to the reader a deity who is engaged both in the life of Jeremiah and in the life of humanity, with her ultimately theological interests reflected in the fact that the analysis culminates in a summary of what these verses reveal about God: that God is personal and a teacher; that God communicates through intuition and imagination, through audition and internal sensibilities; that God is present in the community and that an individual's encounter with the divine is in service of this presence; and that God will not tolerate infidelity.

Although Dempsey consistently refers to Jeremiah as a "character," there is a tendency to elide the distinction between the literary and the historical Jeremiahs. An explicit goal of the work is to "present Jeremiah as a gifted and skilled preacher"; Jeremiah is said to have a "strong sense of self" and is the constant subject of active verbs ("Jeremiah

12. Lundbom applies the method most comprehensively in his commentary on Jeremiah: Jack R. Lundbom, *Jeremiah: A New Translation with Introduction and Commentary* (3 vols; AB 21; New York: Doubleday, 1999, 2004), drawing on his earlier Jack R. Lundbom, *Jeremiah: A Study in Ancient Hebrew Rhetoric* (2nd ed., Winona Lake, IN: Eisenbrauns, 1997). He has written on ch. 1 specifically in Jack R. Lundbom, "Rhetorical Structures in Jeremiah 1," *ZAW* 103 (1991): 193–210, where he is explicitly concerned to argue that the rhetorical structure of the chapter allows the majority of it to be attributed to the historical prophet.

13. Dempsey, *Jeremiah*, xviii.

emphasizes," "Jeremiah reveals," "Jeremiah makes known," etc.).[14] This clearly arises from a desire to emphasize the "timeless" character of the message attributed to Jeremiah by the book which bears his name, but it runs the risk of obscuring the critical methodological point which prompted the literary reading in the first place, namely, that the Jeremiah of the book does not exist in some direct correlation to a Jeremiah of history. Similar slippage between the literary and the historical is visible in the way that Rochester takes the superscription's dating of the prophet's activity and his familial information as they stand, with the suggestion that the attribution of a priestly lineage may be supported by "Jeremiah's sophisticated use of the Hebrew language, his knowledgeable use of the theological tradition and his personal relationship with God."[15] This kind of slippage is not uncommon, but may also be found in other canonical, theological, and synchronic readings of the book of Jeremiah.

From a methodological point of view this may be variously interpreted. On some occasions it seems to reveal an underlying desire, especially among more conservative scholars, to circumvent the distance between present and past which diachronic analyses of the text's complexity have brought to the fore, but it also—and this seems more likely the case for Dempsey and Rochester—highlights a real methodological challenge for canonical and other synchronic analyses. Such studies are increasingly prone to acknowledge that history, however difficult to discern, is somehow important for understanding the text. Texts are difficult to interpret entirely in the abstract; though they may obscure, distort, or otherwise play with history, they assume a living audience in a concrete political, social, and theological world. The challenge is how to grasp the significance of history for both the original and ongoing meaning of the text, without becoming entirely bogged down in it.

The difficulty, in no small part, is: "Which history?" Although the book of Jeremiah may set the activity of a prophet called Jeremiah in the historical context of the late seventh and early sixth centuries, it is quite apparent from even a cursory reading of the book that at least some parts of the book were written after that time and are colored in their theological interests and in their theological perspectives by the particularities of those later historical contexts.[16] So while the political,

---

14. Dempsey, *Jeremiah*, xvi, xxxi, 2–3.
15. Rochester, *Prophetic Ministry*, 14.

social, and theological world of the late seventh and early sixth centuries is obviously significant for the interpretation of the book of Jeremiah, the political, social, and theological worlds of the fifth, fourth, or third centuries may be just as important.

A notable recent effort to integrate the historical, literary, and theological aspects of the study of the book of Jeremiah is that of Kathleen O'Connor, who approaches ch. 1 as part of a sustained reading of the book of Jeremiah from the perspective of trauma studies.[17] As will by now be apparent, one of the major challenges posed by the book is its apparently chaotic and disorganized structure: it skips around in time (when it bothers to provide chronological information at all); it bounces back and forth between poetry and prose; and it addresses first one audience, then another, and then again the first, before turning to yet a third or fourth. One approach to this textual pandemonium is to attempt to dissect and thereby account for it in terms of the book's formation over a long period. Another is to take the final text and work from the assumption that, as it exists in this form, it must be coherent in this form. O'Connor's approach seeks to recognize both the existence of the text as it stands while also acknowledging the disparate and inchoate contents of that text. She does this by arguing that the book's impression of chaos makes sense when it is understood as a response to a massive social trauma, such as the death, destruction, and displacement which occurs in war and its aftermath. O'Connor draws attention to the fact that traumatic violence constitutes "a terrifying disruption of normal mental

16. A well-known analogy, if not a perfect one, is the plays of William Shakespeare. Though these plays (especially the histories) ostensibly dealt with long-past events, they also served as commentary on current ones. Thus, for example, *Macbeth* contains a number of references—and historical alterations in deference—to James I/VI, the sitting English and Scottish monarch at the time the play was written and first performed, while *Richard II* is written with an eye to contemporary royal successions and issues of dynastic legitimacy. Though Shakespeare was writing plays rather than prophecies and felt perhaps less compunction about altering his sources than did the inheritors of the Jeremiah traditions (though, given the complexity of the book of Jeremiah, perhaps not!), the influence of current events on his depictions of the past is a salutary reminder of the relevance of the author's (or editor's) historical context for interpretation.

17. Kathleen M. O'Connor, *Jeremiah: Pain and Promise* (Minneapolis, MN: Fortress, 2011).

processes, distorting reality, even as it becomes the only reality."[18] One of the effects of such trauma is that its victims are unable to address what they have experienced head-on; they can begin to process it only in pieces and only from an oblique angle. The book of Jeremiah, O'Connor contends, contributes to the resuscitation and rebuilding of the community after the disaster by enabling it to cope with its experience by addressing it indirectly "at a slant."[19]

Chapter 1 contributes to this project of community restoration insofar as it forms a part of the book's unusual focus on the life of the prophet, rather than just his words (compare, for example, the books of Isaiah or Amos, which contain very little information of this kind). This interest in the life of the prophet arises from its potential as a symbol for and embodiment of the experience of the community as a whole: "His life illuminates the disaster, embodies it, and signifies survival beyond it."[20] At the same time, the prophet is not merely a mirror for the people, because his suffering is a direct result of their rejection. O'Connor draws attention to the way in which ch. 1 emphasizes the separation between Jeremiah and the people, from his antenatal summons to service (v. 5) to the message he is sent to deliver (v. 10). This functions to assert, from the very beginning of the book, that the disaster which the people have undergone was not the result of divine recklessness or whim, but a comprehensible consequence of their rejection of the words of Jeremiah (and Yhwh). However theologically problematic this explanation may be, it functions to create order out of the chaos which is the world postdisaster by answering the question, "Why did this happen?"[21]

18. O'Connor, *Jeremiah*, 3.

19. O'Connor, *Jeremiah*, 33.

20. O'Connor, *Jeremiah*, 71.

21. Much of the biblical literature concerned with the destruction of Judah articulates a form of theodicy in which blame for the disaster is laid in the lap of the people—an "our fault" theology, in Daniel Smith-Christopher's phrasing. Though this self-blame jars with many modern readers, Smith-Christopher argues that it is more sophisticated than it may at first appear: it "not only shifts the weight of responsibility but ironically empowers … by offering the hope of cultural recovery. *Our own* mistakes offer hopeful possibilities in ways that outside imperial conquest does not" (Daniel L. Smith-Christopher, "Reading Jeremiah as Frantz Fanon," in *Jeremiah (Dis)Placed: New Directions in Writing/ Reading Jeremiah*, ed. A. R. Pete Diamond and Louis Stulman [LHBOTS 529; London: T&T Clark, 2011], 116–17, italics in the original).

One of the most recent discussions of ch. 1 picks up this emphasis on the traumatic impact of large-scale disaster and applies it as a means of thinking about the development of the text. Explicitly setting her analysis apart from those older studies that "value the authentic, original, and primary text over the redacted and secondary copy," Yosefa Raz suggests that ch. 1 is "a pastiche of prophetic vocabulary and conventions," which is targeted at "an anxiety about time, transmission, and lineage in a time of catastrophe."[22] In other words, the text of ch. 1 has developed as it has—with all its awkward difficulties for the modern interpreter—because it is responding to issues raised by traumatic experience. For example, the opening of the book is designed to emphasize continuity and stability in the face of discontinuity and instability: the lineages of both Jeremiah and the kings of Judah in 1:1-3, with their attention to the passage in each case from father to son, are a way of emphasizing the social continuity of progression from generation to generation and the political continuity of the royal house—even though, in the case of the royal lineages, this is at the cost of an accurate account of the complicated progression of Judah's final kings. It omits, for example, the brief reigns of Jehoahaz and Jehoiachin (deposed by Necho and Nebuchadrezzar, respectively) and obscures the awkward reversal in the royal succession embodied by Zedekiah, Jehoiachin's uncle. This illusion of continuity helps to stabilize the inherent instability of exile, as represented by the atypical double dating of Jeremiah's activity (the usual list of the kings in whose reign he was active, but also the catastrophic destruction of Jerusalem). Last but not least, the call and commissioning work as stabilizers, invoking the authority of the Mosaic prophetic tradition and creating for the prophet a divine parentage which circumnavigates ordinary gestation and birth by appealing to literary conventions designed to emphasize royal legitimacy in cases of broken succession. As it does this, the text reveals its deep anxiety about the exile's disruption of Judah's social and political lineages. Moses and monarchy are invoked by the book of Jeremiah's editors in support of Jeremiah's prophetic authority because they represent a patchwork—a pastiche—of divine and civil authority. The final form of the chapter is driven by the need

22. Yosefa Raz, "Jeremiah 'Before the Womb': On Fathers, Sons, and the Telos of Redaction in Jeremiah 1," in *Prophecy and Power: Jeremiah in Feminist and Postcolonial Perspective*, ed. Christl M. Maier and Carolyn J. Sharp (LHBOTS 577; London: Bloomsbury, 2013), 87, 91.

to bring order and explanation to chaos—both the chaos of the exile and the chaos of the book.

As the approaches of these four scholars imply, there is a strong sense in current work on ch. 1 that it cannot be interpreted or understood apart from the book which it begins. The prophet it introduces is a figure whose character is only hinted at in these opening verses, waiting to be fleshed out in greater depth and complexity in the chapters to follow. The language and imagery employed in this preliminary sketch is part and parcel of the literary structuring of the book in its entirety, introducing key theological concepts—the word of YHWH and the struggles faced by the one chosen to convey it, a dominant theme of judgment which is nevertheless accompanied by hope in a minor key, and the international reach of YHWH's power and the work of his prophet—which resonate to varying degrees throughout all of what follows.

Chapters 11–20

A Lamenting Prophet and a Traumatized Community

The Text

Unlike the other parts of the book highlighted in this chapter, chs. 11–20 are a large section rather than a single chapter. These chapters are generally taken together because they contain a series of laments or "confessions," in which the prophetic voice howls at YHWH on account of the suffering which he undergoes as a result of his efforts to convey the divine message to the people. These laments are identified as such in part because of their obviously distressed content but also because of their relationship to similar material in the Psalms, where individual and communal laments are an established form by which human petitioners may protest against perceived injustices and plead with YHWH to intervene on their behalf to punish the wicked and vindicate the righteous (i.e., themselves). Though opinion about the exact extent of the lament material in the book of Jeremiah varies somewhat, it is generally considered to include 11:18-20; 12:1-4; 15:10-18; 17:14-18; 18:18-23; 20:7-13, 14-18. Several of these passages, though not all, are immediately followed by or otherwise incorporate what appear to be divine responses (11:21-23; 12:5-6; 15:19-21).

The laments themselves are among the most powerful speech of the prophetic texts. The first-person voice of the one who speaks on Yʜᴡʜ's behalf has the audacity to rail furiously at the deity, accusing Yʜᴡʜ of having knowingly called him into a form of life which renders him the target of malicious rumors and murderous schemes, in the face of which the deity has abandoned him to his own devices. The prophet accuses Yʜᴡʜ of having deceived him as to the true nature of this calling, describing himself as an innocent lamb, naïvely led to the slaughter (11:19), whom Yʜᴡʜ lured—seduced, or even took by force, if the verb's associations with sexual assaults are intended— into his service without having fully disclosed its dangers (20:7).[23] The plea of 12:3 explicitly inverts the image, as it demands that those who persecute the prophet be themselves put out like sheep for the slaughter. Though the prophet's intimacy with Yʜᴡʜ, even the message itself, is described in positive terms as a joy and delight (15:16), this is followed by a description of the dismal perspective on his compatriots which it occasions (15:17). These passages depict the effects of divine service on the prophet as an almost unmitigated disaster: his audience conspires to kill him (11:19; 18:20), heaps insults upon him (15:15), and mocks him (17:15; 20:7-8). This existence is so unbearable that the prophet laments that he was ever born, in language which echoes the book of Job: it would have been better to have died at birth than to live like this (20:14-18).[24]

Yʜᴡʜ's deceitfulness in having brought the prophet into this grim situation is compounded now by Yʜᴡʜ's failure to provide adequate support for him. Rather than the source of living water (2:13; 17:3),

23. On the language and interpretation of 20:7, see Terence E. Fretheim, *Jeremiah* (Smyth & Helwys; Macon, GA: Smyth & Helwys, 2002), 198–200; Angela Bauer, *Gender in the Book of Jeremiah: A Feminist-Literary Reading* (SBL 5; New York: Peter Lang, 1999), 113–17; Stuart Macwilliam, "The Prophet and His Patsy: Gender Performativity in Jeremiah," in *Prophecy and Power: Jeremiah in Feminist and Postcolonial Perspective*, ed. Christl M. Maier and Carolyn J. Sharp (LHBOTS 577; London: Bloomsbury, 2013), 173–88; and Kathleen M. O'Connor, *The Confessions of Jeremiah: Their Interpretation and Role in Chapters 1–25* (SBLDS 94; Atlanta, GA: Society of Biblical Literature, 1988), 70–2.

24. Katharine Dell, "'Cursed Be the Day I Was Born': Job and Jeremiah Revisited," in *Reading Job Intertextually*, ed. Katharine Dell and Will Kynes (London: T&T Clark, 2012), 106–17.

Yhwh is for the prophet a "deceitful brook, like waters that fail" (15:18). The prophet's attempts to preserve himself by ceasing to convey Yhwh's message are futile and only compound his misery (20:8-9). Adding insult to all this injury, the prophet's opponents continue merrily in their wicked ways, without consequence; repeatedly he demands how this can be and implores Yhwh to intervene, to vindicate the prophet through judgment on his opponents (11:20; 12:1-4; 17:15-18; 18:21-23; 20:11). Though punctuated by occasional declarations of confidence in Yhwh's ultimate justice (11:20; 17:14) or acknowledgment that the prophet's perspective can be nothing to that of Yhwh's (12:1; 20:12), some of these border on the desperate (17:17; 20:11) and the overall tone of the material is that of an individual in *extremis*, brought to his knees by the demands the deity has heaped upon him.

These poetic laments are strung together by multiple sections of prose and are interspersed with some poetic material which does not fit neatly into the lament genre, such as 13:15-27; 14:1-10; 15:5-9. A large proportion of the prose, though not all of it, recounts a series of symbolic actions or sign acts, in which the prophet is instructed to act in a particular way or to observe the actions of someone else. These actions are then interpreted as having symbolic significance, as illustrations of the divine message (13:1-11, 12-14; 16:1-9; 18:1-11; 19:1-13). Though not exclusive to this section of the book, these sign-act narratives are notably concentrated here.[25]

One of the challenges of these sign-acts is apparent immediately from the first in the series, in which the prophet is commanded to wear a linen loincloth, to bury it near the river Euphrates, and then in due course to dig it back up again, whereupon it is discovered to be ruined and useless. It is not immediately obvious whether the text envisions the prophet carrying out this symbolic action in real time and space, or if it is presumed to be a vision or other work of the prophetic imagination.[26]

---

25. Chapters 25; 27–28; 32; and 51 also reflect the attribution of significance to symbolic actions.

26. Reviews of the range of approaches which have been taken to this issue may be found in Kelvin J. Friebel, *Jeremiah's and Ezekiel's Sign-Acts: Rhetorical and Nonverbal Communication* (JSOTSup 283; Sheffield: Sheffield Academic, 1999), 11–78, and Pamela Scalise, "Vision beyond the Visions in Jeremiah," in *'I Lifted my Eyes and Saw': Reading Dream and Vision Reports in the Hebrew Bible*, ed. Elizabeth R. Hayes and Lena-Sofia Tiemeyer (LHBOTS 584; London: Bloomsbury, 2014), 47–58.

If the prophet is supposed to have buried and unburied a real loincloth next to the Euphrates, undertaking two separate trips in order to do so, this presents certain practical difficulties—hence the decision by some commentators to understand *prt* in 13:7 not as the distant river Euphrates but as a location near Jerusalem.

Whether real or imagined, the ultimate point of each of these sign-acts is its interpreted meaning. The ruined loincloth signifies the ruination of Jerusalem and Judah (13:1-11); the full jars of wine presage the people's drunk-like staggering, crashing one into the other, as they experience the weight of judgment (13:12-14). The prophet's lack of wife or children foreshadows the destruction of families through death, to the point that no one is left to mourn (16:1-9). The malleability of the potter's clay mirrors the malleability of the people's fate in YHWH's hands (18:1-11); the broken earthenware jug symbolizes the irrecoverable consequences of a broken people (19:1-13). Though such symbolic activity is known from elsewhere—Isaiah and Hosea bestow portentous monikers upon their children, Isaiah wanders the streets of Jerusalem naked, and Ezekiel plays with bricks, lies on his side for months on end, and bakes on excrement—it is especially prominent in the book of Jeremiah. These actions, carried out by the prophet under divine imperative, render the prophet inextricable from his message.

In addition to these sign-acts, the prose in chs. 11–20 also includes passages which typify the "prose sermon" label often used as shorthand for the book's deuteronomistic prose (11:1-17; 17:19-27). Some of this prose takes the form of instructions from YHWH to convey a particular message to the people. The first of these, for example, introduces the following with: "The word that came to Jeremiah from YHWH ... speak to the people of Judah and the inhabitants of Jerusalem ... say to them, 'Thus says the Lord'..." (11:1; similarly 16:1; 17:19; 18:1). Though the following words take the form of prose, the content is essentially oracular. These and other, shorter deuteronomistic-type prose in chs. 11–20 have been especially significant for their role in identifying the unnamed enemies of the poetic material. Though the poetry refers to these people in general terms, the prose speaks of the opposition of several specific groups or individuals: people from the town of Anathoth, with which Jeremiah is associated (11:21-23), as well as conspirators in Jerusalem (11:9) and other prophets claiming to speak in YHWH's name, with much more optimism and much greater success (14:13-16). Though frustration with the unresponsiveness of the people appears in many of the prophetic books, especially characteristic of the book of Jeremiah is the opposition of other prophets who claim to speak in YHWH's name. After the Greek rendering of these other prophets as *pseudoprophetes*, these are often referred to as "false" prophets. Last but not least is the priest Pashur, whose antagonism merits an oracle addressed directly to him (20:1-6). This prose material also serves to identify the prophetic voice as Jeremiah, who is otherwise an anonymous first-person speaker. The laments are expressed in the first person, with no explicit indication of who is speaking, and the sign-acts are similarly expressed in the first person ("the word of YHWH came to me"). A relatively small number of third-person references (11:1; 14:1; 18:1, 18; 19:14; 20:1-3) prompt the reader to understand the "I" of the laments as the "I" of the prophet.

The treatment of the material in these ten chapters as a single collection hinges largely on the perception that the poetic laments form a cohesive group, though the repeating use of sign-acts and the consistent deuteronomistic style of the prose material also contribute to this. Though not addressed systematically, as such, the material in these chapters speaks persistently to the challenges faced by YHWH's prophet, as both the prophet and his message are rejected by the very people to whom he has been sent.

Approaches to Interpretation

Chapters 11–20 have been the focus of extensive attention in the interpretive history of the book of Jeremiah—as an insight into the personal emotional and mental anguish of the prophet himself, as a case of substantial cross-genre influence within the prophetic literature, and as a locus of investigations into the formation and purpose of the book.

The foundations of current discussions of these chapters rest with a concentrated flurry of monographs, authored by Norbert Ittmann, Pete Diamond, O'Connor, Karl-Friedrich Pohlmann, and Mark Smith.[27] Each approached these chapters from a strongly literary perspective, deploying considerations of the genre of the poetic material as laments in combination with redaction-critical tools in order to discern the origins of this material, as well as the means by which and purpose for which the laments came to be part of the book of Jeremiah.

---

27. Norbert Ittmann, *Die Konfessionen Jeremias: Ihre Bedeutung für die Verkündigung des Propheten* (WMANT 54; Neukirchener-Vluyn: Keukirchener Verlag, 1981); A. R. Pete Diamond, *The Confessions of Jeremiah in Context: Scenes of Prophetic Drama* (JSOTSup 45; London: T&T Clark, 1987); Kathleen

Over the course of the decade in which these studies appeared, it is possible to see a shift in the underlying assumptions which these scholars were making about the origins of this material as well as in their own objectives in dissecting it. Ittmann's investigations were designed to provide insights into the historical prophet's message and work, trying to undo the later editorial uses to which the early words of Jeremiah were put and ultimately producing a detailed analysis of which parts of the text were or were not likely to stem from the prophet's own preaching. Appearing just a few years later, Diamond's work is much more cautious. Although he concluded in favor of the laments' "basic authenticity" as the words of an historical Jeremiah—suggesting that such origins could account for the material's stylistic cohesion and the rationale for its inclusion in the book—his overall purpose was to draw attention to the way in which material concerning the prophet and his life had been used by editors to construct a theodicy justifying the destruction of Judah as the manifestation of Yнwн's judgment on the people. O'Connor's study was conducted along similar lines, using rhetorical and form-critical methods to suggest that this poetry originated in efforts to legitimate Jeremiah's prophetic calling and message to a circle of his disciples. This semi-public function explains why a series of apparently private conversations between prophet and deity came to exist outside the mind of the prophet. It was subsequently incorporated into the wider structure of chs. 1–25, in which it plays a critical role in the depiction of conflict between Jeremiah and his

M. O'Connor, *The Confessions of Jeremiah: Their Interpretation and Role in Chapters 1–25* (SBLDS 94; Atlanta, GA: SBL, 1988); Karl-Friedrich Pohlmann, *Die Ferne Gottes—Studien zum Jeremiabuch: Beiträge zu den "Konfessionen" in Jeremiabuch und ein Versuch zur Frage nach den Anfängen der Jeremiatradition* (BZAW 179; Berlin: de Gruyter, 1989); Mark S. Smith, *The Laments of Jeremiah and Their Contexts* (SBLMS 42; Atlanta, GA: Scholars, 1990). For an accessible summary of research on these chapters prior to this point, see Diamond, *Confessions*, 11–16, or O'Connor, *Confessions*, 149–54. The mode of enquiry reflected in these studies—a combination of literary, redaction-critical, and ultimately historical methods—has most recently been pursued by Jenö Kiss, *Die Klage Gottes und des Propheten: ihre Rolle in der Komposition und Redaktion von Jer 11–12, 14–15 und 18* (WMANT 99; Neukirchen-Vluyn: Neukirchener Verlag, 2003).

opponents, including their rejection of his message and his desire for vengeance upon them.

Smith, whose volume was the last of these major studies to appear, focused almost exclusively on the wider editorial function of this material. Like O'Connor he noted the legitimating function of the laments, highlighting the way in which the divine speeches and the prose stories further transform this material into a theodicy of divine judgment. This is achieved in part through the intense focus on the relationship between Jeremiah and Yʜᴡʜ which, Smith suggests, "serves as a vehicle for expressing the breakdown in the relationship between Yahweh and Israel."[28] In the preceding chapters, Jeremiah had been linked more closely with the people; chs. 11–20 signal his shift away from the people and toward Yʜᴡʜ, contributing to a presentation of Jeremiah in which the people's opposition to the prophet is tantamount to opposition to Yʜᴡʜ. By the end of the decade, the working assumption of an historical prophet—and a default position attributing much of the book to him—had gone. Pohlmann would reject outright the suggestion that the laments could be attributed to Jeremiah, arguing that they should be seen as late postexilic creations expressing the interplay of present suffering, future hope, and delayed expectations, akin to certain late parts of the books of Isaiah and Malachi. He describes their outlook as eschatological, reflecting the experience and particular concerns of a subgroup within the wider community of Israel. The voice of the prophet represents the voice of a group of people who feel themselves persecuted by their own people, in the manner of the persecuted prophet who is presented elsewhere in the Jeremiah traditions.

The use of the traditions associated with Jeremiah over successive generations is an area of research which has made particular use of the twofold preservation of these traditions in the LXX and the MT. Following up on his earlier work, Diamond has argued that the differences between the LXX and the MT are the result of divergent reading traditions of the same underlying Hebrew text (or two very similar texts).[29] Rather than a sign that there were significant differences between the *Vorlage* of the LXX and what is now the

---

28. Smith, *The Laments of Jeremiah*, 61.

29. A. R. Pete Diamond, "Jeremiah's Confessions in the LXX and MT: A Witness to Developing Canonical Function?" *VT* 40 (1990): 33–50.

MT, Diamond contends that the points at which the two editions now differ are points at which their respective editors made different interpretive decisions regarding the consonantal Hebrew text with which they were faced.[30] The MT, he suggests, tends to interpret the text with reference to the prophet, Jeremiah: it reads the laments as the prophet giving voice to his own frustrations. The LXX, by contrast, tends to read them more generically, with a less obvious identification of the prophet as the speaker and thus a greater emphasis on their communal potential. Diamond suggests that this decision on the part of the LXX relates to an interpretive tradition which portrayed Jeremiah as an intercessor on behalf of the community, whereas the MT's focus on Jeremiah is connected to a growing interest in the personal biographies of the prophets and in their depiction as rejected messengers of Yʜᴡʜ. The interpretive contexts and consequent expectations of the LXX and MT readers, in other words, have affected the way in which they understood the text. Because these interpretive decisions affected the translation choices made by the LXX translator, they are visible in the text of the LXX.

The function of the prophet as a representative of the people has been taken up in a number of influential works by O'Connor.[31] These works draw especially heavily on the insights of trauma and disaster studies,

---

30. Until the Middle Ages, Hebrew was written using consonants only and with very little indication of punctuation or word divisions. (The system of vowels used by the MT was devised by the Masoretes toward the end of the first millennium.) While efficient in terms of space, the system suffers from a degree of ambiguity; the same sequence of consonants may be vocalized in different ways and thereby produce different meanings. Context will limit the number of (plausible) options for dividing and vocalizing a given sequence of consonants, but it may not eliminate all possibilities. An example may be found in Timothy M. Law, *When God Spoke Greek: The Septuagint and the Making of the Christian Bible* (Oxford: Oxford University Press, 2013), 22.

31. Chs 11–20 are the focus of Kathleen M. O'Connor, "Figuration in Jeremiah's Confessions with Questions for Isaiah's Servant," in *Jeremiah Invented: Constructions and Deconstructions of Jeremiah*, ed. Else K. Holt and Carolyn J. Sharp (LHBOTS 595; London: Bloomsbury, 2015), 63–73; a more systematic analysis of the book as a whole from this perspective is O'Connor, *Jeremiah*. See also Kathleen M. O'Connor, "Terror All Around: Confusion as Meaning-Making," in *Jeremiah (Dis)Placed: Kathleen M. New Directions in Writing/Reading Jeremiah*, ed. A. R. Pete Diamond and Louis Stulman (LHBOTS 529; London: T&T Clark, 2011), 67–79.

which attempt to characterize and understand the way in which people respond to traumatic violence and social upheaval. It is in this context, she suggests, that the book's peculiar interest in the life of the prophet may be explained. As the story of a single individual, it offers a level of narrative coherence which is lacking in the community's collective experience, insofar as the individual narrative—in which there is cause and effect and in which events have explanations and therefore have meaning—contrasts with and provides an alternative to the communal experience of chaos and upheaval. Biography possesses significant symbolic potential, with the figure of Jeremiah able to "express and mirror traumatic sufferings of Judah after the Babylonian invasions."[32] The lamentations are important because they provide language drawn from the cultic traditions, represented elsewhere by the psalms of individual and communal lament, with which victims of this disaster can articulate their experience. The voice of Jeremiah, agonizing over the extremity of his suffering, becomes the voice of the community and a means by which its members can express their desperation and fury at the God they call(ed) their own.[33] At the same time, the people's rejection of the prophet and his message is presented as a cause of their demise; the prophetic biography thus also provides an explanation for the people's suffering. "Jeremiah," O'Connor observes, "is both the people and not the people."[34]

Mary Callaway picks up on this ambiguity in a discussion of the lamenting voice in ch. 20, with its accusation that YHWH has enticed the speaker unto disaster (v. 7).[35] Usually these words are read as the words of Jeremiah, full of agitation at the grim consequences of his submission to YHWH. Callaway complicates this by interrogating the text's voice from the vantage point of the text's preservation. Though many have observed that the laments' extant location in the book contribute to an exilic theodicy for the disaster—a justification of YHWH's judgment by emphasizing the guilt of the people—Callaway points out that this implies that they were preserved by the very people

32. O'Connor, "Figuration," 64.

33. "They convey in the most vulnerable terms a grasping for faith and a desperate clutching toward God despite massive discontent with God's treatment of the world" (O'Connor, *Jeremiah*, 82).

34. O'Connor, "Figuration," 70.

35. Mary C. Callaway, "Seduced by Method: History and Jeremiah 20," in *Jeremiah Invented: Constructions and Deconstructions of Jeremiah*, ed. Else K. Holt and Carolyn J. Sharp (LHBOTS 595; London: Bloomsbury, 2015), 16–33.

who had previously heard Jeremiah's proclamations but refused to listen to them. It was only in the aftermath of Jerusalem's destruction that Jeremiah's warnings of judgment were acknowledged as legitimate; only in Babylonia that Jeremiah's words were taken up to express the deportees' feeling that Yʜwʜ had betrayed their trust. How might it affect our reading of this outburst, she asks, "if Jeremiah's anguished lament was preserved because it helped those who had fiercely opposed Jeremiah in Jerusalem make sense of what had happened, and gave voice to their despair in Babylon?"[36] In a remarkable case of polyvalence, the text "presents us *simultaneously* with the voices of the prophet in Jerusalem before 587 and of those who tried to silence him, now speaking in his voice ... [it] merges the voice of the tormented with that of his tormentors."[37]

The extent to which the book of Jeremiah is characterized by this kind of interpretive ambiguity is central to Corinne Carvalho's analysis of its depiction of the prophet as permanently single (16:1-9).[38] Though much attention has been paid to the symbolic significance of this divine imperative, far fewer interpreters have noted that for Jeremiah not to marry constitutes a significant deviation from the social norms reflected elsewhere in the biblical texts. Gender theory (also queer theory) emphasizes the social expression of gender identity. By approaching the text from the perspective of its construction (and deconstruction) of gender, Carvalho is able to recognize just how exceptional—even subversive—this sign-act really is. Jeremiah's failure to marry functions as the centerpiece of an image of an isolated prophet: a man who is not a husband and thus not truly or fully a man, whose single state prevents him from engaging with his community in the ways expected of a man (procreation, mourning rituals, etc). The laments, among which this command not to marry is found, depict a prophet reduced to passivity, unable to resist Yʜwʜ: a man whose masculinity is undermined by his inability to act. The association of lamentation with women compounds Jeremiah's alienation; the genre

36. Callaway, "Seduced by Method," 28.
37. Callaway, "Seduced by Method," 29.
38. Corinne L. Carvalho, "Sex and the Single Prophet: Marital Status and Gender in Jeremiah and Ezekiel," in *Prophets Male and Female: Gender and Prophecy in the Hebrew Bible, the Eastern Mediterranean, and the Ancient Near East*, ed. Jonathan Stökl and Corrine L. Carvalho (AIIL 15; Atlanta, GA: SBL, 2013), 237-67.

is one of transition and liminality (including the transition from life to death) and, as such, invokes instability and change.

Carvalho is ultimately interested in the way that this depiction of Jeremiah—as having failed to perform according to the social expectations of a masculine identity, while also being associated with social performances of womanhood—undermines the text's implied assumptions about gender as a stable and binary phenomenon. Jeremiah's singleness complicates his personal social identity, to be sure, insofar as it impedes his ability to interact with other members of his community in an ordinary way. But beyond this, it undermines the stability of gender identities in general, because it projects Jeremiah into an ambivalent and intermediate space where he is neither male nor female. Yet, Carvalho emphasizes that the ambiguity of Jeremiah's gender performance is not random: "The text projects Jeremiah as a liminal figure" specifically because "this liminality mirrors the situation of the ideal readers of the text: refugees of the war with Babylon."[39] As in Ezekiel, where the prophet is forbidden to mourn the death of his wife, the prophet's personal life is invoked in order to comment on the social consequences of Babylonian conquest.

Far be it, however, for the book of Jeremiah to be the same in all its parts. In contrast to the instability observed by Carvalho, Amy Kalmanofsky's analysis of ch. 13 suggests that that chapter does conform to gendered expectations in its depiction of naked male and female bodies.[40] The loincloth with which the prophet initially covers himself in ch. 13 draws attention to his masculinity through its intimate association with his genitalia. When the loincloth eventually deteriorates, it does so away from his body (vv. 4–7), such that neither the potency of the prophet nor the potency of YHWH is endangered. Jeremiah's nakedness is also merely a means to an end; the point of the narrative is to direct the audience's gaze toward the image of rotten

39. Carvalho, "Sex and the Single Prophet," 253. Carvalho subsequently questions whether this use of gender deviance to signify chaos ultimately reinforces gender dichotomies but, on the basis of the material in chs. 30–31, ultimately concludes that gender "disorder" constitutes part of the book's vision of an ideal society (Carvalho, "Sex and the Single Prophet," 264–5).

40. Amy Kalmanofsky, "Bare Naked: A Gender Analysis of the Naked Body in Jeremiah 13," in *Jeremiah Invented: Constructions and Deconstructions of Jeremiah*, ed. Else K. Holt and Carolyn J. Sharp (LHBOTS 595; London: Bloomsbury, 2015), 49–62.

Israel, not upon the prophet's naked body. His nudity is never explicitly articulated; thus the shame which might accrue to the prophet (or, by extension, the deity) as a result of the exposure of his private parts is avoided. The female body of the personified Israel, by contrast, is on full frontal view.[41] Unlike Jeremiah's nakedness, Israel's nakedness is explicit, leaving her standing before the audience whose gaze is directed to her most intimate parts. The rhetorical power of this image, Kalmanofsky suggests, lies in the gendered associations of female nakedness, linked in ancient Near Eastern iconography to sex and erotic desire. The naked female body is used to shock, shame, and titillate the audience. The exposure of Israel's genitalia ("your skirts are lifted up and you are violated," v. 22; "I myself will lift up your skirts over your face and your shame will be seen," v. 26) signifies her vulnerability in the wake of the withdrawal of divine protection and the humiliation of her punishment at YHWH's hand. Though Kalmanofsky ultimately concludes that the imagery of the naked Israel in ch. 13 is obscene (meant to disturb or disgust) rather than pornographic (meant to arouse and excite), its rhetorical power to achieve this effect is grounded in the gendered social construction of female nudity.

Perhaps the most notable feature of work on chs. 11–20 at the end of the twentieth century and the beginning of the twenty-first century is how relatively little of it there is. The flurry of monograph length studies which appeared at the beginning of this period may be interpreted as having arisen out of the last gasp of earlier research's focus on the historical prophet, even if many of those studies— influenced by the historiographical turn of which they were a part— ultimately concluded that these chapters could provide only limited and tentative, if any, information about that prophet. As the interests of scholarship on the book of Jeremiah have turned in the intervening years away from history and toward new modes of interpretation, the confessions—once viewed as the ultimate locus of insight into the mind and life of the prophet—have fallen into a period of neglect. With the occasional exception, it is only very recently that attention has returned to the poems and prose of these chapters, as some of these newer approaches to the book of Jeremiah have been applied to them. These

41. Elsewhere Kalmanofsky discusses this passage from the perspective of horror theory; see Amy Kalmanofsky, "The Monstrous-Feminine in the Book of Jeremiah," in *Jeremiah (Dis)Placed: New Directions in Writing/Reading Jeremiah*, ed. A. R. Pete Diamond and Louis Stulman (LHBOTS 529; London: T&T Clark, 2011), 190–208.

most recent explorations have often taken the form of articles and essays, rather than the more systematic treatment required of those earlier monographs. This is very much in keeping with wider trends in research on the book of Jeremiah, which is at present largely dominated by focused studies on individual chapters—aptly reflecting the often experimental nature of much of this current work.

Chapter 25 (MT) and Chapters 25 and 32 (LXX)

Judah, Judgment, and the Nations

The Text

A summary of the contents of ch. 25 poses an immediate challenge, because it requires a decision of whether the contents in question are those of the MT or those of the LXX. The latter more or less parallels MT through the first thirteen verses, but the material contained in vv. 15–38 of the MT appears in the LXX only in ch. 32, after six intervening chapters containing the oracles against the nations.[42] The MT's v. 14 has no counterpart in the LXX's ch. 32 at all, while both parts of the remaining material exhibit significant and notable differences between the versions. Because of the importance of these differences in scholarly discussions of this material (in both MT and LXX), it will be useful to begin with a twofold summary: first the contents of MT ch. 25, as this is most likely to be the more familiar version and the one to hand, and then the contents of LXX ch. 25 together with LXX ch. 32.

---

42. For the sake of easier comparison to the MT's ch. 25, some editions of LXX ch. 32 number their verses as vv. 15–38, even though there are no other verses in that chapter. In these editions, the LXX of ch. 32 begins with 32:15 instead of beginning with 32:1, such that, for example, MT 25:21 = LXX 32:21. The addition of chapter and verse numbers is quite a late feature of biblical texts and mainly a matter of convenience, even though these breakdowns usually reflect real features in the text. The numbering of LXX ch. 32 in this way reflects this practical purpose. NETS, however, numbers ch. 32 in its own right, beginning with v. 1 (though it does give the MT verse numbers alongside for reference). See Appendix A for further details about the contents and numbering of MT and LXX; here LXX ch. 32 will be numbered following the latter half of MT ch. 25, with the NETS numbering in brackets.

Chapter 25 (MT)

The chapter begins with a word-formula. The fourth year of Jehoiakim (v. 1) equates to 605 and is significant at other key points in the book (36:1; 45:1; 46:2). Though the text never refers explicitly to the event, this was the year of a key battle between the Babylonian and Egyptian armies at Carchemish on the Euphrates River. This battle proved to be the tipping point in the struggle for dominance over the southern Levant. Though it may not have been immediately obvious at the time—hence the persistence of rebellions and alliances, especially with Egypt—Babylonian authority in the region was never really in question after this point. The book of Jeremiah, including ch. 25, interprets this event theologically, seeing in Babylon's decisive military and political ascendance a sign that Judah's disobedience and infidelity to Yʜwʜ had finally reached a similarly decisive moment. "For twenty-three years," Jeremiah says, he and others have tried to persuade the people to repent and return to obedience and loyalty, without success (vv. 3–7). Now this opportunity has passed; Yʜwʜ is decided on judgment. The agent(s) of punishment will come from the north; this anonymous threat has been a recurring theme in this first half of the book (1:13-15; 4:6; 6:1, 22; 10:22; 13:20; 15:12; and by implication in 16:15 and 23:8, where it refers to the destination of the people's exile). Its use here hearkens back to those earlier warnings. MT ch. 25 explicitly identifies this northern foe as "Nebuchadrezzar of Babylon, my servant" (v. 9), a description which is theologically remarkable; the epithet is normally reserved for Yahwists, not foreign kings.[43]

Not only Judah will be subject to the devastation wrought by Babylon; "all these nations around" will also suffer the consequences of Judah's disobedience. Despite the comprehensiveness of v. 9, v. 11 puts a time limit on these nations' service to the king of Babylon: seventy

43. On the identification of Nebuchadrezzar as Yʜwʜ's "servant" in the MT, see Klaas A. D. Smelik, "My Servant Nebuchadnezzar: The Use of the Epithet 'My Servant' for the Babylonian King Nebuchadnezzar in the Book of Jeremiah," *VT* 64 (2014): 109–34; Raymond de Hoop, "Perspectives after the Exile: The King, עבדי, 'My Servant' in Jeremiah—Some Reflections on MT and LXX," in *Exile and Suffering: A Selection of Papers Read at the 50th Anniversary Meeting of the Old Testament Society of South Africa OTWSA/OTSSA Pretoria August 2007*, ed. Bob Becking and Dirk Human (OudSt 50; Leiden: Brill, 2008), 105–21.

years. Then the Babylonians too will be punished. Though nothing explicit is said of what will become of Judah at that time, the promised destruction of the destroyer perhaps contains a hint of hope. It is certainly interpreted as such in the subsequent tradition, as the motif of seventy years is picked up by the book of Daniel as well as by 2 Chr. 36:21 in attempts to identify an eventual end to Judah's enduring exile.

The articulation of Babylon's fate as recompense ("I will repay them according to their deeds") is unique to the MT, in part because v. 14 exists only there. In the MT, this verse works to connect the first part of ch. 25 to what immediately follows: a lengthy description of punishment in terms of the distribution of the "cup of the wine of wrath" (v. 15). This image for punishment—an image which appears also in Isa. 51:17—evokes the figure of the staggering, incoherent drunk, in order to depict the disjointed and unintelligible horror which will arise in reaction to Yнwн's punishment for those who suffer it, accompanied by the loss of bodily control spurred by extreme grief. Delivered by the hand of the prophet (the first-person "me" and "I"), this cup of wrath will be offered to all in turn; though Judah will be first, it will by no means be last. Judah, then all the other nations and peoples known to the ancient world, will drink from the cup—from Egypt in the south to Elam and Media in the far east (vv. 18–26). Last of all will be "the king of Sheshak," that is, the king of Babylon (v. 26).[44] There is no chance of evasion (v. 28). The decree that all must drink is linked to the destruction of Jerusalem; if Yнwн's own city cannot escape neither can any other (v. 29). The final section of the chapter transitions to a pair of poetic oracles which speak in general terms of the coming judgment on "all flesh" (v. 31). The second of the two (vv. 34–38) uses a metaphor of the shepherds able

44. "Sheshak" is a coded reference to Babylon, using a simple substitution cipher known, from its origins in the biblical Hebrew context, as "atbash." This is one of the simplest kinds of code and works by substituting for each letter the letter which is equidistant from the opposite end of the alphabet. The first letter is replaced by the last letter, the second letter is replaced by the second to last letter, and so on. If the coder were using the Roman alphabet, the letter A would be replaced by the letter Z, B would be replaced by Y, C by X, and so on. With the Hebrew alphabet, *aleph* is replaced by *tau*, *bet* is replaced by *shin*, and so on (this is where the name *atbash* comes from: **a**leph-**t**au-**b**et-**sh**in). Through this system of letter replacements, "Babylon," which in Hebrew is written *b-b-l* (Hebrew is traditionally written using only the consonants), becomes *sh-sh-k*.

to defend neither their flock nor themselves from a leonine Yᴴᴡᴴ, drawing on the pastoral imagery often used to depict the ideal king in order to drive home the catastrophic failures of Judah's leadership.

Chapter 25 and Chapter 32 (LXX)

The LXX of ch. 25 differs from the MT in several ways. The first and one of the most notable is that the MT's identification of the agent of Yʜᴡʜ's punishment as Nebuchadrezzar, king of Babylon, is absent from the LXX. Thus in the very first verse the MT locates "the word that came to Jeremiah" not only with reference to the regnal year of Judah's king but also by the regnal year of Nebuchadrezzar, whereas the LXX refers only to Jehoiakim. Though the LXX text perhaps implies a looming judgment from its opening verses—and certainly only a reader who had been paying no attention for the preceding twenty-four chapters would be surprised by its explicit pronouncement in vv. 8–11—it leaves the future far more to the reader's imagination. (Perhaps this is worse.) By contrast, any element of suspense is eliminated in the MT by the double dating.

The LXX and MT also differ in whom they present as the speaker in vv. 3–5. In the LXX the "I" who "spoke to you" (v. 3), who sent the prophets (v. 4), and who implored the people to turn from evil (v. 5) is Yʜᴡʜ, whereas the MT engages a circumlocution such that "the word of Yʜᴡʜ" (v. 3) comes to Jeremiah and it is Jeremiah who is the "I" who has "spoken persistently to you" (v. 3); a Yʜᴡʜ referred to in the third person who sent the prophets (v. 4); and these collective and unnamed prophets who sought the people's repentance (v. 5). The MT's emphasis in ch. 25 both on the "word" of Yʜᴡʜ and on Jeremiah as a prophet sent by Yʜᴡʜ is typical of MT Jeremiah as a whole. The MT's locution in v. 3 works to emphasize this point, in conjunction with the reference to "his [Yʜᴡʜ's] servants the prophets" in v. 4. That the LXX's consistent first-person voice of Yʜᴡʜ—or, rather, an underlying Hebrew *Vorlage* with a consistent first person—was probably altered in the development of the MT (rather than the other way around) seems to be suggested by the persistence of the divine first person in vv. 6–7. Most of v. 7, from "says Yʜᴡʜ" onwards, is only in MT.

The pronouncement of judgment in vv. 8–11 warns in the LXX of an anonymous enemy from the north, whom the MT again names as Nebuchadrezzar (v. 9). The narrowly defined service to the king of Babylon in MT v. 11 is in the LXX a broader pronouncement of service "amongst the nations," though the LXX's declaration that at the end of seventy years "that nation" will be punished perhaps hints at the singularity which in the MT is transformed into "the king of Babylon and that nation, the land of the Chaldeans."

At this point, MT appends to v. 13 a note that the contents of "this book" are Jeremiah's prophesies against all the nations and a summative statement about the fate of "many nations and great kings" (MT v. 14). In LXX, these are unnecessary because the text immediately proceeds from "everything written in this book" (v. 13) to the oracles against the nations, beginning with an oracle against Elam (contained in MT at 49:34-39).[45]

To pick up the rest of the material contained in MT ch. 25 requires jumping forward in the LXX several chapters, to LXX ch. 32. Here too, YHWH offers the wine cup from which all nations are to drink. Unlike MT ch. 25, in which v. 15 [NETS 32:1] already emphasizes that the divine speech is "to me," that is, the prophet (though unnamed), LXX delays this prophetic first person until v. 17 [v. 3]. As noted earlier, this emphasis on the close relationship between YHWH and prophet, though present in LXX Jeremiah, is particularly strong in the MT.

LXX ch. 32 then lists the nations which the prophet, on behalf of YHWH, makes drink from this cup of judgment. Coming in the LXX at the end of the OANs, both this list and the episode as a whole serve to recapitulate the judgment which has been proclaimed upon the nations in the preceding chapters. The relatively lesser role of Babylon in the LXX—most obvious in the location of the oracles against Babylon in the middle of the OANs, rather than at their climax, as well as their substantially shorter length—is apparent in its absence from this list; though it might be perceived to be implied in v. 26 [v. 12], which refers to "all the kings from the east wind, those far and those near" and "all the kingdoms that are on the surface of the earth," it is nowhere explicitly named. As with MT, however, the inclusion of the nations in YHWH's coming judgment is attendant on a judgment that begins with Jerusalem. Though YHWH's own city is the first to drink, it is only the first among equals; "all flesh" (v. 31 [v. 17]) has offended against YHWH.

---

45. There are a few minor differences between the MT and the LXX in the Elam oracle: MT dates the oracle to the beginning of the reign of Zedekiah (49:34); YHWH is given the title "of hosts" (v. 35); "says YHWH" occurs twice in MT where it does not in LXX (vv. 37, 38). All of these are typical of MT. For the overall order of the OANs, which differ in the MT and the LXX, see Appendix A.

The passage speaks of Y<small>HWH</small> in the third person throughout, save a reference to "my anger" in v. 37 [v. 23].

Approaches to Interpretation

The differences between the MT and the LXX have long been a focus for attempts to understand the process by which the traditions associated with a prophet called Jeremiah came to be preserved in the two forms now extant. The particularly obvious nature of these differences with regard to MT's ch. 25 has made this chapter an especially prominent feature of this discussion.

In a typical collocation of such investigations with traditionally historical interests about the origins of the book(s), Richard Steiner seeks to identify the editors of the two versions with the two sons of Neriah: Baruch and Seraiah.[46] His starting point is the widely (though not universally) accepted proposal that the *Vorlage* of the LXX represents an earlier, first edition of the Jeremiah traditions, which was later expanded into a second edition and gave rise in due course to the extant MT.[47] Steiner then draws attention to the two individuals who appear at the end of each of these editions: LXX concludes with an oracle addressed to Baruch (MT ch. 45), while MT concludes with instructions addressed to Baruch's brother, Seraiah (MT ch. 51, excluding ch. 52 as an appendix). On this basis, he argues that the version of the Jeremiah traditions which is preserved by the LXX is mainly attributable to Baruch, while the version preserved by the MT is attributable to Seraiah. He suggests that this would explain several aspects of the MT tradition, including the authority on which the MT's editor—for him, Seraiah—felt able to alter and supplement his material so significantly; the MT's stronger focus on and prioritization of the Babylonian exiles (because this is the community in which Seraiah was living and working); and the greater degree of explicitness in the MT regarding the ultimate destruction of Babylon.

Steiner pays particular attention to ch. 25, noting that the MT explicitly identifies the northern enemy as Babylon and that the relocation and reordering of the OANs have the effect of making the

46. Richard C. Steiner, "The Two Sons of Neriah and the Two Editions of Jeremiah in the Light of Two Atbash Code-Words for Babylon," *VT* 46 (1996): 74–84.

47. Especially J. Gerald Janzen, *Studies in the Text of Jeremiah* (HSM 6; Cambridge, MA: Harvard University Press, 1973); Emanuel Tov, "Exegetical Notes on the Hebrew Vorlage of the LXX of Jeremiah 27 (34)," *ZAW* 91 (1979): 73–93.

oracle(s) against Babylon the climactic conclusion of the entire book. Coded references to Babylon in v. 14 ("Sheshak") and to the Chaldeans in 51:1 ("Leb Qamai") are a result of Seraiah's presence in Babylon where, Steiner suggests, these terms would have been in common use for the exiles' Babylonian overlords.[48] He concludes from the Babylonian orientation of MT that the editor of this so-called second edition (the MT or something close to it) was Seraiah ben Neriah.

That the MT of the book of Jeremiah betrays a more strongly Babylonian orientation than the LXX, however, need not necessarily mean that its editor is individually identifiable as Seraiah. Attending especially to vv. 1–14, Anneli Aejmelaeus observes that there are strong similarities between this section and a number of other passages in the book. Verse 3, with its declaration that Jeremiah has spoken the word of YHWH for 23 years, since the thirteenth year of Josiah, links to the dating scheme of 1:2-3 in order to give Jeremiah a forty-year ministry; vv. 3–7 draw on a variety of other passages, including 35:14-15 and ch. 7; and the "utter destruction" of v. 11 presupposes a concept of the empty land which characterizes late passages such as ch. 24.[49] On the basis of these links Aejmelaeus argues that 25:1-13(14) was already serving an editorial purpose in the earlier edition represented by the LXX, having been designed to pick up various threads from other material in the book. The purpose of this composition was to provide "*an introduction for a collection of oracles against the nations* which [the editor] wished to insert in the Book of Jeremiah."[50] In other words, Aejmelaeus envisions a version of the book of Jeremiah that included material now in chs. 7, 24 and 35 and an editor drawing elements out of that existing material in order to provide a segue into several chapters of additional material. Aejmelaeus also observes that ch. 1, in which Jeremiah is presented as a "prophet to the nations," makes very little sense unless the OANs are part of the book to follow. She therefore concludes that both ch. 1 and ch. 25 are part of an editorial effort to include a collection of OANs in the book and identifies this effort with a late, deuteronomistic stage in the book's development.

48. Given that the name of Babylon is not otherwise obscured in either ch. 25 or in the oracles against Babylon in chs. 50–51, however, he has to suggest that they are being used to flout the usual attempt to be covert about anti-Babylonian sentiments.

49. Anneli Aejmelaeus, "Jeremiah at the Turning-Point of History: The Function of Jer. xxv 1–14 in the Book of Jeremiah," *VT* 52 (2002): 459–82.

50. Aejmelaeus, "Jeremiah at the Turning-Point of History," 473 (italics in the original).

As reflected in the language Aejmelaeus uses, ch. 25's concern with the worship of other gods (v. 6), the elevated role of prophets (v. 4), and the notion that the land was a conditional gift (v. 5) are typical of deuteronomistic language and theology, very similar to the exhortative sections of Deuteronomy as well as the explanations for the exile which are given by 2 Kings. It is not surprising, therefore, to find that this chapter has been especially discussed from the perspective of deuteronomistic involvement in the formation of the book. One of the most prominent contemporary scholars of the deuteronomistic literature is Thomas Römer, who has turned his attention to the location of ch. 25 in the formation and structure of the book of Jeremiah specifically from the perspective of its deuteronomistic characteristics.[51] The background of his argument is the suggestion made by a number of scholars over the course of the twentieth century that the deuteronomistic features of the book are of little, if any, help for understanding its formation. Weippert, for example, argued that the language, style, and theology identified by scholars as deuteronomistic is little more than the typical prose style of the seventh and sixth centuries.[52] Its appearance in the book of Jeremiah is therefore of no particular significance.

If this were the case, Römer argues, then this deuteronomistic style should also be typical of other books from the same time period. Yet, though traces of deuteronomistic language and theology appear sporadically in many books in the Hebrew Bible, it is only the book of Jeremiah and parts of the Deuteronomistic History (Deuteronomy, Joshua, Judges, 1–2 Samuel, and 1–2 Kings) which contain extensive amounts of it.[53] This suggests a particular interest in the book of Jeremiah among a group of deuteronomistic scribes and

---

51. Thomas C. Römer, "How Did Jeremiah Become a Convert to Deuteronomistic Ideology?" in *Those Elusive Deuteronomists: The Phenomenon of Pan-Deuteronomism*, ed. Linda S. Schearing and Steven L. McKenzie (LHBOTS 268; Sheffield: Sheffield Academic, 1999), 189–99.

52. Helga Weippert, *Die Prosareden des Jeremiabuches* (BZAW 132; Berlin: de Gruyter, 1973).

53. On deuteronomistic features in Jeremiah and other prophetic books, see Robert A. Kugler, "The Deuteronomists and the Latter Prophets," in *Those Elusive Deuteronomists: The Phenomenon of Pan-Deuteronomism*, ed. Linda S. Schearing and Steven L. McKenzie (LHBOTS 268; Sheffield: Sheffield Academic, 1999), 127–44.

editors. However, it complicates matters that this interest is reflected in more than one stage of the book. This is apparent from the two versions: although there are already significant deuteronomistic characteristics in LXX, much of the additional material in MT also reflects deuteronomistic style and theology. The existence of multiple layers of deuteronomistic material in the book makes it harder to tell whether it was added as part of a coherent editorial strategy or if it was added ad hoc, in bits and pieces (the rolling corpus concept advocated by McKane). Carroll and McKane argued that there is no coherence discernable in this material, whereas Römer wishes to argue that there is.

Focusing first on the prose sermons, where the deuteronomistic features are most widely recognized, Römer argues that these passages are not just similar in theology, language, and style but are actually interrelated. He pays special attention to chs. 7, 25, and 35, highlighting the idea of the land as a gift to the ancestors from YHWH which is conditional on the people's ethical and theological behavior. Each of these chapters implores its audience to "turn now, every one of you, from your evil way and wicked doings" (25:5; similarly 7:5; 35:15). Römer observes that the Deuteronomistic History uses a similar technique—a series of interrelated prose discourses that act as structural markers—and argues that these chapters form a "literary vault," spanning a first deuteronomistic edition of the book which contained chs. 7–35. He suggests that this first edition was undertaken as an attempt by the deuteronomists to co-opt the Jeremiah tradition, which was too prominent in their community to be ignored but contrary to their own interpretation of the exile (insofar as it supported the possibility of continued life in the land—as, for example, in ch. 32). This first edition was then expanded by the addition of a scribal chronicle about Jeremiah in chs. 37–44, by the collection of oracles in chs. 2–6, and by an editorial frame in chs. 1 and 45.[54] Chapter 36, with its story of the two scrolls, was developed to legitimate this second edition of the book.

Römer's account of the book's development is quite different from the construction of the book in two "halves"—chs. 1–25 and

---

54. The notion of a scribal chronicle is associated especially with Christopher Seitz, though it has since been widely taken up (Christopher R. Seitz, *Theology in Conflict: Reactions to the Exile in the Book of Jeremiah*, [BZAW 176; Berlin: de Gruyter, 1989]).

chs. 26–52—which has been advocated by other scholars and which is often reflected in the division of multivolume commentaries. Central to these differences are disagreements over the nature and extent of the deuteronomistic features of the book. Where Römer sees such characteristics across the book, albeit in varying degrees of intensity, others have followed the divisions of Duhm and Mowinckel in seeing the strongest deuteronomistic influences in chs. 1–25, in the prose sermons which appear in these chapters. Louis Stulman, for example, argued that these sermons work to organize and structure the first half of the book—balancing the increasing chaos of the poetry, in which the various physical and ideological institutions of Judah's existence are rejected and destroyed.[55] Stulman focused especially on the function of chs. 1 and 25 as bookends, arguing that they prepare (ch. 1) and reinforce (ch. 25) the reader's interpretation of the intervening material in terms of the prophetic word and the sovereignty of Yhwh. Chapter 25 asserts the legitimacy of Jeremiah's prophetic office and the guilt of the people, as well as identifying the enemy from the north as Nebuchadrezzar, servant of Yhwh. Stulman's interpretation of these connections is influenced by his decision to focus on the MT of ch. 25 which, because it includes vv. 15–38, has more connections with ch. 1 than does the briefer ch. 25 in the LXX. In a study specifically focused on the role of ch. 25 in the book's formation and meaning, this decision has the effect of magnifying both the importance of ch. 25 and the significance of the differences between MT ch. 25 and LXX ch. 25.

Given the significant challenges facing any attempt to juggle both the MT and the LXX of ch. 25, it is perhaps no great surprise that it

55. Louis Stulman, *The Prose Sermons of the Book of Jeremiah: A Redescription of the Correspondences with the Deuteronomistic Literature in the Light of Recent Text-Critical Research* (SBLDS 83; Atlanta, GA: Scholars, 1986); Louis Stulman, *Order Amid Chaos: Jeremiah as Symbolic Tapestry* (BS 57; Sheffield: Sheffield Academic, 1998); and, in shorter summary, Louis Stulman, "The Prose Sermons as Hermeneutical Guide to Jeremiah 1-25: The Deconstruction of Judah's Symbolic World," in *Troubling Jeremiah*, ed. A. R. Pete Diamond, Kathleen M. O'Connor, and Louis Stulman (JSOTSup 260; Sheffield: Sheffield Academic, 1999), 34–63. Though his conclusions differ somewhat from Stulman's, Clements also sees the deuteronomistic material as structuring chs. 1–25 (Ronald E. Clements, "Jeremiah 1–25 and the Deuteronomistic History," in *Understanding Poets and Prophets: Essays in Honor of George Wishart Anderson*, ed. A.G. Auld [JSOTSup 152; Sheffield: JSOT, 1993], 93–113).

has been the subject of particular attention by scholars working with synchronic and canonical approaches. Sometimes this can be quite polemical; Martin Kessler, for example, condemns the "excessive preoccupation with historical criticism" for its "results that can only be called meager," advocating instead a synchronic approach which minimizes historical considerations.[56] He argues that the apparent disorganization of the book, rather than provoking diachronic attempts to account for its formation, should promote synchronic readings: the book "deliberately ignore[s]" chronological considerations and readers should therefore also abandon their attempts to discern the chronology of the book's formation.[57] As for almost all scholars working from a canonical or synchronic perspective, Kessler works from the MT rather than the LXX.

From this perspective Kessler highlights the issue of true and false prophecy, interpreting the appearance of this issue in ch. 25 in relation to the texts preceding, especially chs. 20–24, and the texts following, especially chs. 26–29. Such an argument would be all but impossible were he working from the LXX, in which chs. 26–29 only follow ch. 25 in the loosest of senses, appearing several chapters later after the OANs. Within MT, however, Kessler argues that vv. 8–14 (within the chapter) and ch. 25 (within the book) function as "hinges," perched between the preceding announcements of judgment on Judah (25:1-11 and chs. 1–24) and the subsequent announcements of judgment on Babylon (25:12-14 and chs. 50–51, with the latter coming after the judgment on Judah has been worked out in chs. 26–45).[58] The climactic position of Babylon in 25:26 echoes the climactic position of the oracles against Babylon in chs. 50–51.

56. Martin Kessler, "Jeremiah 25,1–29: Text and Context: A Synchronic Study," *ZAW* 109 (1997): 45.

57. Kessler, "Jeremiah 25,1–29," 47. Elsewhere he describes this theme as an emphasis on the prophetic *persona* (Martin Kessler, "The Function of Chapters 25 and 50–51 in the Book of Jeremiah," in *Troubling Jeremiah*, ed. A. R. Pete Diamond, Kathleen M. O'Connor, and Louis Stulman [JSOTSup 260; Sheffield: Sheffield Academic, 1999], 68).

58. Kessler, "Jeremiah 25,1–29," 61. This proposal to focus on chs. 1, 25, and 50–51 as the three pillars which hold up the structure of the book of Jeremiah is further developed in Kessler, "The Function of Chapters 25 and 50–51" and Martin Kessler, "The Scaffolding of the Book of Jeremiah," in *Reading the Book of Jeremiah: A Search for Coherence*, ed. Martin Kessler (Winona Lake, IN: Eisenbrauns, 2004), 57–66; in the latter Kessler argues that this structure supports the inclusion of the OANs in the book.

Theologically, Kessler's focus on ch. 25 as a key turning point in the transition from judgment against Judah to judgment against Babylon highlights a kind of reciprocal relationship between Judah and Babylon: judgment for one implies salvation for the other, and vice versa. This conception of the relationship between Babylon's downfall and Judah/ Israel's eventual restoration is more common in discussions of the structure of the LXX of the book of Jeremiah, in which the book's structure is sometimes seen to reflect a progression from judgment on Judah, to judgment on the nations, to salvation for Judah.[59] By focusing on ch. 25, Kessler is able to identify a similar concept in MT.

Though Kessler has a strong dislike for Carroll's ideological approach to the text, they draw similar attention to ch. 25's location and function as both the end of chs. 1–25 and the introduction to chs. 26–52. Carroll describes the chapter as "a Janus text" that looks both backwards and forwards at once.[60] Unlike Kessler, however, Carroll attends to certain ways in which ch. 25 complicates or contradicts other passages in the book. For example, he draws attention to the fact that 25:1-7 blames the people for having refused to listen to the prophets—a complaint which comes close on the heels of accusations that the people are to blame for

59. This schema highlights the hopeful material at the beginning of the section (MT chs. 30–33, LXX chs. 37–40) over the more subdued material which follows. A similar arc has also been perceived in some other prophetic books, especially Isaiah, Ezekiel, and Zephaniah, in which the OANs are preceded by oracles of judgment against Israel and then followed by oracles of salvation for Israel, after oracles of judgment against the nations. The fact that the LXX order mirrors that of these other books has been interpreted both as a sign of the originality of the LXX order (this is how prophetic books were usually structured and it was the later editorial interests of the MT which disrupted it) and as a sign of the originality of the MT order (by virtue of its peculiarity MT is more likely to be original, as the LXX represents an attempt to conform the book of Jeremiah to Isaiah and Ezekiel). However, the identification of such a schema and its depiction in eschatological terms stems more from the interests of Christian systematic theology than the structure of the biblical prophetic books themselves. See Marvin A. Sweeney, "The Masoretic and Septuagint Versions of the Book of Jeremiah in Synchronic and Diachronic Perspective," in *Form and Intertextuality in Prophetic and Apocalyptic Literature* (FAT 45; Tübingen: Mohr Siebeck, 2005), 65–77.

60. Robert P. Carroll, "Halfway through a Dark Wood: Reflections on Jeremiah 25," in *Troubling Jeremiah*, ed. A. R. Pete Diamond, Kathleen M. O'Connor, and Louis Stulman (JSOTSup 260; Sheffield: Sheffield Academic, 1999), 73–86.

listening to the prophets (23:9-40)! Interpreters usually conclude that the former accusation refers to the failure to listen to Jeremiah, the right or true prophet, whereas the latter concerns those who have listened to false or the wrong kind of prophets, but Carroll points out that this is clarity brought to the text, rather than clarity inherent within it.[61] Carroll also observes the way in which Nebuchadrezzar is domesticated by the MT through the depiction of him as YHWH's servant and in the limitation of Babylonian dominance: "the destructive force of the Babylonian hegemony becomes but *a moment* in YHWH's positive treatment of Jerusalem and Judah."[62] He suggests that this ultimately positive depiction of Judah's future was created by the editors and redactors of the tradition and that it effectively subverted much of what was originally conveyed by prophetic voices of judgment. Though equally synchronic and canonical, Carroll's reading is thus of a very different kind than that of Kessler.

As these diverse efforts indicate, there is much to be gained from synchronic and canonical approaches to the book of Jeremiah. Underlying such approaches is often a frustration with the inaccessibility for nonspecialists of many of the common scholarly methods of reading biblical texts, such as redaction criticism. Thus Kessler advocates nonhistorical reading with the declaration that this is how "to serve the faithful community best."[63] More problematic is his contention that this means that "we should try to shape the picture that is consistent with the literature itself, let the text speak for itself and refrain from value judgments or overlay[ing] the text with extrinsic ideologies."[64] As other approaches to the book of Jeremiah make clear, however, the meaning of the text is sometimes obscure and frequently multivalent, if not downright self-contradictory. While a synchronic, close-reading approach has a contribution to make, so too do these other methods. In Carroll's words, "the more readings the better, because every reading is a rereading which affords all other readers a further opportunity for rethinking."[65]

---

61. For the suggestion, however, that Jeremiah was not originally a prophet at all, see Matthijs J. de Jong, "Why Jeremiah Is Not among the Prophets: An Analysis of the Terms נביא and נביאים in the Book of Jeremiah," *JSOT* 35 (2011): 483–510.

62. Carroll, "Halfway through a Dark Wood," 79.

63. Kessler, "The Function of Chapters 25 and 50–51," 72.

64. Kessler, "The Function of Chapters 25 and 50–51," 72.

65. Carroll, "Halfway through a Dark Wood," 85.

Chapter 32

Jeremiah Acquires a Field

The Text

Chapter 32 commences with a demand from the king to Jeremiah: why does the prophet speak of Yнwн's intentions to hand over the city and Zedekiah to the power of the Babylonians (vv. 3–5)? In the wider narrative this query is located in the midst of the Babylonian siege of Jerusalem. For the first time—there will be several such notices in the following chapters—we are told that Jeremiah was imprisoned, though with no reason given for his imprisonment (v. 2).

Jeremiah's response to the king's question is not obviously a response. Rather than providing a direct explanation, he reports a divine word (v. 6) presaging an opportunity to acquire a field in Anathoth (v. 7), the town from which he is elsewhere said to have come (1:1; 29:27). The opportunity duly comes about and Jeremiah proceeds with the acquisition of the property (vv. 8–9). Given that the offer comes from a relative of Jeremiah—his cousin, the son of his uncle—and is couched by him in terms of "the right of possession and redemption" (v. 8), it is generally considered that the transaction is proposed and undertaken against a legal and cultural background in which land was not freely bought and sold private property, in the way that most Western property transactions are today, but rather a matter of familial inheritance, in which the retention of the property within the family was of utmost importance.[66] Although the details of the system are not entirely clear from the biblical texts which address it (Leviticus 25; Ruth) the "right" (or obligation) of redemption probably arose in circumstances where property had been used as collateral for a loan, but then the debt could not be paid off by the original debtor. In such a scenario, the property is in danger of passing out of the hands of the family; to prevent this from happening, another family member could be called upon to settle the debt and take over the property.

The acquisition of the field is not merely reported in summary but detailed at some length: Jeremiah weighs out money to give to his cousin, has legal paperwork drawn up and witnessed, and hands these

---

66. William R. Domeris, "The Land Claim of Jeremiah—Was Max Weber Right?" in *Jeremiah (Dis)Placed: New Directions in Writing/Reading Jeremiah*, ed. A. R. Pete Diamond and Louis Stulman (LHBOTS 529; London: T&T Clark, 2011), 136–49.

documents to Baruch, instructing him to have them sealed up in a ceramic jar so that they might be preserved (vv. 10–14). Finally there is an explanation—of sorts—for all of this palaver: it is meant to represent a divine guarantee that "houses and fields and vineyards shall again be bought in this land" (v. 15).

That the logic of this is not entirely clear even to Jeremiah is apparent from his reaction: a lengthy prayer which, albeit in a rather roundabout fashion, enquires just what Yhwh is up to (vv. 17–25). The prayer is couched as a recitation of Yhwh's past powerful deeds, with specific attention paid to Yhwh's role as creator (v. 17) and as the one who brought Israel out of Egypt and into the promised land (vv. 20–22). Only then does the prayer reach the crux of the matter: the people's disobedience has precipitated divine punishment in the form of the Babylonians, yet Jeremiah has been told to go and acquire a field (vv. 23–25)! Though the long run-up, with its manifold praises of the mighty acts of Yhwh, suggests a degree of self-professed prophetic ignorance concerning the divine logic, the climax of the prayer is a demand for an explanation of how the inevitability of judgment, which has thus far been the focus of the divine and prophetic word, is meant to sit alongside this declaration of hope. Perhaps, too, it implies a certain frustration on the part of the prophet, or the doom-laden tradition which he represents, with the apparent divine failure to stay on message: rather than backing Jeremiah's stubbornly persistent proclamations of judgment and looming destruction at the hand of the Babylonians, at the critical moment Yhwh suddenly changes the tune and promises salvation.

Yhwh's response to Jeremiah consumes the latter half of the chapter. Insofar as it provides an explanation for Jeremiah's bafflement, it says that judgment and hope are both/and, rather than either/or. An initial reminder of Yhwh's dominion (over "all flesh," in a notably universalistic phrase; v. 27) segues into an affirmation that judgment is indeed imminent and inevitable, a consequence of the people's disobedience and especially their worship of other gods (vv. 28–35). Juxtaposed with this is a declaration that despite the city being given over to the Babylonians, its dispersed inhabitants will be gathered back by Yhwh to the land (vv. 36–37). Echoing the language of the covenant formula ("you will be my people and I will be your God"), this return will be marked by a renewed and now eternal covenant, from which the people will be unable to turn (vv. 38–41).

Finally v. 42 brings judgment and promise into a nearer relation than mere juxtaposition: "Just as I have brought all this great disaster upon this people, so I will bring upon them all the good fortune that I now promise them." Both are the result of divine intention, not random or happenstance. Just as YHWH promised judgment and destruction, fulfilling it with the siege and destruction of the city by the Babylonians, now YHWH promises—and will fulfil—a return to and renewal of everyday life in the land. The acquisition of fields, the transfer of money, and the signing, sealing, and witnessing of the requisite legal papers represent the eventual return to normal life, in all the far corners of Judah (vv. 43–44).

Approaches to Interpretation

Like the rest of the book of Jeremiah, ch. 32 has a variety of differences in its MT and LXX versions. Andrew Shead divides the variants between MT and LXX into two types: variations attributable to the process of formation of the MT and variations attributable to the process of formation of the *Vorlage* of the LXX (LXX[V]).[67] To the former, Shead attributes the expansion of several names and titles; repetition of certain words and phrases in order to improve or clarify the structure of the narrative (such as "says YHWH" in vv. 5, 30, and 44 and the addition of "therefore" in v. 36); additions from parallel passages (such as the addition of "according to the fruit of their doings" in v. 19 on the basis of the similar passage at 17:10); and a few places where an addition helps to clarify the sense (such as the addition of "all" in vv. 12 and 19). Notably, he argues that most of this material is "concerned with improving the clarity and tightening the structure."[68] That is, the changes are only very rarely exegetical in nature. Though matters with regard to the LXX[(V)] are less certain because of the inevitably imperfect process of retroversion, Shead argues that several of the differences between the LXX and the MT relate to similar efforts to clarify and improve the structure of the chapter by the editor of the Hebrew *Vorlage* of the LXX. However, he also argues that some of the differences are the result of mistakes on the part of the Greek translator, such as accidentally skipping a line or two (vv. 5–6, 30b) or jumping from a letter or combination of letters in one word to the next time that letter or combination of letters occurs

67. Andrew G. Shead, *The Open Book and the Sealed Book: Jeremiah 32 in Its Hebrew and Greek Recensions* (JSOTSup 347; Sheffield: Sheffield Academic, 2002), 260.

68. Shead, *The Open Book*, 247.

and dropping out the material in between.[69] Sometimes these mistakes caused further changes in the text, in order to make the remaining material make sense.

Shead's analysis of these two versions of ch. 32 relates to a significant point of scholarly argument over the relationship between LXX and MT: is the MT longer because it has added material, or because the LXX has dropped material out? The latter—often assumed to be result of a careless or unskilled translator—was the most common opinion until the last third of the twentieth century, when the discovery at Qumran of a few fragments of a Hebrew text of Jeremiah revealed the existence of a shorter Hebrew version of Jeremiah, similar to the text of LXX. The existence of this shorter Hebrew version of Jeremiah, though only preserved in a few verses, has been widely taken as evidence in support of the argument that LXX's Hebrew *Vorlage* was just such a text. In other words, the extant LXX is shorter than the extant MT because the text that the Greek translator was using for his translation was a shorter Hebrew text, rather than because he had a long text akin to the MT and did a poor job of translating it or intentionally abbreviated it. The generally expansionist tendencies of the MT are now widely acknowledged and the relationship between the two surviving versions of the book of Jeremiah usually understood as the result of a more prolonged process of development on the part of the MT. However, the idea that some of the differences between the two versions reflect omissions or alterations by the LXX, rather than additions to the MT, was never entirely abandoned and has recently been attracting attention again. Shead's close analysis of ch. 32 warns against making overly broad generalizations regarding the relationship of the MT to LXX^V, or the translation habits of LXX.

---

69. This kind of accidental omission occurs also in the recopying of Hebrew texts and should not be considered a particular fault of the Greek translator. This also means that something which looks like an accidental omission in LXX might be the result of an earlier accidental omission by a copyist of its *Vorlage*. Depending on the extent and cause of the omission, it may be referred to as *haplography*, *homoioteleuton*, *homoioarcton*, or *parablepsis*. For descriptions of these and other kinds of scribal errors, see Emmanuel Tov, *Textual Criticism of the Hebrew Bible* (3rd ed., Minneapolis, MN: Fortress, 2012), 219–39.

The long process of revision which gave rise to the MT has been an enduring feature of the book's analysis over the last century and, though no longer quite so dominant as it once was, such redactional investigations continue to shed light on the text. One of the most enduring such studies is the work of Christopher Seitz, who argued that the latter half of the book reflects significant disagreements over which of the post-597 communities represented the locus of future hope and restoration.[70] More specifically, Seitz sees in these chapters the results of a redaction undertaken in favor of the Babylonian exiles, often called the *golah*.[71] The particular interests of this editor (or editors) were to disparage the possibility of a theologically defensible continuation of life in the land and so to prioritize the Babylonian exile community over other diaspora groups (especially the one in Egypt).

This basic premise is taken up by Dalit Rom-Shiloni in her analysis of how the promise of an "eternal covenant" in 32:36-41 contrasts the fate of Jerusalem with the extension of hope to the exiles and fits into this picture of the development of the book of Jeremiah.[72] As is generally the case with redactional studies, identifying this kind of addition involves differentiating it from other texts. To this end Rom-Shiloni identifies five features of vv. 36–41, which she argues reflect their dependence on (and therefore their independence

70. Most extensively, Seitz, *Theology in Conflict*, which focuses on chs. 37–43; discussion of ch. 32 appears in his earlier Christopher R. Seitz, "The Crisis of Interpretation over the Meaning and Purpose of the Exile: A Redactional Study of Jeremiah xxi–xliii," *VT* 35 (1985): 78–97; note also the earlier work of Karl-Friedrich Pohlmann, *Studien zum Jeremiabuch: Ein Beitrag zur Frage nach der Entstehung des Jeremiabuches* (FRLANT 118; Göttingen: Vandenhoeck & Ruprecht, 1978) and the subsequent Carolyn J. Sharp, *Prophecy and Ideology in Jeremiah: Struggles for Authority in the Deutero-Jeremianic Prose* (Old Testament Studies; London: T&T Clark, 2003). For a recent argument that the tensions seen and interpreted in redactional terms by Seitz and others are the result of the rhetorical (e.g., sarcastic) use of existing material by the author(s) of these chapters for his own purposes, see Mark Leuchter, *The Polemics of Exile in Jeremiah 26–45* (Cambridge: Cambridge University Press, 2008).

71. Though the word simply means "exile," *golah* is commandeered by the biblical texts and subsequently by scholarship to refer to the Babylonian exiles more specifically.

72. Dalit Rom-Shiloni, "The Prophecy for 'Everlasting Covenant' (Jeremiah xxxii 36–41): An Exilic Addition or a Deuteronomistic Redaction?" *VT* 53 (2003): 201–23.

from) both the received oracles of the prophet and the main pro-*golah* redaction of those oracles.[73] First, she argues, v. 36 combines two formulae—"into the hand of the king of Babylon" and "by the sword, by famine, and by pestilence"—which otherwise occur only separately. Second, v. 37 uses idioms typical of exilic prophecies in the book of Jeremiah, such as the verb *ndh*, "to drive out." Third, the five verses of vv. 37–41 have far more hapax legomena—words which occur only one time in the entire text of the Hebrew Bible—than any other part of the book of Jeremiah. Fourth, these verses use elements of oracles of judgment, but reverse them in order to forecast salvation. Fifth and finally, though the idea of a new or renewed covenant appears elsewhere in the book of Jeremiah, it is quite different here than, for example, in 31:31-34. Methodologically, the cumulative effect of these is stronger than any one of them would be alone. On the basis of these features, Rom-Shiloni contends that vv. 36–41 are designed to buttress the argument favoring the Babylonian exiles, but that they were not written by the main editor responsible making that argument. Rather, they were added by an editor as a minor supporting addition.

John Applegate points out that these kinds of redactional enquiries into the hopeful passages of the book of Jeremiah are usually prompted by the assumption that the oldest core of the book was overwhelmingly characterized by negative proclamations of judgment and destruction, with hopeful messages of salvation minimal, if present at all.[74] Indeed, the problem as perceived by Seitz was that the historical Jeremiah had proclaimed complete and unremitting judgment—yet this had been only partially fulfilled by the events of 597, resulting in disagreements over whether life in the land was theologically still an option. This attitude goes back to Duhm's contention that the prophet Jeremiah spoke only words of doom, arising from a common belief in the exclusively negative message of ("true") seventh and sixth-century prophets. This legacy still persists in the conception of the preexilic prophets as proclaiming primarily judgment, although there is now

73. Rom-Shiloni, "The Prophecy for 'Everlasting Covenant,'" 208–21.

74. John Applegate, "'Peace, Peace, When there Is No Peace': Redactional Integration of Prophecy of Peace into the Judgement of Jeremiah," in *The Book of Jeremiah and Its Reception: Le livre de Jérémie et sa réception*, ed. Adrian H. W. Curtis and Thomas C. Römer (BETL 78; Leuven: Leuven University Press, 1997), 51–90.

more willingness to allow some possibilities of hope and salvation alongside such proclamations.[75]

If the original message of the Jeremiah traditions was fundamentally negative, however, it raises the question of how later editors were able to integrate more hopeful elements into those traditions. Applegate focuses on ch. 32 as an example of how this could be undertaken: by grafting messages of hope onto episodes in the life of the prophet. He sees this episode as depicting a turning point in Jeremiah's message, part of a strand of hopefulness about the future which may be traced through chs. 26–36. This redactional process, however, is not Applegate's primary interest. Instead, he uses the redactional history of the text as a springboard to literary and rhetorical questions: he is interested in the way that the final edition works on and with the reader, in order to persuade him or her that hope has a legitimate place in the Jeremiah tradition.

Applegate draws attention to a number of features of the text which contribute to its rhetorical effectiveness. First, he argues that ch. 32 raises the question of future hope immediately from its opening verses, couching Zedekiah's question in terms which focus on Jeremiah's prophetic activity up to and including the current moment. By not speaking immediately about the future, the text draws attention to it. The convoluted way that the question is presented—Zedekiah quoting Jeremiah quoting YHWH—also attracts attention to the various characters' and to the reader's uncertainty about the message under discussion. Though the word comes to Jeremiah from YHWH (v. 6), it is only later (vv. 7–8) that Jeremiah recognizes it as such and only in v. 25 that the fact that the word included instructions to "buy the field for money and get witnesses" is revealed to the audience. Applegate argues that this forces the reader to ask whether he or she (or anyone) really knows what is happening as events unfold. The reader is told up front what Jeremiah only realizes later (that the word is from YHWH),

---

75. A more fundamental challenge to the presentation of Jeremiah as a prophet of judgment has been put forward by de Jong, "Why Jeremiah Is Not among the Prophets," 483–510; and Matthijs J. de Jong, "Biblical Prophecy—A Scribal Enterprise: The Old Testament Prophecy of Unconditional Judgement Considered as a Literary Phenomenon," *VT* 61 (2011): 39–70. Applegate's essay has a useful review of the history of scholarship since Duhm on the question of how—or whether—the hopeful material fits into the book of Jeremiah (" 'Peace, Peace, When there Is No Peace,' " 53–71).

but denied until v. 25 what Jeremiah must have already known (that the word included instructions). The effect is "to draw the reader into the dilemmas of [Jeremiah] through the dilemmas of the narrative itself."[76]

Only with the divine speech in vv. 26–44 is YHWH's intention in instructing apparently contradictory proclamations of both hope and judgment finally revealed. Just as Jeremiah's question was a juxtaposition of two statements (vv. 24–25), YHWH's answer reiterates the juxtaposition of both judgment and hope. Though the motive for judgment is detailed at length, restoration derives simply from divine desire. The effect, Applegate argues, is to introduce hope by deliberately highlighting its incongruity with judgment, aligning the reader's skepticism with that of the prophet but enabling the extension of the message to include salvation by attributing it to divine initiative.

Questions about the legitimacy of life in the land and an emphasis on the divine word recur in the wider narrative of which ch. 32 forms a part. Although hopeful material in chs. 32–33 has meant that they have often been read with the poetic hope of chs. 30–31, the links between ch. 32 and the subsequent chapters have increasingly led to its interpretation as an introduction to the following narrative.[77] Elena Di Pede, for example, is interested in how the rather unusual contents of ch. 32 work as an introduction to this larger section of narrative.[78]

76. Applegate, " 'Peace, Peace, When there Is No Peace,' " 81.

77. How far this section goes is less agreed. Hardmeier, for example, thinks it stops with 40:6, while Di Pede thinks it goes as far as ch. 45 (Christof Hardmeier, "Jeremia 32,2–15* als Eröffnung der Erzählung von der Gefangenschaft und Befreiung Jeremias in Jer 34,7; 37,3–40,6*," in *Jeremia und die "deuteronomistiche Bewegung*," ed. Walter Groß [BBB 98; Weinheim: Beltz Athenäum, 1995], 187–214; Elena Di Pede, "Jer 32, exergue du récit des chapitres 32–45?" *ZAW* 117 [2005]: 559–73). Adding to the complexity are ch. 32's connections with ch. 36, which comes in the middle of this section, and ch. 26, which lies outside it. Some of this, as Hardmeier suggests, may come from the use of older materials by later editors for their own purposes.

78. Di Pede, "Jer 32"; see also Elena Di Pede, "Jérémie et les rois de Juda, Sédécias et Joaqim," *VT* 56 (2006): 452–69, and Barbara Green, "Sunk in the Mud: Literary Correlation and Collaboration between King and Prophet in the Book of Jeremiah," in *Jeremiah Invented: Constructions and Deconstructions of Jeremiah*, ed. Else K. Holt and Carolyn J. Sharp (LHBOTS 595; London: Bloomsbury, 2015), 34–48, for discussions of the way in which the encounters between prophet and king shape these chapters.

Though the chapter begins with an announcement that what follows is a word of YHWH, what actually follows is a question from Zedekiah; then comes Jeremiah's "response" to this question, which is not really an answer at all. The divine word which was promised in v. 1 is only finally reported in vv. 26–44. Although this peculiar progression has often been seen as a sign of additions to an original core text, Di Pede argues that it is a deliberate way of addressing the tension between judgment and salvation. The reader joins Jeremiah in his confusion and, like Jeremiah, awaits an explanation from YHWH. The ultimate clarity of the divine purpose sets the tone for what follows, while simultaneously warning the reader that the narrative may not make any more sense in the first instance than did Jeremiah's activities vis-à-vis the field in Anathoth. By beginning with the apparently convoluted series of "words" of ch. 32, whose coherence is nevertheless ultimately revealed, the narrative reassures the reader that the key players in what follows may be relied upon: Jeremiah, YHWH, and the narrator. Similarly, Josef Oesch argues that the chapter is concerned to show its audience how they are to identify and respond to this divine word in difficult situations, even when they are not entirely sure that they understand it, with Jeremiah shown responding to the divine word even before he is sure that it is a divine word, as well as asking YHWH for clarification.[79] The text thus presents Jeremiah as a model for an uncertain audience. This narrative

79. Josef M. Oesch, "Zur Makrostruktur und Textintentionalität von Jer 32," in *Jeremia und die "deuteronomistiche Bewegung,"* ed. Walter Groß (BBB 98; Weinheim: Beltz Athenäum, 1995), 215–24. Though it does not form the main focus of his argument, he also notes a good example of the natural ambiguities of certain texts. In this case, the ambiguity lies with the Hebrew word 'ôd in v. 15 and whether it should be understood in this context to mean "again" or "still." Either would be an acceptable translation of the Hebrew, but the theological implications are very different. Does the verse say that houses and vineyards will be bought in the land *again*—that is, that these activities will resume after they have stopped for a certain length of time? Or does it say that houses and vineyards will *still* be bought in the land—that is, that these activities will not cease at any point, despite the judgment which will be brought down on the land? If it means the latter, then it implies the open-ended possibility of continued life in the land—perhaps intending to support the legitimacy of a community in the land under Gedaliah, for example. If it means that these activities will resume, but only after they have stopped, it seems to suggest that such continuity is not an option.

is not just a sign of hope about the renewed acquisition of property, but addresses a much more fundamental question about the people's discernment of the divine word.

A quite different approach to ch. 32 is the recent application of postcolonial theory to highlight its potential multivalence. As the name suggests, postcolonial theory developed in the latter half of the twentieth century as a way of theorizing experiences of and responses to colonial and imperial power from the perspective of the colonized. Its use as a tool for interpreting Hebrew Bible texts is based on the recognition that the experience of Judah and its population under the Babylonian and then Persian empires might be usefully investigated from a similar point of view. As with some other recent approaches, such as queer theory and gender theory, postcolonial theory focuses especially on the construction and exertion of authority, with special attention for the ways in which colonized individuals and groups may resist such authority, either overtly or covertly.

From this perspective, Steed Davidson identifies several problems with the traditional interpretation of these chapters as a message of hope.[80] First, such interpretations preemptively interpret vv. 6–14 in light of v. 15 and v. 44 and as part of an overall message of hope in chs. 30–33, rather than on their own merits. Second, a hopeful interpretation of ch. 32 is a version of the "myth of the empty land," in which the exiles are presented as returning to and (re-)occupying a land which has been empty in their absence. This ignores the reality of those who remained in the land and turns the returnees into an incoming imperial power.[81] In the process, it ignores that the backdrop of the siege of Jerusalem places all the real power in the hands of the Babylonians—an imperial project which is itself legitimated by the divine *imprimatur*. Indeed the chapter strangely obscures the Babylonians' involvement in the whole scenario, implicitly denying any Babylonian claim to the land. The justification for the devastation of Judah and the (temporary) exile of its population (vv. 29–35) in terms of punishment for bad behavior also problematically "authorizes acts of aggression insofar as they have redemptive consequences for subject peoples."[82]

80. Steed V. Davidson, *Empire and Exile: Postcolonial Readings of the Book of Jeremiah* (LHBOTS 542; London: T&T Clark, 2011).

81. On the myth of the empty land, see Hans M. Barstad, *The Myth of the Empty Land: A Study in the History and Archaeology of Judah during the "Exilic" Period* (Oslo: Scandinavian University Press, 1996).

While Davidson acknowledges that the final form of the text renders a hopeful interpretation normative, he suggests that postcolonial theory creates space for and draws attention to these alternative emphases. He ultimately interprets ch. 32 "as an act of nationalist resistance to the empire," in which Jeremiah's "purchase of ancestral property represents an example of the strategic choice not to engage imperial power in the material domain but rather to protect and assert national sovereignty in the spiritual domain."[83] Unlike analyses which rely on the text's own interpretation of the land acquisition (in v. 15 and v. 44), Davidson prioritizes the symbolic action itself, which relies on the idea that the land is inalienable, legally and perpetually bound within the family. The land cannot ever truly belong to the Babylonians; family overrides nation and empire.

Carolyn Sharp picks up where Davidson leaves off, subjecting vv. 16–44 to a feminist gaze.[84] Like Davidson, she highlights the narrative context of ch. 32 in the "crucial liminal moment" of the Babylonian siege, when judgment has begun but not yet ended, as well as its position at the point where prose narratives overlap with the hopefulness of the Book of Consolation; it shares these characteristics with the material in both directions.[85] Sharp associates this liminality with interpretive ambiguity, arguing that vv. 16–44 reflects both Jeremiah's rejection of the people and his prophetic resistance to normative theology—as well as YHWH's angry response to this resistance. The feminist perspective from which Sharp approaches the text brings specific attention to the morally problematic way in which Judah is

82. Davidson, *Empire and Exile*, 61.

83. Davidson, *Empire and Exile*, 56.

84. Carolyn J. Sharp, "Buying Land in the Text of Jeremiah: Feminist Commentary, the Kristevan Abject, and Jeremiah 32," in *Prophecy and Power: Jeremiah in Feminist and Postcolonial Perspective*, ed. Christl M. Maier and Carolyn J. Sharp (LHBOTS 577; London: Bloomsbury, 2013), 150–72. Elsewhere Sharp discusses the complementary objectives of feminist and postcolonial criticisms, arguing that feminist criticism should operate with an appreciation of and engagement with postcolonial, gender, and ideological approaches, insofar as all of these approaches are attentive to the social and cultural distribution of power (Carolyn J. Sharp, "Mapping Jeremiah as/in a Feminist Landscape: Negotiating Ancient and Contemporary Terrains," in *Prophecy and Power: Jeremiah in Feminist and Postcolonial Perspective*, ed. Christl M. Maier and Carolyn J. Sharp [LHBOTS 577; London: Bloomsbury, 2013], 38–56). Sharp and Maier are currently co-authoring a major two-volume commentary integrating these complementary approaches.

85. Sharp, "Buying Land in the Text of Jeremiah," 161.

"abjected" (marked as "horrifying, decadent, or repulsive").[86] Both Jeremiah's prayer and Yʜwʜ's response, she argues, depict Judah as an "unthinkably corrupt, despicable Other."[87] Yet, crucially, this abjection is not limited to Judah/Israel; any interpretation of the text as simply the condemnation and rejection of Judah/Israel by Jeremiah/Yʜwʜ is complicated by Jeremiah's challenge to Yʜwʜ, which amounts to an accusation of divine incomprehensibility. The laudatory praise rings hollow, the insinuation that Yʜwʜ is not really in control hovering just below the surface: "the prophet implies that God is impotent … [and] threatens to cast God himself out of the history of salvation."[88] Yʜwʜ's response to this challenge creates a schism between deity and prophet; Yʜwʜ derides Jeremiah, putting Jeremiah's words in the mouth of the rebellious people (vv. 36, 43) and thereby lumping him together with despicable Judah.

Sharp's attention to this brutal circle of rhetoric both confirms and rejects elements of earlier interpretations. Though the promise of restoration remains, the all-encompassing language used to describe the people (v. 30, for example) has the effect of turning the audience against itself, forcing its members to reject their own history of sin. Yet this same language also collectivizes the people, demanding an equally comprehensive restoration rather than engaging in the petty disputes between exiles and nonexiles. At the same time that these approaches draw attention to the problematic and challenging aspects of the text, in other words, they widen the interpretive scope for constructive engagement with them.

Chapter 36

Baruch Writes a Scroll

The Text

Jeremiah 36 recounts the creation of two scrolls. The second of these is necessitated by the destruction of the first. Both are produced in

---

86. Sharp, "Buying Land in the Text of Jeremiah," 158. The language is drawn from the work of the feminist philosopher Julia Kristeva (Julia Kristeva, *Powers of Horror: An Essay on Abjection*, trans. Leon S. Roudiez [New York: Columbia University Press, 1982]).

87. Sharp, "Buying Land in the Text of Jeremiah," 164.

88. Sharp, "Buying Land in the Text of Jeremiah," 166.

response to divine instruction, if not quite according to it. On two occasions YHWH instructs Jeremiah to "take a scroll and write on it" (vv. 2, 28); each time Jeremiah summons Baruch to write at Jeremiah's dictation. The instructions for the first scroll are that it should include "all the words that I [YHWH] have spoken to you [Jeremiah] against Israel and Judah and all the nations, from the day I spoke to you, from the days of Josiah until today" (v. 2). The second scroll is to contain "all the former words that were in the first scroll" (v. 28). The final verse also reports that "many similar words were added to them" (v. 32). It is only in the final scene that the contents of the (first) scroll are in any way revealed; according to words put in the mouth of the king, it proclaimed "that the king of Babylon will certainly come and destroy this land, and will cut off from it human beings and animals" (v. 29).

According to v. 1, the episode begins in the fourth year of Jehoiakim (again, the year of the battle at Carchemish), with a commission from YHWH to Jeremiah to write a scroll containing the divine words— though the real action is delayed until the fifth year in the MT and the eighth in the LXX (v. 9). The object of this scriptural exercise is to turn the "house of Judah" from "their evil ways" from "their iniquity and their sin" (v. 3), though the nature of these offenses are not detailed. Jeremiah dictates the contents of this scroll to Baruch.

Though the public proclamation of the scroll's contents was not explicitly mentioned in the commission of its creation, arrangements for its "public-ation" are immediately the focus of the following narrative.[89] Again putting a certain distance between himself and the scroll, Jeremiah declares himself unable to enter the temple; in his stead he orders Baruch to go and read their scroll out in the hearing of the people, on an unspecified fast day (vv. 5–6). Baruch carries out this commission in the fifth (eighth) year, in the ninth month, in a room belonging to a fellow member of the family of Shaphan (vv. 9–10). The son of this room's owner hears Baruch's recitation—no mention is made of the people who were its ostensible object—and reports to a rather long list of royal officials, who promptly demand that Baruch bring this scroll and read it to them in turn (vv. 11–15). Alarmed at its contents, they enquire as to their origins; Baruch emphasizes that

89. For the argument that this is very much the purpose of the episode, see Joachim Schaper, "On Writing and Reciting in Jeremiah 36," in *Prophecy in the Book of Jeremiah*, ed. Hans M. Barstad and Reinhard G. Kratz (BZAW 388; Berlin: de Gruyter, 2009), 137–47.

the words have come directly from Jeremiah (vv. 17–18). Unlike Greek and most English translations, the Hebrew is explicit about this, sourcing the words "from his mouth" (v. 18). Having agreed that the king must be told of these words, but apparently not very sanguine about his response, the officials advise Baruch to hide himself and Jeremiah (v. 19).

Sure enough, the king does not react positively to the words of the scroll. To the contrary, he hacks it off in sections as they are read out and throws them into the fire to burn (v. 23). Having completely destroyed the scroll, he orders the arrest of its authors (v. 26), who are nowhere to be found. Though the scroll and its human creators, Baruch and Jeremiah, are the immediate objects of Jehoiakim's rejection, the king's failure to respond positively to the words contained in the scroll reflects his ultimate rejection of YHWH and the divine word. Indeed, YHWH himself is said to hide Jeremiah and Baruch from the king (v. 26). The battle lines are drawn unmistakably, with YHWH and his prophetic word arrayed against the king and his refusal to listen.

Despite the king's destruction of the scroll, the story is not yet over. Rather, Jeremiah is instructed to "take another scroll and write on it" (v. 28). He is also given a specific word to proclaim concerning the king, denying his throne to his descendants, promising him an ignominious death, and extending the king's punishment to include the whole population, who are now finally said to have also refused to heed YHWH's threats (vv. 29–31). Again Jeremiah commissions Baruch to write on his behalf: "all the words of the scroll that King Jehoiakim of Judah had burned in the fire." The episode ends with the tantalizing note that "many similar words were added to them" (v. 32).

Approaches to Interpretation

For perhaps obvious reasons, this episode has attracted intense scholarly attention. It appears to tell of the origins of a written scroll of oracles, received by Jeremiah from YHWH over the course of the first part of his prophetic career and dictated from the mouth of the prophet himself to a scribe who is sufficiently identified with Jeremiah as to necessitate his own disappearance in anticipation of the royal displeasure. It then tells of the creation of a second scroll, comprising the same contents as the first but apparently also containing additional material. Given the dearth of information regarding the production and expansion of biblical books, prophetic or otherwise, the chapter appears a gold mine of details about the occasion of and rationale for the beginnings of at least one. Especially notable is the role of Baruch the scribe, who is said to act as the prophet's amanuensis and to have diligently taken the dictation of the scrolls' contents directly from his mouth. Surely a stronger case for the origins of the Jeremiah tradition with the prophet Jeremiah himself, and for the involvement of Baruch in this process, could hardly be conceived.

Indeed this was taken largely for granted until the latter part of the twentieth century, with most scholarly attention concerned with identifying the contents of each of these scrolls within the extant book (the contents of the first having been preserved through their duplication in the second, per v. 32). Holladay, for example, proceeded on the basis that the scroll dictated by Jeremiah could be duplicated by the prophet on two occasions, apparently identically, and concluded that it must therefore have had some sort of structure or shape by which its contents and sequence could be readily recalled.[90] He contended that this shape might yet be discerned in the extant text and proceeded to attempt to do so, finding the first scroll preserved in chs. 1–7 and the second in chs. 1–11. Operating from the same basic standpoint—that the scrolls of ch. 36 may still be identified in the book of Jeremiah, provided scholars are able appropriately to determine the correct parameters of the search—Lansing Hicks set out an investigation of the likely size and length of the scroll destroyed by Jehoiakim. Drawing on a wide range of archaeological and ancient Near Eastern evidence about the dimensions of the pieces of leather used to create ancient scrolls, the average number of columns written on such scrolls, the number of lines per column, and so on, he finally concluded that Jeremiah's/Baruch's scroll would have contained somewhere between eighteen and twenty-four chapters of the extant book of Jeremiah.[91] Remarkably enough, this corresponds to approximately the length of the first half of the book (chs. 1–25), in which the words most likely to be attributable to Jeremiah are most usually located.

Much of an investigation into the wider context of the chapter, however, begins to raise questions about its historical veracity—and thus about the ability of scholars to locate the scroll(s) in the extant

---

90. William L. Holladay, "The Identification of the Two Scrolls of Jeremiah," *VT* 30(1980): 453.

91. R. Lansing Hicks, "*delet* and *megillāh*: A Fresh Approach to Jeremiah xxxvi," *VT* 33(1983): 44–66.

book. The first sign of trouble is that the episode appears in the so-called biographical material. This material is quite obviously not written by Jeremiah; it is written in the third person. It also often leaves the prophet to follow the action elsewhere, suggesting that its interests go beyond merely the life and activity of Jeremiah. Until the last quarter of the twentieth century, however, the majority of scholars considered these chapters to stem from his amanuensis and friend, the scribe Baruch. Indeed the plausibility of these narratives having originated with Baruch seems to be reinforced by ch. 36, in which the text grants him the writer's role (unlike any of the other references to Jeremiah's words being written down, in 29:1; 30:2; and 51:60), even though the text is not written in the first person voice. The action also follows Baruch far longer than it follows Jeremiah—though eventually he too disappears, leaving only the scroll in view. In a typical summation of the situation, Holladay concluded that "since Baruch took part in the events narrated, one may presume that it is composed by him."[92] Though not supposed to stem from the hand of Jeremiah himself, therefore—a point which indeed the narrative implies was not the case for any part of the book—it could nevertheless be considered an eyewitness account of the earliest stage in the formation of the book of Jeremiah.

A number of challenges for interpretation in these terms arose as scholars began to ask more probing questions about the nature and origins of material with which ch. 36 exhibits strong similarities, especially the prose narratives of chs. 26–45. Though commonly described as biographical, ch. 36 is a typical example of the inaptness of the description. Chapter 36, like the other narratives in this category, shows actually very little interest in Jeremiah himself. It is the fate of the scroll, not the fate of Jeremiah or Baruch, which is the primary focus. Following on from this is that nonbiographical and not-necessarily-historical interests may be at play in these narratives. Indeed in ch. 36 it is readily apparent that the point of the story is primarily theological: the reaction of the king to the word of YHWH. Jeremiah, Baruch, and the scroll are merely the vehicles for that word. The king's and the people's reactions to the scroll are not significant in and of themselves; they are significant only as representations of their response to YHWH. Although the emphasis on Baruch having

92. William L. Holladay, *Jeremiah 2: A Commentary on the Book of the Prophet Jeremiah (26-52)* (Hermeneia; Philadelphia, PA: Fortress, 1989), 253–54.

written the scroll at the dictation of Jeremiah belies a concern with the authority of the prophetic word, the focus is on the word rather than the man.

The staging of the story—Baruch's threefold recitation of the scroll, the danger implied by the advice that Baruch and Jeremiah hide, and the suspense occasioned by the official leaving the scroll behind when they first go to the king—also suggests that ch. 36 has been written with drama in mind. Drawing attention to the literary design of the narrative, Geert Venema has noted how the book uses concrete details to create an illusion of historicity, like the way that historical fiction might use real people, places, or events to tell an otherwise imagined narrative.[93] This illusion, however, is ultimately betrayed by its vagueness, which is revealed on closer inspection. The purportedly intense conflict between Jeremiah and Jehoiakim, for example, never involves any actual contact between the two men. In fact, it is the lack of any direct contact between the king and the prophet in ch. 36 which makes the story work, as a depiction of Jehoiakim's response to the divine word manifest in the form of a scroll. These sorts of observations on the literary and theological features of the text suggest that ch. 36's design and intentions are more complex than a simple historical recitation.

If the narrative of ch. 36 is as much a literary construction as anything else, however, this raises questions of who wrote it and why. The exceptional attention paid to Baruch as Jeremiah's amanuensis seems to imply some particular purpose in this respect and, indeed, the prominence of Baruch and other members of the family of Shaphan in ch. 36 has attracted particular attention with regard to this question. Although Baruch is not necessarily seen as the actual scribe involved in the production of an actual scroll in these discussions, it is nevertheless suggested that the peculiar focus on the role of scribes in the production and transmission of the two scrolls of ch. 36 is in some way significant to the narrative's existence and purpose.

One factor in these discussions is the apparent connection between ch. 36 and the account of the discovery of the book of the law during the reign of Josiah, recounted in 2 Kings 22–23. These two episodes have significant points of similarity which suggest that they might be meant to be interpreted together, or that ch. 36 might be meant to be

93. Geert J. Venema, *Reading Scripture in the Old Testament: Deuteronomy 9–10; 31, 2 Kings 22–23, Jeremiah 36, Nehemiah 8* (OudSt 48; Leiden: Brill, 2004).

interpreted in light of 2 Kings 22–23. Aside from the well-known, book-level connections involving Josiah and deuteronomistic phraseology, Venema has observed a number of further similarities between these texts. Both narratives recount the reading of a scroll three times, including in the house of Yʜᴡʜ. Both give prominence to the family of Shaphan and the mediating role of scribes. Both involve a prophet, a scribe, and a king and both include an oracle for the king which is predicated on his response to the prophet and the divine word.[94] Venema therefore concludes that ch. 36 was meant to be interpreted in light of 2 Kings 22–23. The particular significance of this relationship is revealed by the several key points at which ch. 36 inverts or reverses specific elements of 2 Kings 22–23. So, for example, the three readings of the scroll in 2 Kings 22–23 are progressively more and more public, while in ch. 36 they become more and more private. Even more significantly, the reactions of the two kings are diametrically opposed: Josiah tears his clothes and immediately obeys the instructions of the written word, whereas Jehoiakim is specifically said to have not torn his clothes, attempting instead to destroy the scroll by burning it.[95]

Contributing to the intrigue is the recurring presence of members of the family of Shaphan: in the 2 Kings 22–23 account of Josiah and the book of the law, as well as in ch. 26, in which a member of the family cites another prophet's words in a bid to create space for Jeremiah's doom-laden proclamations; in ch. 29, in which a member is sent with Jeremiah's letter to the exiles in Babylon; in ch. 32, in which Baruch is involved in the documentation of Jeremiah's land acquisition; in ch. 51, in which Baruch's brother, Seraiah, is sent to Babylon with another scroll of oracles and commissioned with a sign-act in connection with them; and of course in ch. 36 itself. The frequency with which members of this family are described as scribes or are depicted as engaged in scribal activities has led to suggestions that ch. 36 is designed to explain and to justify the involvement of a group of scribes in the production, transmission, and development of the book of Jeremiah—perhaps even the prophetic literature as a whole. A significant early voice in this quarter was Hermann-Josef Stipp, who saw the family of Shaphan, or the "aristocratic" circles they represent, as having been involved in

94. Venema, *Reading Scripture*, 95–137.

95. Venema, *Reading Scripture*, 127–29. Wahl describes ch. 36 as "a negative impression" of 2 Kings 22–23 (Harald M. Wahl, "Die Entstehung der Schriftprophetie nach Jer 36," *ZAW* 110 [1998]: 375).

the book of Jeremiah at a relatively early stage.[96] Similarly, Andrew Dearman reckons that the chapter remembers the contributions of a family group of scribal officials "who were primarily responsible for the contents and shape of the Jeremiah scroll."[97] He identifies this extended family of Shaphan with the deuteronomistic scribes and suggests that this group was responsible for the multiplicity of texts which reflect deuteronomistic theology and style, including the book of Jeremiah. In a variation on this theme, Harald Wahl argued that the chapter preserves memories of literary activities in the context of the temple and the court and, more specifically, of the involvement of the family of Shaphan in the preservation, transmission, and redaction of the Jeremiah traditions in the period immediately following the fall of Jerusalem.[98] In contrast to the working assumptions of Holladay and others who sought to identify the origins of the Jeremiah tradition on the basis of hints discerned from ch. 36, Wahl declares that the *Urrolle* ("original [sc]roll," the German term often used to refer to the first or second version of the scroll) never existed.[99] Rather, ch. 36 provides an etiology for the formation of the book of Jeremiah.

96. Hermann-Josef Stipp, *Jeremia im Parteienstreit: Studien zur Textentwicklung von Jer 26, 36–43 und 45 als Beitrag zur Geschichte Jeremias, seines Buches und judäischer Parteien im 6. Jahrhundert* (BBB 82; Frankfurt-am-Main: Anton Hain, 1992) and (later and much more briefly) Hermann-Josef Stipp, *Jeremia, der Tempel und die Aristokratie: Die patrizische (schafanidische) Redaktion des Jeremiabuches* (Kleine Arbeiten zum Alten und Neuen Testament 1; Waltrop: Hartmut Spenner, 2000).

97. J. Andrew Dearman, "My Servants the Scribes: Composition and Context in Jeremiah 36," *JBL* 109 (1990): 403–21; compare Mark Leuchter, *Josiah's Reform and Jeremiah's Scroll: Historical Calamity and Prophetic Response* (HBM 6; Sheffield: Sheffield Phoenix, 2006), who argues that Jeremiah himself was intimately associated with deuteronomistic circles.

98. This is on the basis that the complete destruction of the monarchy would have been inconceivable prior to that point (Wahl, "Die Entstehung der Schriftprophetie"). How Wahl sees the historically inaccurate oracle of judgment against Jehoiakim—that he would have no offspring on the throne of Judah (v. 30)—fitting into this late conception of ch. 36 is not clear. With regard to the deuteronom(ist)ic connection, he notes especially the work of Christopher R. Seitz, "The Prophet Moses and the Canonical Shape of Jeremiah," *ZAW* 106 (1989): 3–27, which will be more accessible for those without German.

99. Wahl, "Die Entstehung der Schriftprophetie," 375.

From this scribal perspective, the crucial detail of ch. 36 occurs in the final phrase of the chapter: "and many similar words were added to them" (v. 32). Though the context might be taken to imply that these additions were made straight away, there is nothing in the text which necessitates such immediacy. Rather, the note leaves the extent and the contents of the scroll entirely open-ended.[100] Given especially the widely recognized and indeed extensive evidence for editorial activity in the book of Jeremiah, such open-endedness seems more than mere coincidence. Here is a declaration of the origins of the tradition with Jeremiah which nonetheless leaves the way clear for the development of this tradition through further additions. The various members of the Shaphan family are not merely described as writing, reading, and preserving the divine word but as interpreting it—and interpretation of the prophetic tradition is exactly what is in progress in the many layers of the book of Jeremiah.[101]

Theologically and sociologically, this focus on writing and on the written word suggests a transition or change in emphasis within the prophetic tradition itself, from social and historical origins in which the locus of prophetic authority was in the spoken words of the prophet himself or herself to a situation in which the locus of authority resides in the written rendition of those words on a scroll.[102] The word from YHWH, through this transition from speech to text, is emancipated from the immediate confines and limitations of the living, breathing prophet. Prophetic authority is transmuted to the transient, transportable, and transformable written word. Though the written words still originate with the prophet—even from his very mouth (v.18 MT)—the prophet's own presence is no longer necessary for their transmission or effectiveness. In the prophet's stead stands the scribe and the scroll which he pens; these become the medium for the ongoing transmission of the divine word. The real star of the show

---

100. Contrast, for example, the so-called "canon formula" of Deut. 13:1 [Eng 12:32], in which the contents of the text are declared immutable and fixed; also Deut. 4:1-2; Prov. 30:5-6.

101. Dearman, "Composition and Context in Jeremiah 36," 411.

102. The role of scribes in the formation of prophetic books is also a topic of recent interest beyond Jeremiah; on the book of Ezekiel, for example, see Ellen F. Davis, *Swallowing the Scroll: Textuality and the Dynamics of Discourse in Ezekiel's Prophecy* (JSOTSup 78; Sheffield: Almond, 1989) and, more generally, Joachim Schaper, "Exilic and Post-Exilic Prophecy and the Orality/Literacy Problem," *VT* 55 (2005): 324–42.

in ch. 36 is not Jeremiah, nor even Baruch, but the scroll. It is not the king's response to the prophet which bears the symbolic weight of his response to Yнwн, but his response to the written word. Despite the book of Jeremiah's exceptional attention to the figure of the prophet Jeremiah, therefore, this critical text effectively decenters him. Jeremiah and even Baruch may vanish into hiding, even die, but the scroll proves in the end indestructible.

The most recent developments in the study of this chapter pick up on this peculiarly ambiguous attitude to the prophet. Stuart Macwilliam, for example, as part of a wider discussion about the figure of Baruch from the perspective of gender theory, has observed the way in which Jeremiah passes on his subordinate status vis-à-vis Yнwн to Baruch.[103] By investigating the "nods and winks" of ch. 36, he draws attention to the way in which the text constructs, plays with, and deconstructs ideas of masculinity and femininity. This is motivated in part by the recognition that the interpersonal relationships in the book frequently problematize ancient constructions of gender (as we have seen already in Carvalho's analysis of ch. 16). The use of language with echoes of sexual seduction, even rape, to describe Jeremiah's inability to resist Yнwн's prophetic imperative (20:7) has a similar effect. With regard to ch. 36, Macwilliam begins by noting, as have others before him, that this is the only occasion on which Jeremiah summons a scribe to write for him. His attention to power relations, however, leads him on to observe that this is merely the beginning of a chapter in which "Jeremiah's dealings with Baruch seem to mirror those between Yнwн and Jeremiah" and in which Jeremiah dictates to Baruch in the same way that Yнwн first dictates to Jeremiah.[104] This results in a narratively and theologically provocative confusion between Jeremiah and Yнwн: most of the time (vv. 6, 8, 11) the words of the scroll are referred to as "the words of Yнwн," yet what Baruch reads in v. 10 are "the words of Jeremiah." Jeremiah mirrors Yнwн's behavior to him in his behavior to Baruch and this results, for Baruch, in a blurring of the identities of Yнwн and Jeremiah. But why would Jeremiah mimic Yнwн in the first place? Macwilliam argues that Yнwн has effectively "unmanned" Jeremiah by rendering him his absolute subordinate— and that Jeremiah compensates for this in ch. 36 by (re-)exerting his

103. Macwilliam, "The Prophet and His Patsy," 173–88.
104. Macwilliam, "The Prophet and His Patsy," 183. The progressive hierarchy of Yнwн-Jeremiah-Baruch begins in ch. 32 and continues in each of Baruch's appearances (chs. 43 and 45).

masculinity vis-à-vis Baruch. As YHWH commands Jeremiah and even endangers him, given the explosive content of his commission, so Jeremiah commands Baruch (and, in ch. 51, Baruch's brother Seraiah), likewise endangering him by sending him to the temple with the incendiary words of the scroll. By introducing questions about the text's construction and deconstruction of gender, Macwilliam is able to articulate and interpret more clearly the ambiguities in the chapter's portrayal of Jeremiah.

In a similar way, Sharp brings the long-standing tradition of redaction criticism together with ideological criticism, rhetorical criticism, and postcolonial theory to address the multiplicity of voices preserved by the book of Jeremiah and by ch. 36 in particular.[105] She argues that the book is conscious about its internal antagonisms and that ch. 36 represents both an internal and external struggle over the writtenness of the final text, in which the potential power of the written word is acknowledged to be undermined by its very writtenness. That is, while the writtenness of the words of Jeremiah represents an expansion of the means of transmission of the prophetic word, it simultaneously opens that word up to its bastardization by others.[106] There is "tremendous risk," she argues, "in abandoning one's writing": "the writing may be ignored; 'otherness' may be scrawled in the margins or spliced into the body of the text; the writing may be mutilated or entirely destroyed."[107] This potential is limned in the tantalizing v. 32: "and many similar words were added to them." The formation of a text may preserve the intentions of its originator(s) but, equally, it may not. The ambiguities of ch. 36, Sharp contends, encourage us to pay attention to those who subsequently engaged with the text—not, she emphasizes, in order to disparage them or strip them away in search of some "original," but to better attend to the multiplicity of marginalized voices which remain, albeit often quietly, in the text.

Yvonne Sherwood and Mark Brummitt also pick up on the chapter's paradoxical presentation of its own textuality, observing the way in which the immutability of the divine word appears in conjunction with

105. Carolyn J. Sharp, "Jeremiah in the Land of Aporia: Reconfiguring Redaction Criticism as Witness to Foreignness," in *Jeremiah (Dis)Placed: New Directions in Writing/Reading Jeremiah*, ed. A. R. Pete Diamond and Louis Stulman (LHBOTS 529; London: T&T Clark, 2011), 35–46.

106. Sharp, "Jeremiah in the Land of Aporia," 39.

107. Sharp, "Jeremiah in the Land of Aporia," 41.

the very destructibility and vulnerability of the scroll/text itself.[108] They point out that the potential of the written word for extending the life of the prophet is immediately endangered, insofar as the life of the word is dependent on a scroll that is subject to the inclinations and decisions of the tradents who preserve and pass it on. Though the prophet dies, his words continue in the scroll which bears his name. Yet this is no guarantee; if the scroll is destroyed after the prophet no longer lives, the prophetic word is dead too. If the scroll survives, the act of committing the prophetic word to writing has rendered it vulnerable to change.[109] "Jer 36," they write, "seems torn between a belief in the extraordinary power and efficacy of writing—and a fear about the inadequacies of the new medium."[110] It is peculiarly concerned with the technicalities of textual transmission: not merely explaining that the words of the scroll were taken by dictation from the mouth of Jeremiah (MT), but written on the scroll "with ink" (v. 18), then chasing the scroll from its creation back and forth (and back again) through the temple and court, as though it were testing its durability. Though they see in ch. 36 a particular obsession with a new communicative medium—an obsession which is implicitly contextual and historical—Brummitt and Sherwood refuse to venture further historical speculation. They conclude that "it would be naïve in the extreme to read this text as an eyewitness account of how the book of Jeremiah actually composed itself, or a fragment of itself, in an event that really happened in the seventh century B.C.E. Rather, the passage is a dream of perfectly capturing the word."[111] No longer is ch. 36—or the book of Jeremiah—a gateway to the life of the prophet, or even to the origins of the book which bears his name, but a meditation on the (im)permanence of divine revelation.

108. Mark Brummitt and Yvonne Sherwood, "The Fear of Loss Inherent in Writing: Jeremiah 36 as the Story of a Self-Conscious Scroll," in *Jeremiah (Dis)Placed: New Directions in Writing/Reading Jeremiah*, ed. A. R. Pete Diamond and Louis Stulman (LHBOTS 529; London: T&T Clark, 2011), 47–66.

109. Oral words are also subject to alteration, but such changes are elided from performance to performance in a way which is difficult, if not impossible, to achieve in texts.

110. Brummitt and Sherwood, "The Fear of Loss," 51.

111. Brummitt and Sherwood, "The Fear of Loss," 53.

Chapter 6

IN(-)CONCLUSIONS

What are we to make of the book of Jeremiah and of the various modes of its current interpretation? There is, as should by now be clear, no single dominant method by which this book is now being interpreted, any more than there is a single dominant theme, style, or theology which characterizes its fifty-two chapters. The last few decades of research on the book of Jeremiah have seen the introduction and development of a number of major new interpretive approaches and methods, ranging from trauma studies to postcolonial theory to queer studies. Alongside these have been forays into horror theory, film studies, constructions of space, intertextuality and inner-biblical allusion, postmodernism, reception history, and reader-response criticism, among others. Many of these have built on and continue to converse with the work of feminist scholars and ideological critics, whose efforts constituted some of the earliest attempts to question our assumptions about and expectations of the text. Among approaches with longer and more traditional pedigrees, such as historical and redactional criticism and theological and canonical approaches, widely held assumptions about the text and its origins have been subject to robust critique. Ongoing research using these methods has required considered responses to, often including the incorporation of, the insights of newer and more varied approaches. In part, this expansion of perspective may be linked to the widening of the guild itself: a community once dominated by clergy from Western Europe and North America, mostly male and Protestant, has diversified to include members who originate in and approach the text from a much wider range of religious and cultural traditions, as well as from none at all.

In many respects, this newfound and hard-won diversity in contemporary research on the book of Jeremiah is typical of the wider discipline, which has increasingly found space within its walls for approaches other than the historical and redaction critical or the confessionally theological. A browse through the shelves of a biblical studies library will quickly reveal the seismic changes which have occurred in the last four decades, as the underlying historical credence granted to the text by studies conducted in the middle of the twentieth century has given way to the healthy historical skepticism of those conducted in the last decade of the twentieth and the first decade of the twenty-first centuries. Though contemporary scholarship does continue to ask historical questions about the origins and intentions of the biblical literature preserved in the canonical collection, the certainty with which these questions are answered has been mitigated by the recognition that the texts which comprise this collection are doing something far more sophisticated and complex than merely recording historical facts for their audiences' edification. While this complexity renders them far more intriguing to the exegete, insofar as it reflects ancient efforts to make theological sense of lived experience and to work out its implications in a particular community context, it also makes the work of the historian far more of a challenge—not impossible, by any means, but demanding of a far more sophisticated historical toolkit than had hitherto been imagined.

Complementing this acknowledgment of the text's complexity has been the development of numerous new mechanisms for plumbing its depths. The biblical literature is now regularly poked and prodded with interpretive tools of the most diverse kind, as the perspectives from which these ancient texts are approached by their modern readers become ever more sophisticated. Though sometimes startling, the capacity of these approaches to elucidate the text in new and insightful ways, for audiences both past and present, makes the widening of the interpretive field a welcome development. Though the preceding chapters have been able to give space to only a small number of individual studies on the book of Jeremiah, they represent a sample of the many ways in which new approaches to the book are enabling interpreters to engage with an old and familiar text in new and unfamiliar ways, rendering it still surprising and new.

Perhaps the most consequential realization to come out of this diversity of approaches to the biblical literature is the multi- and polyvalence of the texts themselves. These are not monolithic texts, whose authors' singular intention will give way if only we chip away long enough. Rather they are repositories of many and multiple meanings—some perhaps intended, others not. On reflection this is, perhaps, obvious; the very preservation of these texts attests to their uncanny ability to speak meaningfully to audiences other than the one for which they were first conceived. Each of one hundred generations has recounted this material to the next—implicitly or explicitly declaring that their significance extends beyond their original time or original space. Though these texts' multivalence may be implicit in their preservation, the multiplication of approaches and methods for the interpretation of biblical texts which has occurred over the last three or four decades has served as a salutary reminder that these texts rarely have one single meaning or one single message or one single point of view. The answers they provide depend on the questions they are asked as well as the point of view from which the question is posed. Even beyond the recognition of the subjectivity of interpretive perspective, however, these approaches have brought to the fore the complexity of the perspective(s) of the text itself. The tradition we call the book of Jeremiah preserves a multiplicity of perspectives on a multiplicity of overlapping and intertwining theological, political, social, historical, and practical issues. Indeed, the book of Jeremiah is perhaps the paradigm example of such multivalence. Does the book of Jeremiah support the theological legitimacy of a remnant in the land? Does the book of Jeremiah offer the prospect of hope for the future? Is repentance a prerequisite? Does it include the nations? Is that future near or far? The answers to these questions and many others depend on which passages we read and how we read the voices they preserve.

For much of the nineteenth and twentieth centuries, the complexity of the book of Jeremiah was viewed as a problem: an unfortunate consequence of a long process of development and an occlusion of the true words of the prophet. The desire for and expectation of a tidy, coherent canonical text—or at least a tidy, coherent message preached by Jeremiah, the seventh–sixth century prophet—prompted herculean efforts to force the book's complexities into some semblance of logical, explicable order. While such order could be achieved, it came at the cost of a cannibalized text, as large portions were thrown out in search of the elusive *ipsissima verba*. The problem of such an approach from a canonical confessional point of view has been noted already. The narrowing of the book of Jeremiah into the historical words of Jeremiah—and the historical words of Jeremiah alone—however, merits protestation on both confessional and nonconfessional grounds; it hamstrings the text, to both its and our detriment. The complexity of the book may be transformed into "the" words and message of Jeremiah only by eliminating those elements not neatly consistent with a singularly conceived prophetic voice—that is, by dulling the colorful richness of the book into a monochrome beige. With this loss of complexity, the fundamental creative challenge which a multivalent Jeremianic text poses to its readers is also lost: that is, its ability to force readers out of simplicity and into sophisticated reflection on complex theological problems, by forcing them into an unresolved (unresolvable?) engagement with its own lack of resolution. Theological creativity, sacrificed at the altar of a tidy, undemanding text.

Is the book of Jeremiah consistent? Not if by "consistent" we mean a monochrome theology, a uniform style, or a singular perspective. In these respects, it has rightly been called chaotic, incoherent, and inconsistent. But if by "consistent" we mean a thoroughgoing fascination—obsession, even—with the working out of the meaning of the past and present for the purposes of the present and future, then surely it is. The complexity of a book like Jeremiah is a testament to its place in the midst of a long-standing and unresolved conversation: about the interpretation of the past, the meaning of the present, and expectations for the future. Though the canonicity of the received text might appear to stop this conversation at one particular point, rendering one particular moment in the discussion decisive for those who follow, the ongoing nature of the conversation is in fact emphasized by the lack of resolution preserved by the canonical text. In the case of Jeremiah, the lack of resolution is made even more emphatic by the preservation of this conversation at not one but two distinct moments, in the Masoretic and the Septuagint traditions. The books of Jeremiah preserve two particular moments in a conversation; rather than either closing the conversation down, both provoke further discussion. Though there is sometimes a dominant voice in the book of Jeremiah, this voice is never absolute. Multiple voices remain in the text and thus remain in the conversation, continually contesting the idea of a final resolution to the ongoing dialogue in which its many authors and editors are engaged. In its multivalence the text generates an interpretive momentum, denying its readers any easy rest; instead, it perpetually pushes them to engage in ever new and imaginative ways with its manifold challenges.

APPENDIX A: CHAPTER AND VERSE IN HEBREW AND GREEK

Masoretic Text (MT)	Septuagint (LXX)
Followed by the New Revised Standard Version (NRSV) and most other English Bible translations	As enumerated by the *New English Translation of the Septuagint* (NETS), following the Göttingen edition
1:1-19	1:1-19
2:1	–
2:2-37	2:2-37
3:1-25	3:1-25
4:1-31	4:1-31
5:1-31	5:1-31
6:1-30	6:1-30
7:1	–
7:2-26	7:2-26
7:27	–
7:28-34	7:28-34
8:1-10	8:1-10
8:11-12	–
8:13-22	8:13-22
9:1-26	9:1-26
10:1-5, 9	10:1-5a, 9, 5b
10:6-8, 10	–
10:11-25	10:11-25
11:1-6	11:1-6
11:7	–
11:8-23	11:8-23
12:1-17	12:1-17
13:1-27	13:1-27

14:1-22	14:1-22
15:1-21	15:1-21
16:1-21	16:1-1
17:1-4	–
17:5-27	17:5-27
18:1-23	18:1-23
19:1-15	19:1-15
20:1-18	20:1-18
21:1-14	21:1-14
22:1-30	22:1-30
23:1-40	23:1-6, 9-40, 7-8
24:1-10	24:1-10
25:1-13	25:1-13
24:14	–
25:15-38	32:1-24
26:1-24	33:1-24
27:1	–
27:2-6	34:1-5
27:7	–
27:8-12	34:6-10
27:13	–
27:14-20	34:11-17
27:21	–
27:22	34:18
28:1-17	35:1-17
29:1-15	36:1-15
29:16-20	–
29:21-32	36:21-32
30:1-9	37:1-9
30:10-11	–
30:12-21	37:12-21

30:22	–
30:23-24	37:23-24
31:1-34	38:1-34
31:35-36	38:36-37
31:37	38:35
31:38-40	38:38-40
32:1-44	39:1-44
33:1-13	40:1-13
33:14-26	–
34:1-22	41:1-22
35:1-19	42:1-19
36:1-32	43:1-32
37:1-21	44:1-21
38:1-28	45:1-28
39:1-3	46:1-3
39:4-13	–
39:14-18	46:14-18
40:1-16	47:1-16
41:1-18	48:1-18
42:1-22	49:1-22
43:1-13	50:1-13
44:1-30	51:1-30
45:1-5	51:31-35
46:1-28	26:1-28
47:1-7	29:1-7
48:1-44	31:1-44
48:45-47	–
49:1-5	30:1-5
49:6	–
49:7-22	29:8-23
49:23-27	30:12-16

49:28-33	30:6-11
49:34-39	25:14-19
50:1-46	27:1-46
51:1-44	28:1-44
51:45-48	–
51:49-64	28:49-64
52:1	52:1
52:2-3	–
52:4-14	52:4-14
52:15	–
52:16-27	52:16-27
52:28-30	–
52:31-34	52:31-34

APPENDIX B: ANCIENT NEAR EASTERN KINGS

Judah	Assyria	Babylonia	Egypt
			Necho I (672–664)
			Psammeticus I (664–610)
Josiah (640–609)	Assurbanipal (669–627?)		
	Ashur-etil-ilani (631–627?)		
	Sin-shumu-lishir (626)	Nabopolassar (626–605)	
	Sin-shar-iskun (627?–612)		
Jehoahaz (Shallum) (609)	Ashur-uballit II (612–608?)		Necho II (610–595)
Jehoiakim (Eliakim) (609–598)		Nebuchadnezzar II (604–562)	
Jehoiachin (Coniah) (598–587)			Psammetichus II (595–589)
Zedekiah (Mattaniah) (597–586)			Apries (589–570)
Gedaliah (governor) (586–?)			Amasis II (570–526)
		Evil-merodach (562–560)	
		Neriglissar (560–556)	
		Labashi-marduk (556)	
		Nabonidus (556–539)	

FURTHER READING

Commentaries

Allen, Leslie C. *Jeremiah: A Commentary*. OTL. London: Westminster John Knox, 2008.

Brueggemann, Walter. *A Commentary on Jeremiah: Exile and Homecoming*. Grand Rapids, MI: Eerdmans, 1998.

Carroll, Robert P. *Jeremiah: A Commentary*. OTL. London: SCM, 1986.

Clements, Ronald E. *Jeremiah*. Interpretation. Louisville, KY: Westminster John Knox, 1988.

Craigie, Peter C., Page H. Kelley, and Joel F. Drinkard, Jr. *Jeremiah 1–25*. Word Biblical Commentary 26. Dallas, TX: Word, 1991.

Fischer, Georg. *Jeremia*. Herders theologischer Kommentar zum Alten Testament. 2 vols. Freiburg: Herder, 2005.

Fretheim, Terence E. *Jeremiah*. Smyth & Helwys. Macon, GA: Smyth & Helwys, 2002.

Holladay, William L. *Jeremiah*. Hermeneia. 2 vols. Philadelphia, PA: Fortress, 1986, 1989.

Jones, Douglas R. *Jeremiah*. New Century Bible. Grand Rapids, MI: Eerdmans, 1992.

Keown, Gerald L., Pamela J. Scalise, and Thomas G. Smothers. *Jeremiah 26–52*. Word Biblical Commentary 27. Dallas, TX: Word, 1995.

Lundbom, Jack R. *Jeremiah: A New Translation with Introduction and Commentary*. AB 21. 3 vols. New York: Doubleday, 1999, 2004.

McKane, William. *A Critical and Exegetical Commentary on Jeremiah*. ICC. 2 vols. Edinburgh: T&T Clark, 1986, 1996.

Schmidt, Werner H. *Das Buch Jeremia*. Das Alte Testament Deutsch 21. 2 vols. Göttingen: Vandenhoeck & Ruprecht, 2008, 2013.

Schreiner, Josef. *Jeremia*. Die Neue Echter Bibel 9. Würzburg: Echter Verlag, 1981, 1984.

Stulman, Louis. *Jeremiah*. AOTC. Nashville, TN: Abingdon, 2005.

Walser, Georg A. *Jeremiah: A Commentary Based on Ieremias in Codex Vaticanus*. Septuagint Commentary Series 9. Leiden: Brill, 2012.

Wanke, Gunther. *Jeremia*. Zürcher Bibelkommentare. 2 vols. Zürich: Theologischer Verlag, 1995, 2003.

Werner, Wolfgang. *Das Buch Jeremia*. Neuer Stuttgarter Kommentar 19. 2 vols. Stuttgart: Verlag Österreiches Katholisches Bibelwerk, 1997, 2003.

Major Essay Collections

Barstad, Hans M., and Reinhard G. Kratz, eds. *Prophecy in the Book of Jeremiah*. BZAW 388. Berlin: de Gruyter, 2009.
Bogaert, Pierre-Maurice, ed. *Le livre de Jérémie*. BETL 54. Leuven: Peeters, 1981.
Curtis, Adrian H. W., and Thomas C. Römer, eds. *The Book of Jeremiah and Its Reception: Le livre de Jérémie et sa réception*. BETL 128. Leuven: Peeters, 1997.
Diamond, A. R. Pete, and Louis Stulman, eds. *Jeremiah (Dis)Placed: New Directions in Writing/Reading Jeremiah*. LHBOTS 529. London: T&T Clark, 2011.
Diamond, A. R. Pete, Kathleen M. O'Connor, and Louis Stulman, eds. *Troubling Jeremiah*. JSOTSup 260. Sheffield: Sheffield Academic, 1999.
Goldingay, John, ed. *Uprooting and Planting: Essays on Jeremiah for Leslie Allen*. LHBOTS 459. London: Bloomsbury, 2007.
Groß, Walter, ed. *Jeremia und die "deuteronomistische Bewegung."* BBB 98. Weinheim: Beltz Athenäum, 1995.
Holt, Else K., and Carolyn J. Sharp, eds. *Jeremiah Invented: Constructions and Deconstructions of Jeremiah*. LHBOTS 595. London: Bloomsbury, 2015.
Kessler, Martin, eds. *Reading the Book of Jeremiah: A Search for Coherence*. Winona Lake, IN: Eisenbrauns, 2004.
Maier, Christl M., and Carolyn J. Sharp, eds. *Prophecy and Power: Jeremiah in Feminist and Postcolonial Perspective*. LHBOTS 577. London: Bloomsbury, 2013.
Perdue, Leo G., and Brian W. Kovacs, eds. *A Prophet to the Nations: Essays in Jeremiah Studies*. Winona Lake, IN: Eisenbrauns, 1984.

Summary Discussions of Recent Research

Brueggemann, Walter. "Next Steps in Jeremiah Studies?" In *Troubling Jeremiah*, edited by A. R. Pete Diamond, Kathleen M. O'Connor, and Louis Stulman, 404–22. JSOTSup 260. Sheffield: Sheffield Academic, 1999.
Carroll, Claire E. "Another Dodecade: A Dialectic Model of the Decentred Universe of Jeremiah Studies 1996–2008." *Currents in Biblical Research* 8 (2010): 162–82.
Carroll, Robert P. "Something Rich and Strange: Imagining a Future for Jeremiah Studies." In *Troubling Jeremiah*, edited by A. R. Pete Diamond, Kathleen M. O'Connor, and Louis Stulman, 423–43. JSOTSup 260. Sheffield: Sheffield Academic, 1999.
Carroll, Robert. "Century's End: Jeremiah Studies at the Beginning of the Third Millennium." In *Recent Research on the Major Prophets*, edited by Alan J. Hauser, 217–31. Sheffield: Sheffield Phoenix, 2008.

Carroll, Robert. "Surplus Meaning and the Conflict of Interpretations:
    A Dodecade of Jeremiah Studies (1984–95)." In *Recent Research on the
    Major Prophets*, edited by Alan J. Hauser, 195–216. Sheffield: Sheffield
    Phoenix, 2008.
Diamond, A. R. Pete. "Introduction." In *Troubling Jeremiah*, edited by
    A. R. Pete Diamond, Kathleen M. O'Connor, and Louis Stulman, 15–32.
    JSOTSup 260. Sheffield: Sheffield Academic, 1999.
Diamond, A. R. Pete. "The Jeremiah Guild in the Twenty-First Century:
    Variety Reigns Supreme." In *Recent Research on the Major Prophets*, edited
    by Alan J. Hauser, 232–48. Sheffield: Sheffield Phoenix, 2008.
Diamond, A. R. Pete, and Louis Stulman. "Analytical Introduction: Writing
    and Reading Jeremiah." In *Jeremiah (Dis)Placed: New Directions in Writing/
    Reading Jeremiah*, edited by A. R. Pete Diamond and Louis Stulman, 1–32.
    LHBOTS 529. London: T&T Clark, 2011.
Perdue, Leo G. "Jeremiah in Modern Research: Approaches and Issues." In *A
    Prophet to the Nations: Essays in Jeremiah Studies*, edited by Leo G. Perdue
    and Brian W. Kovacs, 1–32. Winona Lake, IN: Eisenbrauns, 1984.

Reflections on Method

Bowman, Barrie. "Future Imagination: Utopianism in the Book of Jeremiah."
    In *Jeremiah (Dis)Placed: New Directions in Writing/Reading Jeremiah*,
    edited by A. R. Pete Diamond and Louis Stulman, 243–9. LHBOTS 529.
    London: T&T Clark, 2011.
Brummitt, Mark. "Troubling Utopias: Possible Worlds and Possible Voices in
    the Book of Jeremiah." In *Jeremiah (Dis)Placed: New Directions in Writing/
    Reading Jeremiah*, edited by A. R. Pete Diamond and Louis Stulman,
    175–89. LHBOTS 529. London: T&T Clark, 2011.
Callaway, Mary C. "Reading Jeremiah with Some Help from Gadamer." In
    Jeremiah (Dis)Placed: New Directions in Writing/Reading Jeremiah, edited
    by A. R. Pete Diamond and Louis Stulman, 266–78. LHBOTS 529. London:
    T&T Clark, 2011.
Carroll, Robert P. "The Book of J: Intertextuality and Ideological Criticism."
    In *Troubling Jeremiah*, edited by A. R. Pete Diamond, Kathleen M.
    O'Connor, and Louis Stulman, 220–43. JSOTSup 260. Sheffield: Sheffield
    Academic, 1999.
Carroll, Robert P. "The Polyphonic Jeremiah: A Reading of the Book of
    Jeremiah." In *Reading the Book of Jeremiah: A Search for Coherence*, edited
    by Martin Kessler, 77–85. Winona Lake, IN: Eisenbrauns, 2004.
Claassens, L. Juliana. "'Like a Woman in Labor': Gender, Postcolonial,
    Queer, and Trauma Perspectives on the Book of Jeremiah." In *Prophecy
    and Power: Jeremiah in Feminist and Postcolonial Perspective*, edited by
    Christl M. Maier and Carolyn J. Sharp, 117–32. LHBOTS 577. London:
    Bloomsbury, 2013.

Davidson, Steed V. "Ambivalence and Temple Destruction: Reading the Book of Jeremiah with Homi Bhabha." In *Jeremiah (Dis)Placed: New Directions in Writing/Reading Jeremiah*, edited by A. R. Pete Diamond and Louis Stulman, 162–71. LHBOTS 529. London: T&T Clark, 2011.

Davidson, Steed V. *Empire and Exile: Postcolonial Readings of the Book of Jeremiah*. LHBOTS 542. London: T&T Clark, 2011.

Erzberger, Johanna. "Prophetic Sign Acts as Performances." In *Jeremiah Invented: Constructions and Deconstructions of Jeremiah*, edited by Else K. Holt and Carolyn J. Sharp, 104–16. LHBOTS 595. London: Bloomsbury, 2015.

Fischer, Irmtraud. "On Writing a Feminist-Postcolonial Commentary: A Critical Evaluation." In *Prophecy and Power: Jeremiah in Feminist and Postcolonial Perspective*, edited by Christl M. Maier and Carolyn J. Sharp, 234–51. LHBOTS 577. London: Bloomsbury, 2013.

Henderson, Joe. "Duhm and Skinner's Invention of Jeremiah." In *Jeremiah Invented: Constructions and Deconstructions of Jeremiah*, edited by Else K. Holt and Carolyn J. Sharp, 1–15. LHBOTS 595. London: Bloomsbury, 2015.

Holt, Else K. "Jeremiah the Lamenter: A Synoptic Reading." In *Jeremiah Invented: Constructions and Deconstructions of Jeremiah*, edited by Else K. Holt and Carolyn J. Sharp, 117–28. LHBOTS 595. London: Bloomsbury, 2015.

Maier, Christl M., and Carolyn J. Sharp. "Introduction: Feminist and Postcolonial Interventions in and with the Book of Jeremiah." In *Prophecy and Power: Jeremiah in Feminist and Postcolonial Perspective*, edited by Christl M. Maier and Carolyn J. Sharp, 1–18. LHBOTS 577. London: Bloomsbury, 2013.

McKinlay, Judith E. "Challenges and Opportunities for Feminist and Postcolonial Biblical Criticism." In *Prophecy and Power: Jeremiah in Feminist and Postcolonial Perspective*, edited by Christl M. Maier and Carolyn J. Sharp, 19–37. LHBOTS 577. London: Bloomsbury, 2013.

O'Connor, Kathleen M. "Terror All Around: Confusion as Meaning-Making." In *Jeremiah (Dis)Placed: New Directions in Writing/Reading Jeremiah*, edited by A. R. Pete Diamond and Louis Stulman, 67–79. LHBOTS 529. London: T&T Clark, 2011.

Seitz, Christopher R. "The Place of the Reader in Jeremiah." In *Reading the Book of Jeremiah: A Search for Coherence*, edited by Martin Kessler, 67–75. Winona Lake, IN: Eisenbrauns, 2004.

Sharp, Carolyn J. "Mapping Jeremiah as/in a Feminist Landscape: Negotiating Ancient and Contemporary Terrains." In *Prophecy and Power: Jeremiah in Feminist and Postcolonial Perspective*, edited by Christl M. Maier and Carolyn J. Sharp, 38–56. LHBOTS 577. London: Bloomsbury, 2013.

Shields, Mary E. "Impasse or Opportunity or …? Women Reading Jeremiah Reading Women." In *Jeremiah (Dis)Placed: New Directions in Writing/Reading Jeremiah*, edited by A. R. Pete Diamond and Louis Stulman, 290–302. LHBOTS 529. London: T&T Clark, 2011.

Smith-Christopher, Daniel L. "Reading Jeremiah as Frantz Fanon." In *Jeremiah (Dis)Placed: New Directions in Writing/Reading Jeremiah*, edited by A. R. Pete Diamond and Louis Stulman, 115–24. LHBOTS 529. London: T&T Clark, 2011.

Stulman, Louis. "Art and Atrocity, and the Book of Jeremiah." In *Jeremiah Invented: Constructions and Deconstructions of Jeremiah*, edited by Else K. Holt and Carolyn J. Sharp, 92–103. LHBOTS 595. London: Bloomsbury, 2015.

Stulman, Louis. "Commentary as Memoir? Reflections on Writing/Reading War and Hegemony in Jeremiah and in Contemporary U.S. Foreign Policy." In *Prophecy and Power: Jeremiah in Feminist and Postcolonial Perspective*, edited by Christl M. Maier and Carolyn J. Sharp, 57–71. LHBOTS 577. London: Bloomsbury, 2013.

Stulman, Louis. "Here Comes the Reader." In *Jeremiah (Dis)Placed: New Directions in Writing/Reading Jeremiah*, edited by A. R. Pete Diamond and Louis Stulman, 99–103. LHBOTS 529. London: T&T Clark, 2011.

Issues in Interpretation

The Relationship between the Book and History

Barstad, Hans M. "Jeremiah the Historian: The Book of Jeremiah as a Source for the History of the Near East in the Time of Nebuchadnezzar." In *Studies on the Text and Versions of the Hebrew Bible in Honour of Robert Gordon*, edited by Geoffrey Khan and Diana Lipton, 87–98. Leiden: Brill, 2012.

Barstad, Hans M. "What Prophets Do: Reflections on Past Reality in the Book of Jeremiah." In *Prophecy in the Book of Jeremiah*, edited by Hans M. Barstad and Reinhard G. Kratz, 10–32. BZAW 388. Berlin: de Gruyter, 2009.

Boadt, Lawrence. "The Book of Jeremiah and the Power of Historical Recitation." In *Troubling Jeremiah*, edited by A. R. Pete Diamond, Kathleen M. O'Connor, and Louis Stulman, 339–49. JSOTSup 260. Sheffield: Sheffield Academic, 1999.

Brueggemann, Walter. "The 'Baruch Connection': Reflections on Jeremiah 43.1–7." In *Troubling Jeremiah*, edited by A. R. Pete Diamond, Kathleen M. O'Connor, and Louis Stulman, 367–86. JSOTSup 260. Sheffield: Sheffield Academic, 1999.

Callaway, Mary C. "Seduced by Method: History and Jeremiah 20." In *Jeremiah Invented: Constructions and Deconstructions of Jeremiah*, edited by Else K. Holt and Carolyn J. Sharp, 16–33. LHBOTS 595. London: Bloomsbury, 2015.

Grabbe, Lester L. "'The Lying Pen of the Scribes'? Jeremiah and History." In *Essays on Ancient Israel in its Near Eastern Context: A Tribute to Nadav*

Na'aman, edited by Yairah Amit, Ehud Ben Zvi, Israel Finkelstein, and
Oded Lipschits, 189–204. Winona Lake, IN: Eisenbrauns, 2006.
Leuchter, Mark. *Josiah's Reform and Jeremiah's Scroll: Historical Calamity and
Prophetic Response*. HBM 6. Sheffield: Sheffield Phoenix, 2006.
Nissinen, Martti. "The Historical Dilemma of Biblical Prophetic Studies." In
Prophecy in the Book of Jeremiah, edited by Hans M. Barstad and Reinhard
G. Kratz, 103–20. BZAW 388. Berlin: de Gruyter, 2009.
Wilson, Robert R. "Historicizing the Prophets: History and Literature in the
Book of Jeremiah." In *On the Way to Nineveh: Studies in Honor of George
M. Landes*, edited by Stephen L. Cook and S. C. Winter, 136–54. Atlanta,
GA: Scholars, 1999.

The Nature of Prophecy

Becking, Bob. "Means of Revelation in the Book of Jeremiah." In *Prophecy in
the Book of Jeremiah*, edited by Hans M. Barstad and Reinhard G. Kratz,
33–47. BZAW 388. Berlin: de Gruyter, 2009.
Berquist, J. L. "Prophetic Legitimation in Jeremiah." *VT* 39 (1989): 129–39.
Bultmann, Christoph. "Jeremiah *Epigrammatistes*: Towards a Typology of
Prophecy in Jeremiah." In *Prophecy in the Book of Jeremiah*, edited by
Hans M. Barstad and Reinhard G. Kratz, 74–79. BZAW 388. Berlin: de
Gruyter, 2009.
Carroll, Robert P. *From Chaos to Covenant: Prophecy in the Book of Jeremiah*.
London: SCM, 1981.
Epp-Tiessen, Daniel. *Concerning the Prophets: True and False Prophecy in
Jeremiah 23:9–29:32*. Eugene, OR: Pickwick, 2012.
Grabbe, Lester L. "Jeremiah among the Social Anthropologists." In *Prophecy
in the Book of Jeremiah*, edited by Hans M. Barstad and Reinhard G. Kratz,
80–88. BZAW 388. Berlin: de Gruyter, 2009.
Hibbard, J. Todd. "True and False Prophecy: Jeremiah's Revision of
Deuteronomy." *JSOT* 35 (2011): 339–58.
Jong, Matthijs J. de. "Biblical Prophecy—A Scribal Enterprise: The Old
Testament Prophecy of Unconditional Judgement considered as a Literary
Phenomenon." *VT* 61 (2011): 39–70.
Jong, Matthijs J. de. "Why Jeremiah Is Not among the Prophets: An Analysis of
the Terms in the Book of Jeremiah." *JSOT* 35 (2011): 483–510.
Leene, Hendrik. "Blowing the Same Shofar: An Intertextual Comparison of
Representations of the Prophetic Role in Jeremiah and Ezekiel." In *The
Elusive Prophet: The Prophet as a Historical Person, Literary Character and
Anonymous Artist*, edited by Johannes C. De Moor, 175–98. OudSt 45.
Leiden: Brill, 2001.
Otto, Eckart. "Scribal Scholarship in the Formation of Torah and Prophets:
A Postexilic Scribal Debate between Priestly Scholarship and Literary

Prophecy—The Example of the Book of Jeremiah and Its Relation to the Pentateuch." In *The Pentateuch as Torah: New Models for Understanding Its Promulgation and Acceptance,* edited by Gary N. Knoppers and Bernard M. Levinson, 171–84. Winona Lake, IN: Eisenbrauns, 2007.

Polk, Timothy. *The Prophetic Persona: Jeremiah and the Language of the Self.* JSOTSup 32. London: T&T Clark, 1984.

Rochester, Kathleen M. *Prophetic Ministry in Jeremiah and Ezekiel.* Contributions to Biblical Exegesis and Theology 65. Leuven: Peeters, 2012.

Sharp, Carolyn J. *Prophecy and Ideology in Jeremiah: Struggles for Authority in the Deutero-Jeremianic Prose.* Old Testament Studies. London: T&T Clark, 2003.

Silver, Edward. "Performing Domination/Theorizing Power: Israelite Prophecy as a Political Discourse beyond the Conflict Model." *JANER* 14 (2014): 186–216.

Sweeney, Marvin A. "The Truth in True and False Prophecy." In *Form and Intertextuality in Prophetic and Apocalyptic Literature,* 78–93. FAT 45. Tübingen: Mohr Siebeck, 2005.

Tarrer, Seth B. *Reading with the Faithful: Interpretation of True and False Prophecy in the Book of Jeremiah from Ancient Times to Modern.* JTIS 6. Winona Lake, IN: Eisenbrauns, 2013.

Thelle, Rannfrid. "MT Jeremiah: Reflections of a Discourse on Prophecy in the Persian Period." In *The Production of Prophecy: Constructing Prophecy and Prophets in Yehud,* edited by Diana V. Edelman and Ehud Ben Zvi, 184–207. London: Equinox, 2009.

Weeks, Stuart. "Jeremiah as a Prophetic Book." In *Prophecy in the Book of Jeremiah,* edited by Hans M. Barstad and Reinhard G. Kratz, 265–74. BZAW 388. Berlin: de Gruyter, 2009.

The Formation of the Book(s)

Applegate, John. "The Fate of Zedekiah: Redactional Debate in the Book of Jeremiah: Part I." *VT* 48 (1998): 137–60.

Applegate, John. "The Fate of Zedekiah: Redactional Debate in the Book of Jeremiah: Part II." *VT* 48 (1998): 301–8.

Applegate, John. " 'Peace, Peace, When there Is No Peace': Redactional Integration of Prophecy of Peace into the Judgement of Jeremiah." In *The Book of Jeremiah and Its Reception: Le livre de Jérémie et sa réception,* edited by Adrian H. W. Curtis and Thomas C. Römer, 51–90. BETL 78. Leuven: Leuven University Press, 1997.

Clements, Ronald E. "Jeremiah 1–25 and the Deuteronomistic History." In *Understanding Poets and Prophets: Essays in Honor of George Wishart Anderson,* edited by A. Graeme Auld, 93–113. JSOTSup 152. Sheffield: JSOT, 1993.

Collins, Terrence. "Deuteronomist Influence on the Prophetical Books." In *The Book of Jeremiah and Its Reception: Le livre de Jérémie et sa réception*, edited by Adrian H. W. Curtis and Thomas C. Römer, 15–26. BETL 78. Leuven: Leuven University Press, 1997.

Gesundheit, Shimon. "The Question of LXX Jeremiah as a Tool for Literary-Critical Analysis." *VT* 62 (2012): 29–57.

Hornkohl, Aaron D. *Ancient Hebrew Periodization and the Language of the Book of Jeremiah: The Case for a Sixth-Century Date of Composition*. Studies in Semitic Languages and Linguistics 74. Leiden: Brill, 2014.

Janzen, J. Gerald. *Studies in the Text of Jeremiah*. HSM 6. Cambridge, MA: Harvard University Press, 1973.

Jong, Matthijs J. de. "Biblical Prophecy—A Scribal Enterprise: The Old Testament Prophecy of Unconditional Judgement considered as a Literary Phenomenon." *VT* 61 (2011): 39–70.

Kessler, Martin. "The Function of Chapters 25 and 50–51 in the Book of Jeremiah." In *Troubling Jeremiah*, edited by A. R. Pete Diamond, Kathleen M. O'Connor, and Louis Stulman, 64–72. JSOTSup 260. Sheffield: Sheffield Academic, 1999.

Kugler, Robert A. "The Deuteronomists and the Latter Prophets." In *Those Elusive Deuteronomists: The Phenomenon of Pan-Deuteronomism*, edited by Linda S. Schearing and Steven L. McKenzie, 127–44. LHBOTS 268. Sheffield: Sheffield Academic, 1999.

Leuchter, Mark. *Josiah's Reform and Jeremiah's Scroll: Historical Calamity and Prophetic Response*. HBM 6. Sheffield: Sheffield Phoenix, 2006.

Leuchter, Mark. "The Medium and the Message, or, What Is 'Deuteronomistic' about the Book of Jeremiah?" *ZAW* 126 (2014): 208–27.

Leuchter, Mark. *The Polemics of Exile in Jeremiah 26–45*. Cambridge: Cambridge University Press, 2008.

Lundbom, Jack R. *Jeremiah: A Study in Ancient Hebrew Rhetoric*. 2nd ed. SBLDS 18. Winona Lake, IN: Eisenbrauns, 1997.

Nicholson, Ernest. *Preaching to the Exiles: A Study of the Prose Tradition in the Book of Jeremiah*. Oxford: Basil Blackwell, 1970.

Noll, K. L. "Deuteronomistic History or Deuteronomic Debate? (A Thought Experiment)." *JSOT* 31 (2007): 311–45.

Pakkala, Juha. "Zedekiah's Fate and the Dynastic Succession." *JBL* 125 (2006): 443–52.

Parke-Taylor, Geoffrey H. *The Formation of the Book of Jeremiah: Doublets and Recurring Phrases*. SBLMS 51. Atlanta, GA: Society of Biblical Literature, 2000.

Person, Jr., Raymond F. "A Rolling Corpus and Oral Tradition: A Not-So-Literate Solution to a Highly Literate Problem." In *Troubling Jeremiah*, edited by A. R. Pete Diamond, Kathleen M. O'Connor, and Louis Stulman, 263–71. JSOTSup 260. Sheffield: Sheffield Academic, 1999.

Pietersma, Albert. "Greek Jeremiah and the Land of Azazel." In *Studies in the Hebrew Bible, Qumran, and the Septuagint Presented to Eugene Ulrich,* edited by Peter W. Flint, Emanuel Tov, and James C. Vanderkam, 402–11. VTSup 101. Leiden: Brill, 2006.

Pietersma, Albert. "Of Translation and Revision: From Greek Isaiah to Greek Jeremiah." In *Isaiah in Context: Studies in Honour of Arie van der Kooij on the Occasion of his Sixty-Fifth Birthday*, edited by Michael N. Van Der Meer, P. Van Keulen, W. Van Peursen, and B. Ter Haar Romeny, 359–87. VTSup 138. Leiden: Brill, 2010.

Rofé, Alexander. "The Arrangement of the Book of Jeremiah." *ZAW* 101 (1989): 390–98.

Römer, Thomas C. "The Formation of the Book of Jeremiah as a Supplement to the So-Called Deuteronomistic History." In *The Production of Prophecy: Constructing Prophecy and Prophets in Yehud*, edited by Diana V. Edelman and Ehud Ben Zvi, 168–83. London: Equinox, 2009.

Römer, Thomas C. "How Did Jeremiah Become a Convert to Deuteronomistic Ideology?" In *Those Elusive Deuteronomists: The Phenomenon of Pan-Deuteronomism*, edited by Linda S. Schearing and Steven L. McKenzie, 189–99. Sheffield: Sheffield Academic, 1999.

Seitz, Christopher R. "The Prophet Moses and the Canonical Shape of Jeremiah." *ZAW* 101 (1989): 3–27.

Sharp, Carolyn J. *Prophecy and Ideology in Jeremiah: Struggles for Authority in the Deutero-Jeremianic Prose*. Old Testament Studies. London: T&T Clark, 2003.

Shead, Andrew G. "Jeremiah." In *The T&T Clark Companion to the Septuagint*, edited by James K. Aitken, 469–86. London: Bloomsbury, 2015.

Soderlund, Sven. *The Greek Text of Jeremiah. A Revised Hypothesis.* JSOTSup 47. London: T&T Clark, 1985.

Steiner, Richard C. "The Two Sons of Neriah and the Two Editions of Jeremiah in the Light of Two Atbash Code-Words for Babylon." *VT* 46 (1996): 74–84.

Stipp, Hermann-Josef. *Jeremia, der Tempel und die Aristokratie: die patrizische (schafanidische) Redaktion des Jeremiabuches*. Kleine Arbeiten zum Alten und Neuen Testament 1. Waltrop: Spenner, 2000.

Stulman, Louis. *Order amid Chaos: Jeremiah as Symbolic Tapestry*. Sheffield: Sheffield Academic, 1998.

Stulman, Louis. "The Prose Sermons as Hermeneutical Guide to Jeremiah 1–25: The Deconstruction of Judah's Symbolic World." In *Troubling Jeremiah*, edited by A. R. Pete Diamond, Kathleen M. O'Connor, and Louis Stulman, 34–63. JSOTSup 260. Sheffield: Sheffield Academic, 1999.

Stulman, Louis. *The Prose Sermons of the Book of Jeremiah: A Redescription of the Correspondences with the Deuteronomistic Literature in the Light of Recent Text-Critical Research*. SBLDS 83. Atlanta, GA: Scholars, 1986.

Thiel, Winfried. *Die deuteronomistische Redaktion von Jeremia 1–25*. WMANT 41. Neukirchen-Vluyn: Neukirchener Verlag, 1973.

Thiel, Winfried. *Die deuteronomistische Redaktion von Jeremia 26–45: mit einer Gesamtbeurteilung der deuteronomistischen Redaktion des Buches Jeremia*. WMANT 52. Neukirchen-Vluyn: Neukirchener Verlag, 1981.

Tov, Emanuel. "Determining the Relationship between the Qumran Scrolls and the LXX: Some Methodological Issues." In *The Hebrew and Greek Texts of Samuel: 1980 Proceedings IOSCS, Vienna*, edited by Emanuel Tov, 45–67. Jerusalem: Academon, 1980.

Tov, Emanuel. *The Greek and Hebrew Bible: Collected Essays on the Septuagint*. VTSup 72. Leiden: Brill, 1999).

Tov, Emanuel. *The Septuagint Translation of Jeremiah and Baruch: A Discussion of an Early Revision of the LXX of Jeremiah 29–52 and Baruch 1 1–3 8*. HSM 8. Missoula, MT: Scholars, 1976.

Tov, Emanuel. "Some Aspects of the Textual and Literary History of the Book of Jeremiah." In *Le livre de Jérémie: le prophète et son milieu, les oracles et leur transmission*, edited by Pierre-Maurice Bogaert, 145–67. BETL 54. Leuven: Peeters, 1981.

Waard, Jan de. *Handbook on Jeremiah*. Textual Criticism and the Translator 2. Winona Lake, IN: Eisenbrauns, 2003.

Weis, Richard D. "The Textual Situation in the Book of Jeremiah." In *Sôfer Mahîr: Essays in Honour of Adrian Schenker Offered by Editors of Biblia Hebraica Quinta*, edited by Yohanan A. P. Goldman, Arie van der Kooij, and Richard D. Weis, 269–93. VTSup 110. Leiden: Brill, 2006.

Williams, Michael J. "An Investigation of the Legitimacy of Source Distinctions for the Prose Material in Jeremiah." *JBL* 112 (1993): 193–210.

The Theology of the Book

Biddle, Mark. *Polyphony and Symphony in Prophetic Literature: Rereading Jeremiah 7–20*. Studies in Old Testament Interpretation 2. Macon, GA: Mercer University Press, 1996.

Brueggemann, Walter. *Hopeful Imagination: Prophetic Voices in Exile*. Philadelphia, PA: Fortress, 1986.

Brueggemann, Walter. *The Theology of the Book of Jeremiah*. Old Testament Theology. Cambridge: Cambridge University Press, 2007.

Conrad, Edgar W. *Reading the Latter Prophets: Toward a New Canonical Criticism*. JSOTSup 376. London: T&T Clark, 2004.

Dempsey, Carol. *Jeremiah: Preacher of Grace, Poet of Truth*. Interfaces. Collegeville, MN: Liturgical, 2007.

Green, Barbara. *Jeremiah and God's Plan of Well-Being*. Studies on Personalities of the Old Testament. Columbia, SC: University of South Carolina Press, 2013.

Joo, Samantha. *Provocation and Punishment: The Anger of God in the Book of Jeremiah and Deuteronomistic Theology*. BZAW 361. Berlin: de Gruyter, 2006.

Kessler, Martin, ed. *Reading the Book of Jeremiah: A Search for Coherence*. Winona Lake, IN: Eisenbrauns, 2004.

Levin, Christoph. "The 'Word of Yahweh': A Theological Concept in the Book of Jeremiah." In *Reading the Scriptures: Essays on the Literary History of the Old Testament*, 221–43. FAT 87. Tübingen: Mohr Siebeck, 2013.

McConville, J. Gordon. *Judgment and Promise: An Interpretation of the Book of Jeremiah*. Leicester: Apollos, 1993.

Mills, Mary E. *Alterity, Pain, and Suffering in Isaiah, Jeremiah, and Ezekiel*. LHBOTS 479. London: T&T Clark, 2007.

O'Connor, Kathleen M. *Jeremiah: Pain and Promise*. Minneapolis, MN: Fortress, 2011.

Perdue, Leo G. "The Book of Jeremiah in Old Testament Theology." In *Troubling Jeremiah*, edited by A. R. Pete Diamond, Kathleen M. O'Connor, and Louis Stulman, 320–38. JSOTSup 260. Sheffield: Sheffield Academic, 1999.

Perdue, Leo G. *Reconstructing Old Testament Theology: After the Collapse of History*. Overtures to Biblical Theology. Minneapolis, MN: Fortress, 2005.

Plant, Robin J. R. *Good Figs, Bad Figs: Judicial Differentiation in the Book of Jeremiah*. LHBOTS 483. London: T&T Clark, 2008.

Shead, Andrew G. *A Mouth Full of Fire: The Word of God in Jeremiah*. New Studies in Biblical Theology 29. Downers Grove, II: Apollos, 2012.

Unterman, J. *From Repentance to Redemption: Jeremiah's Thought in Transition*. JSOTSup 54. Sheffield: JSOT, 1987.

Its Relationship to Other Biblical Books

Avioz, Michael. "*I Sat Alone*": Jeremiah among the Prophets*. Piscataway, NJ: Tigris, 2009.

Beuken, Willem A. M. "Common and Different Phrases for Babylon's Fall and Its Aftermath in Isaiah 13–14 and Jeremiah 50–51." In *Concerning the Nations: Essays on the Oracles against the Nations in Isaiah, Jeremiah and Ezekiel*, edited by Andrew Mein, Else K. Holt, and Hyun C. P. Kim, 53–73. LHBOTS 612. London: Bloomsbury T&T Clark, 2015.

Dell, Katharine. "'Cursed Be the Day I Was Born': Job and Jeremiah Revisited." In *Reading Job Intertextually*, edited by Katharine Dell and Will Kynes, 106–17. London: T&T Clark, 2012.

Dell, Katharine J. "The Suffering Servant of Deutero-Isaiah: Jeremiah Revisited." In *Genesis, Isaiah and Psalms: A Festschrift to Honour Professor John Emerton for His Eightieth Birthday*, edited by Katharine J. Dell, Graham Davies, and Yee Von Koh, 119–34. Leiden: Brill, 2010.

Halpern, Baruch. "The New Names of Isaiah 62:4: Jeremiah's Reception in the Restoration and the Politics of 'Third Isaiah.'" *JBL* 117 (1998): 623–43.

Lee, Nancy C. "Exposing a Buried Subtext in Jeremiah and Lamentations: Going after Baal and … Abel." In *Troubling Jeremiah*, edited by A. R. Pete Diamond, Kathleen M. O'Connor, and Louis Stulman, 87–122. JSOTSup 260. Sheffield: Sheffield Academic, 1999.

O'Connor, Kathleen M. "Figuration in Jeremiah's Confessions with
Questions for Isaiah's Servant." In *Jeremiah Invented: Constructions
and Deconstructions of Jeremiah*, edited by Else K. Holt and Carolyn J.
Sharp, 63–73. LHBOTS 595. London: Bloomsbury, 2015.

Rom-Shiloni, Dalit. "Facing Destruction and Exile: Inner-Biblical Exegesis in
Jeremiah and Ezekiel." *ZAW* 117 (2005): 189–205.

Sommer, Benjamin D. *A Prophet Reads Scripture: Allusion in Isaiah 40–66*.
Contraversions. Stanford, CA: Stanford University Press, 1998.

Sweeney, Marvin A. "Jeremiah's Reflection on the Isaian Royal Promise:
Jeremiah 23:1–8 in Context." In *Reading Prophetic Books: Form,
Intertextuality, and Reception in Prophetic and Post-Biblical Literature*,
154–66. FAT 89. Tübingen: Mohr Siebeck, 2014.

Sweeney, Marvin A. "The Reconceptualization of the Davidic Covenant in
the Books of Jeremiah." In *Reading Prophetic Books: Form, Intertextuality,
and Reception in Prophetic and Post-Biblical Literature*, 167–81. FAT 89.
Tübingen: Mohr Siebeck, 2014.

Venema, Geert J. *Reading Scripture in the Old Testament: Deuteronomy 9–10;
31, 2 Kings 22–23, Jeremiah 36, Nehemiah 8*. OudSt 48. Leiden: Brill, 2004.

Vieweger, Dieter. *Die literarischen Beziehungen zwischen den Büchern Jeremia
und Ezechiel*. BEATAJ 26. Frankfurt: Lang, 1993.

Jeremiah's Afterlife

Barton, John. "Jeremiah in the Apocrypha and Pseudepigrapha." In *Troubling
Jeremiah*, edited by A. R. Pete Diamond, Kathleen M. O'Connor, and
Louis Stulman, 306–17. JSOTSup 260. Sheffield: Sheffield Academic, 1999.

Curtis, Adrian H. W. "'Terror on Every Side!'" In *The Book of Jeremiah and Its
Reception: Le livre de Jérémie et sa réception*, edited by Adrian H. W. Curtis and
Thomas C. Römer, 111–18. BETL 78. Leuven: Leuven University Press, 1997.

Dimant, Devorah. "From the Book of Jeremiah to the Qumranic Apocryphon
of Jeremiah." *DSD* 20 (2013): 452–71.

Goldstein, Ronnie. "Jeremiah between Destruction and Exile: From Biblical to
Post-Biblical Traditions." *DSD* 20 (2013): 433–51.

Hill, John. "'Your Exile Will Be Long': The Book of Jeremiah and the Unended
Exile." In *Reading the Book of Jeremiah: A Search for Coherence*, edited by
Martin Kessler, 149–61. Winona Lake, IN: Eisenbrauns, 2004.

Koenen, Klaus. *Die Klagelieder Jeremias: eine Rezeptionsgeschichte*. Biblisch-
theologische Studien 143. Neukirchen-Vluyn: Neukirchener Verlag, 2013.

Leuchter, Mark. "The Exegesis of Jeremiah in and beyond Ezra 9–10." *VT* 65
(2015): 62–80.

Leuchter, Mark. "Remembering Jeremiah in the Persian Period." In
*Remembering Biblical Figures in the Late Persian and Early Hellenistic
Periods: Social Memory and Imagination*, edited by Diana V. Edelman and
Ehud Ben Zvi, 384–414. Oxford: Oxford University Press, 2013.

Textual Studies

Chapter 1

Auld, Graeme. "Jeremiah—Manasseh—Samuel: Significant Triangle? Or Vicious Circle?" In *Prophecy in the Book of Jeremiah*, edited by Hans M. Barstad and Reinhard G. Kratz, 1–9. BZAW 388. Berlin: de Gruyter, 2009.

Harris, Scott L. "The Second Vision of Jeremiah: Jer 1:13–15." *JBL* 102 (1983): 281–2.

Hayes, Elizabeth R. "Of Branches, Pots and Figs: Jeremiah's Visions from a Cognitive Perspective." In *Prophecy in the Book of Jeremiah*, edited by Hans M. Barstad and Reinhard G. Kratz, 89–102. BZAW 388. Berlin: de Gruyter, 2009.

Levin, Christoph. "The 'Word of Yahweh': A Theological Concept in the Book of Jeremiah." In *Reading the Scriptures: Essays on the Literary History of the Old Testament*, 221–43. FAT 87. Tübingen: Mohr Siebeck, 2013.

Lundbom, Jack R. "Rhetorical Structures in Jeremiah 1." *ZAW* 103 (1991): 193–210.

Olyan, Saul M. "To Uproot and to Pull Down, to Build and to Plant: Jer 1:10 and Its Earliest Interpreters." In *Hesed Ve-Emet: Studies in Honor of Ernest S. Frerichs*, edited by Jodi Magness and Seymour Gitin, 63–72. Atlanta, GA: Scholars, 1998.

Raz, Yosefa. "Jeremiah 'Before the Womb': On Fathers, Sons, and the Telos of Redaction in Jeremiah 1." In *Prophecy and Power: Jeremiah in Feminist and Postcolonial Perspective*, edited by Christl M. Maier and Carolyn J. Sharp, 86–100. LHBOTS 577. London: Bloomsbury, 2013.

Jeremiah 2–6

Abma, Richtsje. *Bonds of Love: Methodic Studies of Prophetic Texts with Marriage Imagery: Isaiah 50:1–3 and 54:1–10, Hosea 1–3, Jeremiah 2–3*. SSN 40. Leiden: Brill, 1999.

Althann, Robert. *A Philological Analysis of Jeremiah 4–6 in the Light of Northwest Semitic*. Biblica et orientalia 38. Rome: Pontifical Biblical Institute, 1983.

Bauer, Angela. "Dress to Be Killed: Jeremiah 4.29–31 as an Example of the Functions of Female Imagery in Jeremiah." In *Troubling Jeremiah*, edited by A. R. Pete Diamond, Kathleen M. O'Connor, and Louis Stulman, 293–305. JSOTSup 260. Sheffield: Sheffield Academic, 1999.

Biddle, Mark E. *A Redaction History of Jeremiah 2:1–4:2*. Abhandlungen zur Theologie des Alten und Neuen Testaments 77. Zürich: Theologischer Verlag, 1990.

Diamond, A. R. Pete, and Kathleen M. O'Connor. "Unfaithful Passions: Coding Women Coding Men in Jeremiah 2–3 (4.2)." In *Troubling Jeremiah*, edited by A. R. Pete Diamond, Kathleen M. O'Connor, and Louis Stulman, 123–45. JSOTSup 260. Sheffield: Sheffield Academic, 1999.

Green, Barbara. "Cognitive Linguistics and the 'Idolatry-Is-Adultery' Metaphor of Jeremiah 2–3." In *Daughter Zion: Her Portrait, Her Response*, edited by Mark J. Boda, Carol J. Dempsey, and LeAnn S. Flesher, 11–38. AIIL 13. Atlanta, GA: SBL, 2012.

Holt, Else K. "'The Stain of Your Guilt Is Still Before Me' (Jeremiah 2:22): (Feminist) Approaches to Jeremiah 2 and the Problem of Normativity." In *Prophecy and Power: Jeremiah in Feminist and Postcolonial Perspective*, edited by Christl M. Maier and Carolyn J. Sharp, 101–15. LHBOTS 577. London: Bloomsbury, 2013.

Moughtin-Mumby, Sharon. *Sexual and Marital Metaphors in Hosea, Jeremiah and Ezekiel*. Old Testament Monographs. Oxford: Oxford University Press, 2008.

O'Connor, Kathleen M. "The Tears of God and Divine Character in Jeremiah 2–9." In *Troubling Jeremiah*, edited by A. R. Pete Diamond, Kathleen M. O'Connor, and Louis Stulman, 387–401. JSOTSup 260. Sheffield: Sheffield Academic, 1999.

Shields, Mary. *Circumscribing the Prostitute: The Rhetorics of Intertextuality, Metaphor and Gender in Jeremiah 3.1–4.4*. JSOTSup 387. London: T&T Clark, 2004.

Sweeney, Marvin A. "Structure and Redaction in Jeremiah 2–6." In *Troubling Jeremiah*, edited by A. R. Pete Diamond, Kathleen M. O'Connor, and Louis Stulman, 200–18. JSOTSup 260. Sheffield: Sheffield Academic, 1999.

Jeremiah 7

Davidson, Steed V. "Ambivalence and Temple Destruction: Reading the Book of Jeremiah with Homi Bhabha." In *Jeremiah (Dis)Placed: New Directions in Writing/Reading Jeremiah*, edited by A. R. Pete Diamond and Louis Stulman, 162–71. LHBOTS 529. London: T&T Clark, 2011.

Lange, Armin. "'They Burn Their Sons and Daughters—That Was No Command of Mine' (Jer 7:31): Child Sacrifice in the Hebrew Bible and in the Deuteronomistic Jeremiah Redaction." In *Human Sacrifice in Jewish and Christian Tradition*, edited by Karin Finsterbusch, Armin Lange, and K. F. Diethard Römheld, in association with Lance Lazar, 109–32. Numen: Studies in the History of Religions 112. Leiden: Brill, 2007.

Leuchter, Mark. "The Temple Sermon and the Term LeAnn in the Jeremianic Corpus." *JSOT* 30 (2005): 93–109.

Tiemeyer, Lena-Sofia. "The Priests and the Temple Cult in the Book of Jeremiah." In *Prophecy in the Book of Jeremiah*, edited by Hans M. Barstad and Reinhard G. Kratz, 233–64. BZAW 388. Berlin: de Gruyter, 2009.

Jeremiah 8-10

Bultmann, Christoph. "Patterns or Poetry in Jeremiah? Introducing a Reader to the Twin Poems in Jeremiah 5 and 8." In *The Centre and the Periphery: A European Tribute to Walter Brueggemann*, edited by Jill Middlemas, David J. A. Clines, and Else K. Holt, 61-78. HBM 27. Sheffield: Sheffield Phoenix, 2010.

Halpern, Baruch. "The False Torah of Jeremiah 8 in the Context of 7th Century BCE Pseudepigraphy: The First Documented Rejection of Tradition." In *From Gods to God: The Dynamics of Iron Age Cosmologies*, edited by Matthew J. Adams, 132-41. FAT 63. Tübingen: Mohr Siebeck, 2009.

Kruger, Paul A. "A World Turned on Its Head in Ancient Near Eastern Prophetic Literature: A Powerful Strategy to Depict Chaotic Scenarios." *VT* 62 (2012): 58-76.

Levtow, Nathaniel B. *Images of Others: Iconic Politics in Ancient Israel*. Winona Lake, IN: Eisenbrauns, 2008.

O'Connor, Kathleen M. "The Tears of God and Divine Character in Jeremiah 2-9." In *Troubling Jeremiah*, edited by A. R. Pete Diamond, Kathleen M. O'Connor, and Louis Stulman, 387-401. JSOTSup 260. Sheffield: Sheffield Academic, 1999.

Pilarski, Ahida C. "A Study of the References to LeAnn in Jeremiah: 8:18-9:2(3): A Gendered Lamentation." In *Why? How Long? Studies on Voice(s) of Lamentation Rooted in Biblical Hebrew Poetry*, edited by LeAnn S. Flesher, Carol J. Dempsey, and Mark J. Boda, 20-35. LHBOTS 552. London: Bloomsbury, 2014.

Jeremiah 11-20

Avioz, Michael. "The Call for Revenge in Jeremiah's Complaints (Jer xi-xx)." *VT* 55 (2005): 429-38.

Bezzel, Hannes. "The Suffering of the Elect: Variations on a Theological Problem in Jer 15:10-21." In *Prophecy in the Book of Jeremiah*, edited by Hans M. Barstad and Reinhard G. Kratz, 48-74. BZAW 388. Berlin: de Gruyter, 2009.

Boda, Mark J. "From Complaint to Contrition: Peering through the Liturgical Window of Jer 14,1-15,4." *ZAW* 113 (2001): 186-97.

Boda, Mark J. " 'Uttering Precious Rather Than Worthless Words': Divine Patience and Impatience with Lament in Isaiah and Jeremiah." In *Why? How Long? Studies on Voice(s) of Lamentation Rooted in Biblical Hebrew Poetry*, edited by LeAnn S. Flesher, Carol J. Dempsey, and Mark J. Boda, 83-99. LHBOTS 552. London: Bloomsbury, 2014.

Callaway, Mary C. "Seduced by Method: History and Jeremiah 20." In *Jeremiah Invented: Constructions and Deconstructions of Jeremiah*, edited by Else K. Holt and Carolyn J. Sharp, 16–33. LHBOTS 595. London: Bloomsbury, 2015.

Carvalho, Corinne L. "Sex and the Single Prophet: Marital Status and Gender in Jeremiah and Ezekiel." In *Prophets Male and Female: Gender and Prophecy in the Hebrew Bible, the Eastern Mediterranean, and the Ancient Near East*, edited by Jonathan Stökl and Corrine L. Carvalho, 237–67. AIIL 15. Atlanta, GA: SBL, 2013.

Dell, Katharine. "'Cursed Be the Day I Was Born': Job and Jeremiah Revisited." In *Reading Job Intertextually*, edited by Katharine Dell and Will Kynes. LHBOTS 572. London: T&T Clark, 2012.

Diamond, A. R. Pete. *The Confessions of Jeremiah in Context: Scenes of Prophetic Drama*. JSOTSup 45. London: T&T Clark, 1987.

Diamond, A. R. Pete. "Jeremiah's Confessions in the LXX and MT: A Witness to Developing Canonical Function?" *VT* 40 (1990): 33–50.

Elgavish, David. "'Concerning the Droughts': Jeremiah 14:1–15:9—Structure and Significance." In *"My Spirit at Rest in the North Country" (Zechariah 6.8): Collected Communications to the XXth Congress of the International Organization for the Study of the Old Testament, Helsinki 2010*, edited by Hermann M. Niemann and Matthias Augustin, 51–64. BEATAJ 57. Frankfurt am Main: Peter Lang, 2011.

Erzberger, Johanna. "Prophetic Sign Acts as Performances." In *Jeremiah Invented: Constructions and Deconstructions of Jeremiah*, edited by Else K. Holt and Carolyn J. Sharp, 104–16. LHBOTS 595. London: Bloomsbury, 2015.

Floyd, Michael H. "Prophetic Complaints about the Fulfillment of Oracles in Habakkuk 1:2–17 and Jeremiah 15:10–18." *JBL* 110 (1991): 397–418.

Foreman, Benjamin A. "Strike the Tongue: Silencing the Prophet in Jeremiah 18:18b." *VT* 59 (2009): 653–57.

Frese, Daniel A. "Lessons from the Potter's Workshop: A New Look at Jeremiah 18.1–11." *JSOT* 37 (2013): 371–88.

Friebel, Kelvin J. *Jeremiah's and Ezekiel's Sign-Acts: Rhetorical and Nonverbal Communication*. JSOTSup 283. Sheffield: Sheffield Academic, 1999.

Ittmann, Norbert. *Die Konfessionen Jeremias: Ihre Bedeutung für die Verkündigung des Propheten*. WMANT 54. Neukirchener-Vluyn: Keukirchener Verlag, 1981.

Johnston, Philip S. "'Now You See Me, Now You Don't!' Jeremiah and God." In *Prophecy and the Prophets in Ancient Israel: Proceedings of the Oxford Old Testament Seminar*, edited by John Day, 290–308. LHBOTS 531. London: T&T Clark, 2010.

Kalmanofsky, Amy. "Bare Naked: A Gender Analysis of the Naked Body in Jeremiah 13." In *Jeremiah Invented: Constructions and Deconstructions of Jeremiah*, edited by Else K. Holt and Carolyn J. Sharp, 49–62. LHBOTS 595. London: Bloomsbury, 2015.

Kalmanofsky, Amy. "The Monstrous-Feminine in the Book of Jeremiah." In *Jeremiah (Dis)Placed: New Directions in Writing/Reading Jeremiah*, edited by A. R. Pete Diamond and Louis Stulman, 190–208. LHBOTS 529. London: T&T Clark, 2011.

Kiss, Jenö. *Die Klage Gottes und des Propheten: ihre Rolle in der Komposition und Redaktion von Jer 11–12, 14–15 und 18.* WMANT 99. Neukirchen-Vluyn: Neukirchener Verlag, 2003.

McBride, Jr., S. Dean. "Jeremiah and the Levitical Priests of Anathoth." In *Thus Says the Lord: Essays on the Former and Latter Prophets in Honor of Robert R. Wilson,* edited by John J. Ahn and Stephen L. Cook, 179–96. LHBOTS 502. London: T&T Clark, 2009.

O'Connor, Kathleen M. *The Confessions of Jeremiah: Their Interpretation and Role in Chapters 1–25.* SBLDS 94. Atlanta, GA: Society of Biblical Literature, 1988.

Pohlmann, Karl-Friedrich. *Die Ferne Gottes: Studien zum Jeremiabuch: Beiträge zu den "Konfessionen" in Jeremiabuch und ein Versuch zur Frage nach den Anfängen der Jeremiatradition.* BZAW 179. Berlin: de Gruyter, 1989.

Smith, Mark S. *The Laments of Jeremiah and Their Contexts.* SBLMS 42. Atlanta, GA: Scholars, 1990.

Jeremiah 21–23

Lemke, Werner E. "The Near and the Distant God: A Study of Jer 23:23–24 in Its Biblical Theological Context." *JBL* 100 (1981): 541–55.

Maier, Christl M. "God's Cruelty and Jeremiah's Treason: Jeremiah 21:1–10 in Postcolonial Perspective." In *Prophecy and Power: Jeremiah in Feminist and Postcolonial Perspective,* edited by Christl M. Maier and Carolyn J. Sharp, 132–49. LHBOTS 577. London: Bloomsbury, 2013.

Schipper, Jeremy. "'Exile Atones for Everything': Coping with Jeremiah 22.24–30." *JSOT* 31 (2007): 481–92.

Seitz, Christopher R. "The Crisis of Interpretation over the Meaning and Purpose of the Exile: A Redactional Study of Jeremiah xxi-xliii." *VT* 35 (1985): 78–97.

Wessels, W. J. "Jeremiah 22,24—30: A Proposed Ideological Reading." *ZAW* 101 (1989): 232–49.

Jeremiah 24

Hayes, Elizabeth R. "Of Branches, Pots and Figs: Jeremiah's Visions from a Cognitive Perspective." In *Prophecy in the Book of Jeremiah,* edited by Hans M. Barstad and Reinhard G. Kratz, 89–102. BZAW 388. Berlin: de Gruyter, 2009.

Scalise, Pamela. "Vision beyond the Visions in Jeremiah." In *I Lifted My Eyes and Saw': Reading Dream and Vision Reports in the Hebrew Bible,* edited by Elizabeth R. Hayes and Lena-Sofia Tiemeyer, 47–58. LHBOTS 584. London: Bloomsbury, 2014.

Seitz, Christopher R. "The Crisis of Interpretation over the Meaning and Purpose of the Exile: A Redactional Study of Jeremiah xxi–xliii." *VT* 35 (1985): 78–97.

Jeremiah 25

Aejmelaeus, Anneli. "Jeremiah at the Turning-Point of History: The Function of Jer. xxv 1–14 in the Book of Jeremiah." *VT* 52 (2002): 459–82.

Carroll, Robert P. "Halfway through a Dark Wood: Reflections on Jeremiah 25." In *Troubling Jeremiah*, edited by A. R. Pete Diamond, Kathleen M. O'Connor, and Louis Stulman, 73–86. JSOTSup 260. Sheffield: Sheffield Academic, 1999.

Hill, John. "The Construction of Time in Jeremiah 25 (MT)." In *Troubling Jeremiah*, edited by A. R. Pete Diamond, Kathleen M. O'Connor, and Louis Stulman, 146–60. JSOTSup 260. Sheffield: Sheffield Academic, 1999.

Holt, Else K. "King Nebuchadrezzar of Babylon, My Servant, and the Cup of Wrath: Jeremiah's Fantasies and the Hope of Violence." In *Jeremiah (Dis)Placed: New Directions in Writing/Reading Jeremiah*, edited by A. R. Pete Diamond and Louis Stulman, 209–18. LHBOTS 529. London: T&T Clark, 2011.

Kessler, Martin. "Jeremiah 25,1–29: Text and Context. A Synchronic Study." *ZAW* 109 (1997): 44–70.

Leuchter, Mark. "Jeremiah's 70-Year Prophecy and the ימק בל/ךשש Atbash Codes." *Bib* 85 (2004): 503–22.

Smelik, Klaas A. D. "My Servant Nebuchadnezzar: The Use of the Epithet 'My Servant' for the Babylonian King Nebuchadnezzar in the Book of Jeremiah." *VT* 64 (2014): 109–34.

Jeremiah 26–29

Aejmelaeus, Anneli. "'Nebuchadnezzar, My Servant': Redaction History and Textual Development in Jer 27." In *Interpreting Translation: Studies on the LXX and Ezekiel in Honour of Johan Lust*, edited by F. García Martínez and M. Vervenne, with the collaboration of B. Doyle, 1–18. BETL 192. Leuven: Peeters, 2005.

Davidson, Steed V. "Ambivalence and Temple Destruction: Reading the Book of Jeremiah with Homi Bhabha." In *Jeremiah (Dis)Placed: New Directions in Writing/Reading Jeremiah*, edited by A. R. Pete Diamond and Louis Stulman, 162–71. LHBOTS 529. London: T&T Clark, 2011.

Davidson, Steed V. *Empire and Exile: Postcolonial Readings of the Book of Jeremiah*. LHBOTS 542. London: T&T Clark, 2011.

Dijkstra, Meindert. "Prophecy by Letter (Jeremiah xxix 24–32)." *VT* 33 (1983): 319–22.

Leuchter, Mark. "Personal Missives and National History: The Relationship between Jeremiah 29 and 36." In *Prophets, Prophecy, and Ancient Israelite*

Historiography, edited by Mark J. Boda and Lissa M. Wray Beal, 275–93.
Winona Lake, IN: Eisenbrauns, 2013.

Pyper, Hugh S. " 'Whose Prophecy Is It Anyway?' What Micah 3:12 Is Doing
in Jeremiah 26." In *Far from Minimal: Celebrating the Work and Influence of
Philip R. Davies*, edited by Duncan Burns and John W. Rogerson, 365–77.
LHBOTS 484. London: T&T Clark, 2012.

Seitz, Christopher R. *Theology in Conflict: Reactions to the Exile in the Book of
Jeremiah*. BZAW 176. Berlin: de Gruyter, 1989.

Silver, Edward. "Performing Domination/Theorizing Power: Israelite Prophecy
as a Political Discourse beyond the Conflict Model." *JANER* 14 (2014):
186–216.

Jeremiah 30–31

Becking, Bob. *Between Fear and Freedom: Essays on the Interpretation of
Jeremiah 30–31*. OudSt 51. Leiden: Brill, 2004.

Bozak, Barbara A. *Life "Anew": A Literary-Theological Study of Jer. 30–31*.
Analecta biblica 122. Rome: Pontifical Biblical Institute, 1991.

Brueggemann, Walter. "The 'Uncared for' Now Cared for (Jer 30:12–17):
A Methodological Consideration." *JBL* 104 (1985): 419–28.

Halvorson-Taylor, Martien A. *Enduring Exile: The Metaphorization of Exile in
the Hebrew Bible*. VTSup 141. Leiden: Brill, 2010.

Kruger, Paul A. "A Woman Will 'Encompass' a Man: On Gender Reversal in
Jer 31,22b." *Bib* 89 (2008): 380–8.

Leene, Hendrik. "Jeremiah 31,23–26 and the Redaction of the Book of
Comfort." *ZAW* 104 (1992): 349–64.

Moon, Joshua N. *Jeremiah's New Covenant: An Augustinian Reading*. JTIS 3.
Winona Lake, IN: Eisenbrauns, 2011.

Rata, Tiberius. *The Covenant Motif in Jeremiah's Book of Comfort: Textual
and Intertextual Studies of Jeremiah 30–33*. SBL 107. New York: Peter
Lang, 2007.

Schmid, Konrad. *Buchgestalten des Jeremiabuches: Untersuchungen zur
Redaktions- und Rezeptionsgeschichte von Jer 30–33 im Kontext des Buches*.
WMANT 72. Neukirchen-Vluyn: Neukirchener Verlag, 1996.

Sweeney, Marvin A. "Jeremiah 30–31 and King Josiah's Program of National
Restoration and Religious Reform." *ZAW* 108 (1983): 569–83.

Jeremiah 32–39

Applegate, John. " 'Peace, Peace, When there Is No Peace': Redactional
Integration of Prophecy of Peace into the Judgement of Jeremiah." In *The
Book of Jeremiah and Its Reception: Le livre de Jérémie et sa réception*, edited
by Adrian H. W. Curtis and Thomas C. Römer, 51–90. BETL 78. Leuven:
Leuven University Press, 1997.

Begin, Ze'ev B. "Does Lachish Letter 4 Contradict Jeremiah xxxiv 7?" *VT* 52 (2002): 166–74.

Biddle, Mark E. "The Redaction of Jeremiah 39–41 [46–48 LXX]." *ZAW* 126 (2014): 228–42.

Brummitt, Mark, and Yvonne Sherwood. "The Fear of Loss Inherent in Writing: Jeremiah 36 as the Story of a Self-Conscious Scroll." In *Jeremiah (Dis)Placed: New Directions in Writing/Reading Jeremiah*, edited by A. R. Pete Diamond and Louis Stulman, 47–66. LHBOTS 529. London: T&T Clark, 2011.

Callaway, Mary C. "Black Fire on White Fire: Historical Context and Literary Subtext in Jeremiah 37–38." In *Troubling Jeremiah*, edited by A. R. Pete Diamond, Kathleen M. O'Connor and Louis Stulman, 171–78. JSOTSup 260. Sheffield: Sheffield Academic, 1999.

Davidson, Steed V. *Empire and Exile: Postcolonial Readings of the Book of Jeremiah*. LHBOTS 542. London: T&T Clark, 2011.

Davidson, Steed V. "'Exoticizing the Otter': The Curious Case of the Rechabites in Jeremiah 35." In *Prophecy and Power: Jeremiah in Feminist and Postcolonial Perspective*, edited by Christl M. Maier and Carolyn J. Sharp, 188–207. LHBOTS 577. London: Bloomsbury, 2013.

Dearman, J. Andrew. "My Servants the Scribes: Composition and Context in Jeremiah 36." *JBL* 109 (1990): 403–21.

Domeris, William R. "The Land Claim of Jeremiah—Was Max Weber Right?" In *Jeremiah (Dis)Placed: New Directions in Writing/Reading Jeremiah*, edited by A. R. Pete Diamond and Louis Stulman, 136–49. LHBOTS 529. London: T&T Clark, 2011.

Green, Barbara. "Sunk in the Mud: Literary Correlation and Collaboration between King and Prophet in the Book of Jeremiah." In *Jeremiah Invented: Constructions and Deconstructions of Jeremiah*, edited by Else K. Holt and Carolyn J. Sharp, 34–48. LHBOTS 595. London: Bloomsbury, 2015.

Hicks, R. Lansing. "*delet* and *megillāh*: A Fresh Approach to Jeremiah xxxvi." *VT* 33 (1983): 46–66.

Hoffman, Yair. "Aetiology, Redaction and Historicity in Jeremiah xxxvi." *VT* 46 (1996): 179–89.

Holladay, William L. "The Identification of the Two Scrolls of Jeremiah." *VT* 30 (1980): 452–67.

Leuchter, Mark. "The Manumission Laws in Leviticus and Deuteronomy: The Jeremiah Connection." *JBL* 127 (2008): 635–53.

Macwilliam, Stuart. "The Prophet and His Patsy: Gender Performativity in Jeremiah." In *Prophecy and Power: Jeremiah in Feminist and Postcolonial Perspective*, edited by Christl M. Maier and Carolyn J. Sharp, 173–88. LHBOTS 577. London: Bloomsbury, 2013.

McKane, William. "Jeremiah and the Rechabites." *ZAW* 100 (1988): 106–23.

Pakkala, Juha. "Zedekiah's Fate and the Dynastic Succession." *JBL* 125 (2006): 443–52.

Rom-Shiloni, Dalit. "The Prophecy for 'Everlasting Covenant' (Jeremiah xxxii 36–41): An Exilic Addition or a Deuteronomistic Redaction?" *VT* 53 (2003): 201–23.

Roncace, Mark. *Jeremiah, Zedekiah, and the Fall of Jerusalem.* LHBOTS 423. London: T&T Clark, 2005.

Schaper, Joachim. "On Writing and Reciting in Jeremiah 36." In *Prophecy in the Book of Jeremiah*, edited by Hans M. Barstad and Reinhard G. Kratz, 137–47. BZAW 388. Berlin: de Gruyter, 2009.

Seitz, Christopher R. *Theology in Conflict: Reactions to the Exile in the Book of Jeremiah.* BZAW 176. Berlin: de Gruyter, 1989.

Sharp, Carolyn J. "Buying Land in the Text of Jeremiah: Feminist Commentary, the Kristevan Abject, and Jeremiah 32." In *Prophecy and Power: Jeremiah in Feminist and Postcolonial Perspective*, edited by Christl M. Maier and Carolyn J. Sharp, 150–72. LHBOTS 577. London: Bloomsbury, 2013.

Sharp, Carolyn J. "Jeremiah in the Land of Aporia: Reconfiguring Redaction Criticism as Witness to Foreignness." In *Jeremiah (Dis)Placed: New Directions in Writing/Reading Jeremiah*, edited by A. R. Pete Diamond and Louis Stulman, 35–46. LHBOTS 529. London: T&T Clark, 2011.

Shead, Andrew G. *The Open Book and the Sealed Book: Jeremiah 32 in Its Hebrew and Greek Recensions.* JSOTSup 347. Sheffield: Sheffield Academic, 2002.

Talstra, Eep, and Reinoud Oosting. "Jeremiah 32: A Future and Its History—Actualisation in Writing and Reading." In *African and European Readers of the Bible in Dialogue: In Quest of a Shared Meaning*, edited by Hans De Wit and Gerald O. West, 199–219. Studies of Religion in Africa 32. Leiden: Brill, 2008.

Venema, Geert J. *Reading Scripture in the Old Testament: Deuteronomy 9–10; 31, 2 Kings 22–23, Jeremiah 36, Nehemiah 8.* OudSt 48. Leiden: Brill, 2004.

Wanke, Gunther. "Jeremias Gebet nach dem Ackerkauf (Jer 32,16–25) und der Pentateuch: Eine Problemanzeige." In *Auf dem Weg zur Endgestalt von Genesis bis II Regum: Festschrift Hans-Christoph Schmitt zum 65. Geburtstag*, edited by Martin Beck and Ulrike Schorn, 273–77. BZAW 370. Berlin: de Gruyter, 2006.

Jeremiah 40–45

Biddle, Mark E. "The Redaction of Jeremiah 39–41 [46–48 LXX]." *ZAW* 126 (2014): 228–42.

Bodner, Keith. *After the Invasion: A Reading of Jeremiah 40–44.* Oxford: Oxford University Press, 2015.

Brueggemann, Walter. "The 'Baruch Connection': Reflections on Jeremiah 43.1–7." In *Troubling Jeremiah*, edited by A. R. Pete Diamond, Kathleen M. O'Connor, and Louis Stulman, 367–86. JSOTSup 260. Sheffield: Sheffield Academic, 1999.

Davidson, Steed V. "Chosen Marginality as Resistance in Jeremiah 40:1–6." In *Jeremiah (Dis)Placed: New Directions in Writing/Reading Jeremiah*, edited by A. R. Pete Diamond and Louis Stulman, 150–61. LHBOTS 529. London: T&T Clark, 2011.

Davidson, Steed V. *Empire and Exile: Postcolonial Readings of the Book of Jeremiah*. LHBOTS 542. London: T&T Clark, 2011.

Davidson, Steed V. "'Every Green Tree and the Streets of Jerusalem': Counter Constructions of Gendered Sacred Space in the Book of Jeremiah." In *Constructions of Space IV: Further Developments in Examining Ancient Israel's Social Space*, edited by Mark K. George, 111–31. LHBOTS 569. London: Bloomsbury, 2013.

Ellis, Teresa A. "Jeremiah 44: What if 'the Queen of Heaven' Is YHWH?" *JSOT* 33 (2009): 465–88.

Harding, James E. "The Silent Goddess and the Gendering of Divine Speech in Jeremiah 44." In *Prophecy and Power: Jeremiah in Feminist and Postcolonial Perspective*, edited by Christl M. Maier and Carolyn J. Sharp, 208–23. LHBOTS 577. London: Bloomsbury, 2013.

Holt, Else K. "The Potent Word of God: Remarks on the Composition of Jeremiah 37–44." In *Troubling Jeremiah*, edited by A. R. Pete Diamond, Kathleen M. O'Connor, and Louis Stulman, 161–70. JSOTSup 260. Sheffield: Sheffield Academic, 1999.

Pakkala, Juha. "Gedaliah's Murder in 2 Kings 25:25 and Jeremiah 41:1–3." In *Scripture in Transition: Essays on Septuagint, Hebrew Bible, and Dead Sea Scrolls in Honour of Raija Sollamo*, edited by Anssi Voitila and Jutta Jokiranta, 401–11. Supplements to the Journal for the Study of Judaism 126. Leiden: Brill, 2008.

Peels, Eric. "The Assassination of Gedaliah (Jer. 40:7–41:18)." In *Exile and Suffering: A Selection of Papers Read at the 50th Anniversary Meeting of the Old Testament Society of South Africa OTWSA/OTSSA Pretoria August 2007*, edited by Bob Becking and Dirk Human, 83–103. OudSt 50. Leiden: Brill, 2008.

Seitz, Christopher R. *Theology in Conflict: Reactions to the Exile in the Book of Jeremiah*. BZAW 176. Berlin: de Gruyter, 1989.

Weinberg, Joel. "Gedaliah, the Son of Ahikam in Mizpah: His Status and Role, Supporters and Opponents." *ZAW* 119 (2007): 356–68.

Jeremiah 46–51

Bellis, Alice O. "Assaulting the Empire: A Refugee Community's Language of Hope." In *Jeremiah (Dis)Placed: New Directions in Writing/Reading*

Jeremiah, edited by A. R. Pete Diamond and Louis Stulman, 219–34. LHBOTS 529. London: T&T Clark, 2011.

Bellis, Alice O. "Poetic Structure and Intertextual Logic in Jeremiah 50." In _Troubling Jeremiah_, edited by A. R. Pete Diamond, Kathleen M. O'Connor, and Louis Stulman, 179–99. JSOTSup 260. Sheffield: Sheffield Academic, 1999.

Bruggemann, Walter. "At the Mercy of Babylon: A Subversive Rereading of the Empire." In _Reading the Book of Jeremiah: A Search for Coherence_, edited by Martin Kessler, 117–34. Winona Lake, IN: Eisenbrauns, 2004.

Graybill, Rhiannon. "Jeremiah, Sade, and Repetition as Counterpleasure in the Oracles against Edom." In _Concerning the Nations: Essays on the Oracles against the Nations in Isaiah, Jeremiah and Ezekiel_, edited by Andrew Mein, Else K. Holt, and Hyun C. P. Kim, 128–41. LHBOTS 612. London: Bloomsbury, 2015.

Hill, John. _Friend or Foe? The Figure of Babylon in the Book of Jeremiah MT_. BIS 40. Leiden: Brill, 1999.

Huwyler, Beat. _Jeremia und die Völker: Untersuchungen zu den Völkersprüchen in Jeremia 46–49_. FAT 20. Tübingen: Mohr Siebeck, 1997.

Kalmanofsky, Amy. "'As She Did, Do to Her!' Jeremiah's OAN as Revenge Fantasies." In _Concerning the Nations: Essays on the Oracles against the Nations in Isaiah, Jeremiah and Ezekiel_, edited by Andrew Mein, Else K. Holt, and Hyun C. P. Kim, 109–27. LHBOTS 612. London: Bloomsbury, 2015.

Kessler, Martin. _Battle of the Gods: The God of Israel versus Marduk of Babylon: A Literary/Theological Interpretation of Jeremiah 50–51_. SSN 42. Leiden: Brill, 2003.

Pyper, Hugh S. "Postcolonialism and Propaganda in Jeremiah's Oracles against the Nations." In _Concerning the Nations: Essays on the Oracles against the Nations in Isaiah, Jeremiah and Ezekiel_, edited by Andrew Mein, Else K. Holt, and Hyun C. P. Kim, 145–57. LHBOTS 612. London: Bloomsbury, 2015.

Sharp, Carolyn J. "Embodying Moab: The Figuring of Moab in Jeremiah 48 as Reinscription of the Judean Body." In _Concerning the Nations: Essays on the Oracles against the Nations in Isaiah, Jeremiah and Ezekiel_, edited by Andrew Mein, Else K. Holt, and Hyun C. P. Kim, 95–108. LHBOTS 612. London: Bloomsbury, 2015.

Sharp, Carolyn J. "'Take Another Scroll and Write': A Study of the LXX and the MT of Jeremiah's Oracles against Egypt and Babylon." _VT_ 47 (1997): 487–516.

Smelik, Klaas A. D. "The Function of Jeremiah 50 and 51 in the Book of Jeremiah." In _Reading the Book of Jeremiah: A Search for Coherence_, edited by Martin Kessler, 87–98. Winona Lake, IN: Eisenbrauns, 2004.

Thelle, Rannfrid. "Babylon as Judah's Doppelgänger: The Identity of Opposites in the Book of Jeremiah (MT)." In _Concerning the Nations: Essays on_ *the Oracles against the Nations in Isaiah, Jeremiah and Ezekiel*, edited by Andrew Mein, Else K. Holt, and Hyun C. P. Kim, 77–94. LHBOTS 612. London: Bloomsbury, 2015.

Woods, Julie. *Jeremiah 48 as Christian Scripture*. Princeton Theological Monograph Series 149. Eugene, OR: Pickwick, 2011.

Jeremiah 52

Person, Raymond F. *The Kings–Isaiah and Kings–Jeremiah Recensions*. BZAW 252. Berlin: de Gruyter, 1997.

INDEX OF SCRIPTURAL REFERENCES

Note: **Bold text** indicates principal discussion.

INDEX OF AUTHORS

INDEX OF SUBJECTS

Septuagint (Greek),   11, 19, 22, 26,
        30–7, 41, 54, 64, 68–9, 72, 80,
        97–8, 103–15, 119–20, 128
Shaphan, family of   23, 29, 128, 132–4
Source criticism   39–45, 47–9, 58–60

text criticism   36–7
theological interpretation   14–16, 20,
        27–8, 52–3, 58, 62, 69–73, 75,
        83–91, 104, 113–14, 120–1, 124,
        131–2, 136

theologies of exile   8–9, 20–1, 23, 27–30,
        47–8, 51–3, 79, 88–91, 104–5, 109,
        110–11, 120–7
trauma studies   63, 74, 88–91, 98–9

visions   12, 21, 29, 46, 78, 81–3, 85, 93

Zedekiah   7, 19–21, 23, 25–8, 31, 40,
        78–9, 90, 107, 116, 122, 124